T0131656

Praise for *The Absent Hand*

"Half memoir, half cri de coeur, Lessard's lambent, thoughtful, exquisitely written collection of interconnected essays dissects—as an art historian would a picture, a literary critic a text, a medical examiner a cadaver—a diverse swath of America, from Gettysburg and the King of Prussia Mall in Pennsylvania to Truth or Consequences, N.M.; from the seat of an airplane, 30,000-odd feet above Alaska, to the stoops and sidewalks of Brooklyn during the 1990s; from Georgetown, in Washington, where the author used to live, to Youngstown, Ohio." —MICHAEL KIMMELMAN, *The New York Times Book Review*

"Unusual and engaging . . . A subjective, Whitmanesque meditation on the way we live today . . . What makes this book compelling is not so much where the author goes, but how she reflects on what she sees when she gets there . . . Her wonderfully trenchant observations cast new light on the everyday." —WITOLD RYBCZYNSKI, *The Wall Street Journal*

"This book of thought-provoking essays queries the nature of place, asking landscapes to reveal their meanings . . . [Lessard] eloquently asks us to look harder at our surroundings, and ask better questions about what we see." —JAMES S. RUSSELL, *Architectural Record*

"In an elegant series of essays, *New Yorker* contributor Lessard (*The Architect of Desire*) explores the American landscape as a metaphor for recent shifts in the national consciousness . . . Throughout, Lessard offers an extraordinary way of examining and understanding the aesthetics of different environments, whether urban, suburban, or bucolic, which will inspire readers to look with new curiosity at the places around them." —*Publishers Weekly* (starred review)

"Part memoir, part examination of the American cultural landscape. Lessard offers a unique and necessary perspective on the deterioration of our society's connection to the landscape, manifested most prominently in the book as sprawl." —AARON KING, *The Dirt*

"In a series of finely tuned essays that track the author's journey from the Hudson Valley into the Midwest and the South, Lessard explores the relationship between humanity and place that once defined us but, she argues, doesn't any longer." —JONATHAN HAHN, *Sierra*

"This genre-blurring work of criticism—part history, part travel diary, part personal narrative—explores the contradictions of the American landscape. In episodic chapters, Lessard probes a medley of places: the mountain villages of upstate New York; Brooklyn housing projects; the sprawl and megamall of King of Prussia, Pennsylvania; and plantations in Natchez, Mississippi . . . As Lessard alternates between narrative and analysis, what begins as a pastiche of vignettes builds into an entrancing reconsideration of America's history, from the spaces of the antebellum South through the landscapes of the Cold War and beyond . . . A stellar work of landscape criticism, a rapturous meditation on the revelatory power of place." —*Booklist*

"*The Absent Hand* is like no other book I have read, narrated by a writer whose perceptions and language are as radically original as they are eloquent. Observed with a gentle irony, an abiding lyricism, and an acute sense of the comfortable pieties we live by, Suzannah Lessard's hybrid creation—part memoir, part history, part literary criticism, and part sociological document—is an elegy to the all-but-lost power of landscape. Whether commenting on an abandoned but still vibrant village in the Hudson River Valley, 'suburbaphobia' among the educated elite, the 'peculiar stillness' of Sheraton hotel rooms, or the complex artifice of the Disney vision, *The Absent Hand* explores the way we inhabit the space around us, physically as well as mentally, individually as well as collectively. It is a wise as well as poignant book, leavened by flashes of humor—one that will make you think about the bargains we have made with our natural surroundings and the price we have paid for them." —DAPHNE MERKIN, author of *This Close to Happy*

"One of Suzannah Lessard's great gifts is that of seeing, of discerning and explaining the details most of us skip past. She is also gifted at conveying this precise view. Everyone who reads this book will see the American landscape differently, in its urban and rural variety and splendor and disrepair. Readers will also have a clearer appreciation for what is beautiful and why—and of how the unlovely might be restored." —JAMES FALLOWS, coauthor of *Our Towns*

"*The Absent Hand: Reimagining Our American Landscape* is a place-based book in the deepest sense. Lessard's keen observations about selected landscapes in which she has thoroughly immersed herself in order to parse their broader underlying meanings ranks her style with Thoreau's experiential mode of writing. The book is pitch-perfect and filled with cogent philosophical interpretations, a loving and shrewd appraisal of the physical fabric of our once- and still-beautiful but fraught country." —ELIZABETH BARLOW ROGERS, president of the Foundation for Landscape Studies

THE ABSENT HAND

Reimagining Our American Landscape

Suzannah Lessard

Counterpoint / California

THE ABSENT HAND

The Library of Congress has cataloged the hardcover as follows:
Names: Lessard, Suzannah, author.
Title: The absent hand : reimagining our american landscape / Suzannah Lessard.
Description: First hardcover edition. | Berkeley, California : Counterpoint, 2019.
Identifiers: LCCN 2018041022 | ISBN 9781640092211
Subjects: LCSH: United States—Description and travel. | Landscape assessment—United States. | Landscape changes—United States. | Geographical perception—United States. | Travelers' writings, American. | Lessard, Suzannah—Travel.
Classification: LCC E169.Z83 L47 2019 | DDC 917.304—dc23
LC record available at https://lccn.loc.gov/2018041022

Paperback ISBN: 978-1-64009-351-5

Cover design by Jenny Carrow
Book design by Wah-Ming Chang

COUNTERPOINT
Los Angeles and San Francisco, CA
www.counterpointpress.com

Printed in the United States of America

For Alida,
who taught me to heed place with body and soul,

and

for Noel,
who backed me with love
throughout the journey that ensued.

With gratitude.

Contents

Part Three
The Absent Hand

AUTHOR'S NOTE

Once the world was wide. Now we live in collapsed space: the chip in our pocket. Once wilderness was beyond society. Now even the storm bears our imprint. We are awed by ourselves. We are frightened by ourselves. We have acquired godlike powers. We can't govern ourselves. Besotted by our grandeur, we consider geo-engineering. Befogged by our data we grope for transcendence. We pretend we are small, a figure in the furrowed field, sowing, woodlots and windrows riding the hills to their crests all around us, as always. But wherever we turn we bump into ourselves. We live as in a walled garden now, walled by ourselves. We have been building this wall for some time, but now it's complete. That is new. And yet our surroundings remain as radiantly mysterious as ever. The connection to place remains deep: touching the core of our being. Landscape is our mirror, our book of revelations, as always. This is where reorientation starts.

Part One

Listening to the Fields

mill, also three stories, where felt was produced. Felt made from sheep's wool was used in the production of paper, and became the great industry of the village. The gnarly little mountains around here are good for sheep. When the woolen mill was in operation, a flume siphoned water from the top of the falls down to the mill at the bottom, a descent of a hundred feet, into the mill, into the turbine, inside of which was a small wheel of vanes turned by the concentrated water, powering the works. Once, even the pitching land around the gorge was pasture. Now all the slopes that enclose the village are wooded.

From the gristmill the village tumbles downhill, above a small widening floodplain, alongside the tumbling stream. A reproduction of a print that I bought at the Historical Society, which now occupies the gristmill, is taped to the wall above the bathtub in my cottage. It shows the floodplain in the nineteenth century, busy with industry: largely lumbering—big tree trunks, some strewn about, some stacked. You can tell it was noisy and dirty. The work of agrarian times was not always as peaceful as we like to imagine. Indeed, there were once five mills along the stream. Today people get upset if a tiny business opens in the village, as if that would ruin its historical character. Midway down Main Street are town-house-style attached dwellings that were once lived in by merchants who ran shops at street level. Some houses along the way are substantial. The village is small, and yet there was substance here, reflecting a time when wealth and political power was in land—those pastures full of grazing sheep whose wool could be turned into felt. When wealth is in the land, then the countryside is less context, more the main thing. It's a spread-out scene, decentered, continuous yet with nodes, like a painting by Kandinsky. That land-wealth gave even a small settlement like the village importance. Other houses are farmhouse-sized with barns in back; others are tiny. Downstream, where Main Street gets steep, sundry houses and cottages are attached to one another to comical effect, as if to keep from falling.

Beyond the last houses, the stream turns into a small valley of fields where it quiets.

The village is Rensselaerville, located in the Helderberg Mountains, a small range in the northwestern corner of the Hudson River Valley, between the Catskills and the Adirondacks in New York State. It's named for one of the Dutch patroon families that first settled the region. The arrangement was feudal, typical of the region. It held back more varied development until overturned by rebellious farmers. As a result, the earliest houses in the village are late eighteenth century— late for the East. People here are place-proud, but in daily parlance Rensselaerville is just "the village," and I will adopt that usage here because it captures a quality of anonymity, of solitude, of being the only village—not quite on the map and perhaps a bit lost in time, too, that is the quality of many villages. Behind the anonymous solitude lies the history of a small productive society, an arrangement out of which the physical form of the village arose, including the specter of a previous feudal arrangement successfully routed. However stratified the architecture, there is a strong "we" in the close clustered physical village: a sense of something earned by all, and lasting—passed on: something modestly, collectively triumphant.

Landscape differs from region to region, but all our landscapes incorporate shifting layers of meaning, some purely personal, sometimes strangely close to the hidden springs of personhood, some familial where lines go back as they do here, intertwining, but always ultimately, to my mind—even when landscape invites us to solitude—recalling our profound social connectedness, a sense of our lives together. Landscape to me is different from nature alone, from wilderness. It is the work of art that results from the collaboration between man and that which has been provided—the gift of providence, you could say, but whatever you say, it is not something man had a hand in at the start. Landscape is what arises from the hand of work as we make our living on the planet and our relation to one another as we do so. The hand of work creates in terrain a kind of syntax, an arrangement of interrelating parts, a composition that has a human meaning that is always, in part, beyond words. Landscape is different from wilderness: Wilderness only has meaning in relation to domesticated environments, while landscape is always part human, though never all human. All our physical surroundings, including the city, are landscapes. Architecture is a component of landscape, a maker of landscape, too. The mill is a landscape maker, literally connecting the parts. The village is a landscape maker, inseparable from its surroundings. The meaning of landscape changes from region to region but our landscapes are all, in one regard, related. The greatest power of landscape is that in expressing our collaboration with the physical world—with that which has been provided—and in that to each other, it becomes the armature of our common interior life; our most social dimension. This is the ultimate, most profound value of landscape.

It's raining today in the village. After a series of spectacular June days, in which the light was so bright and the shadows so dark one felt blinded, the rain is a relief. On June days of that sort, heaven seems to have come down and occupied the landscape, leaving us dazed and a bit embarrassed by our inadequacy. Without the wherewithal to take it in, we are stupid. When the sun begins to sink into the long evening we are reprieved. A rainy day is something different: just us. I like the lowered demands of a rainy day. Here in my cottage the sound of the rain is lost in the sound of the falls, but I can see its pattern against the side of the mill. The pattern is veil-like, a loose weave, but what has my attention are the spaces. The wind blows and the veil billows. The trees are blowing, too. I love a windy rain.

What I see in the moving weave of spaces is the gorge, the floodplain, the valley beyond before the village was built. That transparency is always part of our American landscapes: still. The mill is old, and this draws me to it, but its age is thin. We Americans have a little to remember now, but part of what we remember is that not very long ago we had nothing to remember.

Suddenly it's raining harder. In its clustering character, the village conveys both exposure and the comforts of shelter, but nothing does this more than rain on a roof. The rain is making so much noise that I can't hear the falls. Now the rain is half turning to hail, rattling in the bird feeder and smoking off the roof of the gristmill, mixed in with curtains of water. I go out on the porch to watch. Hail lands in the grass by the road: unseemly white in the green. Now it's raining harder yet, almost too hard. Hail in June is a marvel, but when common rain gets uncommonly heavy these days, a question arises. Suddenly the rain subsides. There are rivulets in the road, and the steady sound of the falls reemerges. The landscape reassembles.

Long ago the dynamo of American agriculture moved on to the Midwest. Later, but still long ago, agriculture itself was replaced by manufacturing as the leading work of American society. The first change was on a continuum, rendering the village merely lesser, but the second severed the continuum. The village was left back in another era, unchanged on the surface but changed in meaning, becoming a pastoral haven for industrialists whose primary home was in the city of Albany and whose wealth was derived from factories there. The village became romantic.

Those city factories reconfigured American society. You could say that they made of us a nation—that is, a people with a common interior life, as opposed to an association of regions. The factories as national form-givers subverted the gravitas of the village, its sense of itself as complete, but also made that very quality, lingering in its physical character, deeply attractive as an escape from the realities of industrial times. The owners of the woolen mill in ruins by the falls in the woods saw opportunity in this change. As the market became national and the economy industrial, they abandoned the village mill, separately building bigger ones in cities on rivers elsewhere. Felt had by that time become a popular fabric for clothing: the felters made fortunes. One later returned to the village, and built a large, very lovely house there for his family in the summers. The gristmill by this time was unable to make a profit but the farmers still needed it, so the felter subsidized it. Other wealthy families, most from Albany, who summered in the village, developed a philanthropic relationship to it as well. The gristmill was in operation until 1945, which is why, in contrast to the almost vanished woolen mill, it is still so sure of its place on the stream.

Today manufacturing has, in turn, been superseded as the first order of American work, once again radically altering the meaning of place, here and elsewhere. Factories, once eyesores, have become beautiful to our eyes. The industrial landscape has become our immediate past, as the agrarian landscape once was. For its part, the village is now separated from its origins by two eras, is now the past of the past: double severance. And yet the form of the village is the same. Landscapes remember, and part of what they can help us remember is the successive armatures of former collective interior lives. In this they pass on what could be the most important part of our history long-term. But it's difficult to see what the meaning of the village has become today, because the romantic interpretation we have inherited from the immediate past has the hold on our imaginations of a fully developed archetype, while the new meaning is undeveloped and elusive. To ask what the village is and means today is to engage with the strangeness of our transitional time, in which place itself seems undercut in meaning. Having no common interpretation of our surroundings, we are, to a degree, lacking in any common interior life with which to orient to one another. In a way we are lost. I find this to be unnerving but also invigorating. It makes me curious about where we are, really. The elemental simplicity of the village landscape provides a reassuring place to start.

In truth, the agrarian landscape around here has been disappearing for a while. The fields down the valley are half gone to brush, even while still used as pasture for sheep, horses, some cattle. In the many forests that are former fields, collapsed stone walls run through: unimaginable labor squandered. Some of this reforestation is more recent than one might think. Ways of life developed in one era inevitably live on into successive ones, and farming is a particularly change-resistant occupation, even in regions unsuited to contemporary agriculture. People went on raising sheep near the village for a long time after industrial scale rendered feltmaking here obsolete. They sheep-farmed because there continued to be a market for wool and lamb chops and because of the momentum of habit—sheep farming is what has always been done here. Americans are attracted to working the land. Farming in the Northeast may have been demoted to a secondary, or even downright marginal, realm a long time ago, but lots of northeasterners have gone on farming anyway. Here in the Helderbergs it was only in the 1980s, when an epidemic of burrs too hard to extract from the wool broke out, that sheep farming faded. Much of the reforestation around the village began at that time.

But corn and hay are also traditional local crops: plenty of fields around here remain clear. I am a lifelong connoisseur of the eastern field as genus, but the local variety was new to me when I first came to the village. Gentleness is lacking. It has to do, perhaps, with the pitch of the land and the fierceness of the winters. Many village fields are odd-shaped and small. You can feel in them still that they were laboriously hacked out from forest, the very forest that pushes back relentlessly at their edges. These irregular, hacked-out fields seem talky to me, as if asking for help or protesting, or unloading memories before it's too late, in contrast to the modest but confident silence of classic eastern fields. Most unrestrained in this way are abandoned apple orchards, where mature, even elderly, long neglected trees gesticulate in openly distraught, pulsatingly intense poses, as if painted by Van Gogh, and at no time more so than in spring, when they blossom, becoming gorgeous King Lears—crazed divas, some already engulfed in returning forests where they bloom in the dark murmuring passionately, Here! Here we still are!

But there are also fields around here that are expansive in size and have the assurance of a reciprocal providential bargain. In these the lay of the land, revealed by the wind blowing through crops, is comfortable, steady. Even the most confident eastern fields are implicitly threatened by development and, under that threat, have about them an elegiac sweetness: next year they could be gone. The eye of the speculator is around here, too, and people looking to build vacation homes with a nice view. Cleared farmed fields are always the best for building and, around here, often have the best views. But the possibility of abandonment is the defining one, and actual, too, in those old pastures that show us the stages of disappearance, from brush-encroached pastures all the way up to mature forest.

In some fields in early winter, corn stubble pokes up through light snow, delineating furrows as if in translation. Unlike the wind in a full-grown crop, also a translation, the stubble in snow accentuates the micro-irregularity of the terrain. Later, serious snowfall once again smooths the lay of the land. As forests become totally leafless the views open up, and the windrows and half-toppled stone walls dividing the fields are like complicated, delicate black sewing. These seams reveal intelligent, unexpected shapes that are obscured by the promiscuous green of summer. Like pieces of cloth that have been cut to conform to the body of the land, the fields in winter reveal the genius of the great couturier of landscape that man at work can unwittingly become.

All approaches to the village are from above; from the surrounding ridges. The first thing you see is a white steeple piercing through trees. This is the Presbyterian church in the center of the village. The spire tapers sharply to a point, directed at the sky. There is, in this, a stretch of the spirit that, though I have seen it many times, always gives me a small leap of heart. Descending into the village you lose sight of the steeple, and then you are in the densest part, near the merchant houses, and there is the church on a knoll, with the steeple so far above you have to crane your neck to see it. The church was built in 1842, in the Greek Revival style that had become popular in America because of identification with a war for independence in Greece, the birthplace of democracy. The simplicity of the style was a statement of opposition to the more ornate styles of Europe, which were seen as celebrating social orders based on privilege of birth. The village church is an especially fine specimen, austerely symmetrical, perfectly proportioned. The church completes the landscape of the village as an expression of the human experience of life on Earth and what we have made of it—what we made of it in this place and at that time. The steeple, with humble precision, introduces a measure beyond measures. It perfects the landscape of gorge, stream, and valley, village and mills, with the human intimation of transcendence. When I see it I feel that no more need be said.

But in truth the congregation is dwindling, and no one would claim that the church expresses a core collective belief of the residents of the village, as once was true. The interior is austere, high, with tall windows. The glass is clear, bringing in the plain light of day. On those rare occasions I attend, I look out the windows at sky; trees blowing. The simplicity of the church and the choice of clear over stained glass remind me of the Puritan tradition, in which the idea of a hierarchy, of priestly intermediaries between God and the individual, was rejected in favor of a direct encounter. The plain interior of the church is attuned to that idea.

The village chorus often sings at services. It's comprised of just who's here who likes to sing, so the quality of the voices varies, but a lot of work, a lot of discipline, goes into the music. I know this first-hand, because I sometimes sing in the chorus. At other times I am a listener. Then I hear the vulnerability of the voices and, in that, the significance of making a mark on the surrounding silence that was this place before it was landscape. Moments of excellence in this lo-cal music move me in a way world-class performers in the great halls never have.

Everything is here, I think, in such moments: everything. Yet, for all this, I get impatient in church. I'm not one who thinks all re-ligion is claptrap, but, sooner or later, I crab to myself that anyone in the congregation could do as well as the person giving the sermon, that we are all just politely pretending to be enlightened because it comforts us, and that, where awe is concerned, or whatever part of ourselves we are exercising here, I could do as well by myself in my garden. In this I am probably more of a piece with the current collec-tive beliefs of the village than not.

A few years ago the steeple began to list. It was determined that if the list was not corrected the steeple would become dangerous and the spire would have to be taken down. Many villages hereabouts have churches with steeples cut off at the belfry. I don't like to see this. Whenever I pass one of these churches, I fleetingly feel trun-cated myself. Like many in Rensselaerville who are not a part of the regular congregation, I was dismayed by the prospect that this could happen to our village. A matriarch from one of the old philanthropic families, a kind of godmother of the village who was dying at that time of a brain tumor—many of her set were coming to the end of their lives in this period—took up the cause. A campaign to raise funds got a lively response—though it must be said too that for some the preservation of a monument to white Christianity did not seem urgent. Still a first-class preservation architect was hired. He found that the steeple had been repaired in the 1930s but in a makeshift way. The godmother was adamant that the job should be done properly for future generations. A meeting was called at which we learned that the outer casing of the spire was connected by supports, called cradles, to a mast that had its footing in the body of the steeple. To do the job properly, the mast had to be taken down. Another group that was disappearing were steeplejacks: the last one in the region had just retired. A crane was brought in that diminished the entire village. Parts of the steeple were removed to a faraway workshop. The mast, meanwhile, was laid alongside the church, peeking out from under a bright blue tarpaulin; rough-hewn, still mostly tree.

Then funds ran out, and there was a long hiatus. I went to visit the godmother at this time: she was at a table with villagers stuffing envelopes with letters signed by herself, soliciting more funds. In the end she had to turn to deep pockets outside the village. She died before the work was completed, but the spire went back up, so straight and true it stops the heart. An inauguration ceremony filled the church as it had not been filled in a long time. At the ceremony, a rumor circulated that the Presbyterian powers were considering letting go of the Rensselaerville church because regular attendance was so small. The closing of churches is hardly a surprising matter but in combination with the completion of the heroic effort to repair the steeple, the rumor created one of those moments of slippage, common in our time of transition, in which you realize you had somehow drifted back into a world that no longer existed. Had we all somehow believed that restoring the steeple would actually stabilize our shifting cultural landscape? The village is convincing. I think perhaps I, for one, did.

When the ceremony was over we all stepped out onto a small flat-stone terrace. I, like many, looked up at the façade and the steeple above, magnificently foreshortened from that perspective. The sky that day was a deep blue, the steeple a brilliant white. I snapped it with my iPhone.

2

Suburbophobia

One summer day a few years ago, when the stream was brown
and racing, I set out across the Hudson River to a village in the
Connecticut Berkshires to visit a friend. Caroline is twenty years my
senior, an interesting interval that makes us a short generation apart.
Generations today are separated by vastly different experiences of
a changing world, but Caroline and I share a language of place-love
that can bridge that gap easily. These languages are not the same as
what linguists look at but are rather skeins of references, usually to
the natural world, regional or even local, that have emotional meaning to people who live there. Paumanok, for example, is my name for
a pre-suburban Long Island place language, a subcategory of mid-
Atlantic, and there are Berkshire and Helderberg, which are related,
belonging to the larger group I think of as Northeastern—but different, like dialects of Italian. If Paumanok speakers say, "The beach
plums are ripe," that evokes not only the dunes where they grow, not
just the plums, and the sweet-sour taste of the deep red-purple jam
that can be made from them, but also continuity going back, not just

through human generations—certain kitchens, certain people, long gone, momentarily alive in the reference to beach plums—but the whole tapestry of a former way of life, now vanished, and, even, the longer history of the place where beach plums grow, back to prehistory as we think of the time of native tribes. (I haven't been able to ascertain whether Long Island tribes used beach plums: they are very sour and require a lot of sugar to become palatable.) There is a special intimacy in using place-language, usually unspoken, and the deepest level of the feeling communicated is of the way place itself transcends, connects. The associations are usually unspoken, their presence more likely conveyed with a glance or an especially tender way of spreading beach plum jam on toast. An equivalent in the Helderbergs might be "The ramps are in," meaning a kind of wild leek that pops up in dense clusters in the forests before almost any other green has arrived, standing out spookily against the dead brown of the forest floor. I'd never heard of ramps when I came here, but knowing beach plum language I had an inkling of what they meant, and that helped me into the local landscape. When a basket of ramps was left anonymously on my porch, I knew that meant more, than, say, zucchinis. Wildness is a part of it. Place-love language can also convey a sense of uncanniness. On a mid-Atlantic coast, crows on the beach, on a windy late October day, are an unusual sight, conveying something reckless afoot, perhaps transgressive. I don't yet know Helderberg well enough to cite an equivalent but am on the lookout.

Caroline and I are both native speakers of mid-Atlantic. Berkshire and Helderberg, respectively, are second languages for each of us: she doesn't know Helderberg at all, while I have only a visitor's smattering of Berkshire. So it was native fluency in mid-Atlantic that provided a language of powerful connection. Yet over time a kind of anxiety, a sense of generational alienation, had begun to undermine this, and not just with Caroline. I had begun to repeatedly have a feeling of my elders, sitting smug, safe, and oblivious in a seemingly

intact world on one side of an abyss, abandoning me to horrid loss
and exile on the other. Caroline perceives the changes in the world
from a perspective that evidently does not require her to question her
beliefs about the landscapes she loves, nor does she feel any necessity
to engage imaginatively with the new one engulfing us. I, in contrast,
feel I have no choice, and that goes deep with me, is indeed the driving force of this whole exploration, an adventure from which I do not
want to turn back. But when I feel generationally abandoned, self-
pity takes over. How could I be stranded in this way, and Caroline
not, when there is only twenty years between us? I can find myself
wanting to strip her beautiful faith in the constancy of the places she
loves from her, forcing her to come with me, even as I keep that faith
for myself in my pocket almost like a secret vice.

And yet, at another time, we will communicate just fine, and I
know that what I really want is company. I want someone to mourn
with me who knows what is being mourned, and maybe a bit of ap-
plause for my struggle to let go of attachments and step into a re-
imagined world from someone who understands the cost. That's not
a longing that goes well with being an explorer.

In the week before going across the river to visit Caroline, I had
been reading *Howards End*, a novel by the English writer E. M. Forster, published in 1910. I hadn't read it since I was a young woman,
when I loved it for affirming the value of the country landscape,
though in English place-love translation. Indeed *Howards End* is a
story written wholly in the language of place-love—and, place-hate,
sometimes. The title is the name of a house and the lands around
it that, while modest enough, represent the old landowning aristocracy of England that originated in feudal times. The novel contains
the phrase for which Forster is most famous: "Only connect!" It is
the deep inner thought of his heroine, Margaret, an urbane person
who learns from Howards End—the place, and the people who live
there—the limits of cultural refinement and, above all, the supreme

importance of a natural connective warmth between human beings that arises out of an older relationship to place and that was fast disappearing in a "commercial age." Human feelings are very much the subject of *Howards End*. The paragon of good in the novel is Ruth Wilcox, the aristocratic owner of Howards End when we first encounter it, who has a mystical connection to the place beyond normal language. Living on the estate, too, are people whose ancestors worked the land, still practicing customs dating from pre-Christian times. The pigs' teeth embedded in the trunk of the wych elm that spreads over the house are the most concise image in the novel of the spiritual vitality of those roots. The foil to that spiritual vitality are Ruth's husband and sons, unsentimental businessmen who don't like Howards End because it has no modern conveniences. The true antagonist, however, the embodiment of the worst of the "commercial age," is the loathsome tide of suburban sameness creeping inexorably out from London toward the house and its lands.

Forster was a humanist and progressive in ways that were daring for his time. And yet for these poor suburbanites he has so little love that he does not even bother to imagine them on the page. When I first read the book, and this second time, too, the question pressed at the edges of my enjoyment: How does he get away with romanticizing feudalism while demonizing democratization, which is surely what that line of approaching sameness was? What struck me this time was the longevity of the attitude. It seems not to have budged one bit in a century, our having passed into an entirely new era notwithstanding. But I saw something else, which I might not have seen had the era not changed: that I loved the village landscape because it was country, but also because of what it wasn't—because it wasn't suburbia, and that not being suburbia had, over time, become a part of the definition of "country" for me. Since I would be spending the night across the river I took *Howards End*, which I had not quite finished, with me.

Soon after my arrival we set out to meet Caroline's friend Kate for lunch at a restaurant in a nearby village. Kate was about twelve years Caroline's junior—that is to say, between us in age—and deeply fluent in Berkshire. Somehow suburban development cropped up in the conversation: how awful it was, and why it is that "Americans"— as if Caroline and Kate and I were not American—feel they have to have a freestanding house on a piece of land. Off they went, the two of them, both with their beautiful old houses and even more soulful gardens, on the emptiness of the suburban dream. All about what a crime the destruction of the countryside was, and not one word about what those houses, those small plots of land, might mean to those who owned them, let alone the fairness of distributing a little to many rather than sticking with a lot for a few. Of course I knew what they meant; they were speaking to my deepest springs of place-love. And yet, wrestling, as I was, with the paradox of *Howards End*, I felt I would blow my top any minute. We were in one of the most fashionable parts of the Berkshires, pastoral though it appeared to be. Didn't they realize that the "countryside" they loved was really a kind of picturesque park, an amenity, a redoubt of privilege? Didn't they see that they hated suburbia because it was an intrusion on that comfortable and exclusive bastion? "Suburbia is an English invention," I said, as a way to catch them off guard in their righteousness—a clever strategy because I knew Englishness had cozy associations of landscape authenticity for them. But then I faltered. I knew from experience that there is no winning against suburbophobia. That night I finished *Howards End*, closing it, for all my quibbles, with satisfaction. Illogical as Forster's assumptions might be, his book had survived the crossing into our new era.

Raymond Williams was a Welsh literary critic who came along a couple of generations after Forster, and who took as his subject the meanings with which we infuse landscape and place. He invented the excellent phrase "structure of feeling," for those powerful combinations of emotions and ideas that we attach to landscape—among other aspects of culture—to the point that we don't even notice them because they have become a part of our emotional and intellectual lives. A structure of feeling to which he paid special attention is the idea, to be found in much literature, of a golden past, as embodied in the memory of an idyllic landscape, in comparison with which the present is degraded. He then showed what the supposedly golden ages really were: never golden. Williams's focus was on landscapes of the past, both real and mythical. The one venture he made into twentieth-century suburbia was coining the trenchant phrase "mobile privatism" for that way of life—but not, as far as I know, examining our contemporary attitudes toward suburbia, or our sense of an earlier golden age, which I find interesting, given that, coming two generations after Forster, he lived well into the period of the suburbanization of England. But that, perhaps, reflects the scholar's wise caution about wading into one's own time. Still, we can surely use Williams's wonderful conception to say that the opinion that country is good and suburbia is bad—which the tone of the phrase "mobile privatism" might be said to reflect—is a structure of feeling deep set in the progressive mind of our times.

Something I admire about Williams is that, despite his commitment to bursting bubbles of illusion with facts, he doesn't mistake his scholarly debunking for the last word. He is engaged with a range of ways of knowing landscape, of which scholarship is just one. For example, he wrote a two-volume novel that begins in geological time, and in which, I have been told, the mountains of Wales are a major character. I confess I have not rushed to read this novel. But I love the way giving the mountains an important part in the novel implicitly acknowledges the ultimately strange yet intimately powerful presence of landscape in our lives, that there is always more to the meaning of landscape than service as a stage set for our doings; that it is always a bit beyond us.

What is especially puzzling to me about the suburbophobic structure of feeling is that it is as rampant in progressive circles as it is among the upper class, especially "old money" landowners who have a natural interest in preserving landscapes not only steeped in family tradition but representing a society in which their position has long been one of privilege. But what could be the roots of suburbophobia in urban progressive people? Forster's political inclinations were courageously advanced for his time, yet he lovingly depicted endangered humanistic values thriving quietly in the aristocratic environment of Howards End. In contemporary America the urban creative class flocks in summertime to country landscapes long beloved as havens by people of wealth, developing Forsteresque attachments to those places alongside a horror of invading suburbia. What could be at stake for them—for us? I ask of myself as much as of anyone else. What is lost for us with the suburban development of the landscape? The answer is many things—beauty, refuge, relief from the city. I wonder, too, if social position doesn't also play a role here, even for this more modest class. Suburbia has been cast by Hollywood as a domain barren of culture and also politically conservative. That's a stereotype, true of some suburbanites and not of others, but it's a widespread assumption. So there is, perhaps, a level on which suburban development says to a creative or intellectual person, "There is no place for you here."

But my guess is that the need for a sense of transcendent providential order that beautiful country can convey is the wellspring of cosmopolitan devotion to pastoral landscapes and antipathy to suburban ones as well. Quite aside from theistic doctrine, the capacity to sense ourselves as part of something larger than ourselves, and, indeed, the need to exercise that capacity, to feed it, to keep it in play in our lives—to be in relation to dimensions of life beyond our comprehension—is an elemental part of our humanity for many of us. It was for Forster surely: I can think of no other explanation for why this atheistic progressive made of a feudal holding a symbol of spiritual health.

The problem with transcendence for progressives is that it is conservative in a profound way. I would venture that *Howards End* expresses a conservativism in Forster, in the sense of valuing what has accumulated over time, and the ways in which it can amount to something more than the sum of its parts, its uses, its price; a conservativism that was at odds with his progressive values yet could be expressed through a relationship to place depicted in *Howards End*; but only because that world was depicted as sufficiently obsolete that issues of power and status, of exclusion and exploitation, were not at play. The actual form of suburbia, in contrast, breaks up landscape into tiny pieces, spreading out indefinitely, undoing the pastoral terrain as context—as something larger than ourselves. It balkanizes an age-old archetype of providential order—much as most progressives would resist that quasi-theistic idea. The pastoral landscape is the last resort of secular humanists in search of a quiet expression of their sense of transcendence—and the suburban formation destroys that. Long-shot speculation? Well, yes. But maybe it opens a tiny chink in the mystery of suburbophobia.

The lecture that was on the tip of my tongue at lunch with Caroline and Kate was about the English origins of American suburbia. In *Bourgeois Utopias*, historian Robert Fishman identifies William Wilberforce, an eighteenth-century British evangelical preacher and crusader for the abolition of slavery, as the founder of the first modern suburban community, outside the farm village of Clapham, not far from London. Its pleasant environment of airy houses surrounded by lawns was an idealized country setting, in an actual working country landscape, but near enough to the city that the men could get there to work. As London grew, becoming an industrial city, it turned, in the eyes of Wilberforce and other religious people, into a cauldron of evil unsuitable for women and children: "The city is bad."

Wilberforce's settlement had communal spaces, but as the suburban idea became more popular these fell away. The prevailing
model became the "villa," surrounded by walls. This was a small-scale
imitation of the aristocratic estate. The driving idea remained that
"the city is bad," physically and also morally: women and children
should be removed to a more wholesome environment. Continental
Europeans, who experienced exactly the same enlargement of their
cities as well as the same cultural changes, didn't recoil in this way
at all. What Anglo-Saxons saw as vices—theater, restaurants, society, and less legitimate activities, too—they saw as attractions. In
Paris, for example, the luxury apartment building, invented for the
rising industrial class, appeared along grand new avenues, such as
the Champs-Élysées. Paris was the arbiter of fashion on the Continent. Suburbanization did not happen in Europe. America, however, though over half a century behind, took up the British moral
loathing of cities: after all, our Puritanism originated in England.
Still, the first waves of suburbanites in twentieth-century America
were of European extraction, descendants of immigrants who had
come across the ocean for jobs. It would seem that just setting foot
on American soil entailed contracting the "city is bad" virus, but then
most nineteenth-century immigrants to America were not coming
from luxury apartments on the Champs-Élysées. Many in fact were
coming from peasant lives in quasi-feudal sectors of Europe, in which
home ownership was beyond the reach of most.

To satisfy my suspicion that the springs of suburbophobia are
lodged in a hidden relationship to providence, I have to trace back
in English history past the villas to the aristocratic model on which
they—unlike Clapham—were based. The villas were not imitating
old landed estates like Howards End. Their model was a new aesthetic, first embraced by some in the old landed aristocracy, and then
taken up in force by the new industrial capitalists, self-made men
who derived their wealth not from the land on which they lived but

from factories in the cities or plantations in faraway colonies. This was an industrial-age severance of work from domestic life, breaking the direct relationship between survival and nature as we live in it. A confusing factor is that, though the industrial barons sought to overthrow the old aristocracy with free-market values and social mobility, they fervently sought to imitate the style of the old estates. On most of these work and life had been intertwined since time immemorial. But it was the newer picturesque style that appealed to the self-made industrialists. This style was the creation of a great generation of British landscape designers who had sprung up in the second half of the eighteenth century; Lancelot "Capability" Brown and Sir Humphry Repton were among the most famous. These geniuses distilled the aesthetic qualities of the older estates, qualities that had evolved out from the requirements of agrarian work and of a feudal social arrangement. Lifting these qualities off their practical foundation, they created idealized facsimiles, evocative landscape romances that looked like the "real thing" but weren't. And indeed there were differences. On older estates, as they had evolved over time, the cow pasture came up to the house, separated from it, perhaps, by only a small formal garden. Villages inhabited by the people who worked the land were located where they had originated in the mists of time. Fields fell out in formations that had, in some instances, first been laid out in prehistoric times. In the new facsimiles, terrain was artificially harmonized and eyesores removed, cows and rough pasture put at a distance at which they are pretty, a lake created where it would improve the composition, fields tailored to visual pleasure, too, less ideal elements excised or made over. Indeed, in one famous case a whole village was removed, because it spoiled the view from the great house. The style was called picturesque, a word that in itself conveys separation, a frame: "picturelike"—not a farmer's term, certainly, but it was entirely suitable for estates that were not in themselves the source of their owners' wealth but principally built for pleasure.

Indeed, pictures literally were the models for the idealizing aesthetic, in particular swooningly romanticized pastoral scenes by the French painter Claude Lorrain.

The villas, the first stabilized model of English suburbia, were, in turn, small-scale imitations of the facsimile estates. Each villa was a compartmentalized landscape, strictly separate from the realm of work. The picturesque aesthetic was miniaturized by British horticulurist John Claudius Loudon. An ocean of such tiny walled landscapes spread out inexorably, enveloping the old countryside, extensions of the ever enlarging industrial cities of England: the gray force that was approaching Howards End. The breakup into miniature units destroyed the continuousness of the natural world and the long evolving relationship of people to it, as evoked by Forster.

This destruction of a world in which work and life are intertwined in an ancient landscape overtly animates Forster's antipathy to suburbia in *Howards End*. He seems to be saying of the modern world, "We need something else, we had something else, and whatever that is we can't live without it as full human beings," and then he cooks up a mysterious world of pigs' teeth in the wych elm and an imbedded relation to nature with its origins in the mists of time, without noticing that he was embracing a remnant of feudalism. Are not we latter-day American suburbophobes of a piece with Forster? Maybe we need something more, too, but don't have a way to define it in our political and social universe. Is not the phobia, at bottom, a fear of exposure to the truths of modern times that finds a quiet, sub rosa expression in the language of feelings about landscape? Forster created a place-language that arose out of a visceral sense that the ancient country of England was good and suburban development was bad. I am no scholar of English attitudes, but it seems likely to me that this structure of feeling had been in the cultural air for some time before Forster brilliantly expressed it in his novel. The social history of our landscape is very different, but it seems likely that in our reaction against suburbia there are strands of the Fosteresque contradictory thirst as well.

Over here in America, Andrew Jackson Downing developed both architectural forms and garden designs for suburban Americans: he is regarded as the founder of landscape architecture in the United States. His first book, which drew heavily on Loudon's designs, was published in 1841. He was a passionate democrat. He hoped his standardized designs for suburban houses—the Italianate, the Gothic, the Bracketed—would bring to the common man a dignity long denied him. He also believed in large urban parks for a similar reason. His partner was Calvert Vaux. Downing died very young, in an accident. After Downing's death Vaux entered a partnership with Frederick Law Olmsted, a landscape designer who became famous for his large pastoral urban parks. Olmsted was also a passionate democrat. On a trip overseas he was impressed by the picturesque aesthetic developed for the English estates, but was repelled by the social inequity of the aristocratic system. With Vaux he designed Central Park in New York in which a picturesque environment was open to all. Olmsted adored the natural landscape, but one could actually argue that, hero today to urbanists and suburbophobes alike, he was a great suburbophile and in fact had a hand in inventing the archetype. Indeed, he laid down the suburban ideal in the creation of Riverside, Illinois, on the outskirts of Chicago, a rolling landscape created from scratch on the flat prairie, planted with quantities of imported trees and bushes and laid out with winding roads that unfolded scenes in the most pleasing, seemingly pastoral way—a creation as severed from the continuous providential world of working country as could be. Toward the end of his life, he lived in Brookline, a rich early suburb of Boston. Brookline is famous for resisting annexation but Olmsted did not see cities and suburbs as opposed but rather as necessary to each other. He did not design Brookline but he admired the qualities that had evolved there of comfortable houses on grassy leafy plots with railroad access to dense central Boston.

Olmsted did not hate cities. He understood that cities, with their economic and cultural dynamism, were essential to the age and sought to civilize them—perfect them—with parks, and also suburban outskirts that provided relief from density. Still, suburbophobe that I am, I have to laugh at the fact that Olmsted not only was a suburbophile but made significant contributions to the suburban aesthetic. I laugh because of the way this embrace of suburban ideals collides with the sacred structure of feeling with regard to cities and suburbia among urbanists and country lovers alike: myself, for example. I laugh because these attributes are so indelible in myself: at the fact that, for all my earnest efforts to unmask old structures of feeling and to reimagine the contemporary landscape in a forward-looking way, it remains that if I were to climb the beautifully refurbished steeple of the village church and, looking down the valley, see McMansions there, I would suffer.

3

Gettysburg

Early one Memorial Day morning, I was walking through the village when a neighbor driving by slowed to a halt to say hello. We chatted and then he exhorted me to attend a gathering at the war monument in the graveyard at eleven. A village can be like that: snagging you. "No way," I thought—I had my plan for the day—but then I went. The civic graveyard of Rensselaerville was established by the township in the second half of the nineteenth century on high land, above the village. It is laid out in the style of idealized country that was perfected by Frederick Law Olmsted: a loose assembly of graves in a grassy, quite hilly expanse under trees. The monument is a small obelisk set at the highest point, at the edge of a steep drop. About fifteen people had already congregated around it when I arrived. After I found my place among them, I noticed that it was specifically a Civil War monument. Only then did I remember that Memorial Day honors the casualties of that war specifically. I had unthinkingly reverted to the notion that the veterans of all wars were equally honored. I say "reverted" because, in fact, I had looked into this matter of the evolution of Memorial Day in some detail. Yet the knowledge had somehow remained abstract, as if in a compartment separate from a Memorial Day observance in the village into which I had been unexpectedly snagged. The Civil War seemed very long ago and far away, and I rather regretted coming.

Then the names of the local casualties were read off and the Civil War didn't feel far away at all. This closeness of past time and people is a characteristic of the village—most villages, probably. "Do you think they knew what they were fighting for?" whispered a friend standing next to me. Then we sang "The Battle Hymn of the Republic," as ever rousing, disconcertingly bellicose, magnificent but slightly off its rocker. Then came the Gettysburg Address. After landscape, we Americans rely on words for identity, another reminder of a shallowness in our history. The Declaration of Independence, the Constitution, the Gettysburg Address are weavings floated over a void. With the reading of the address the Gettysburg battlefield was suddenly present, as if, in a game of historical mother-may-I, it had taken a huge step toward us behind our backs. Then someone read Whitman's "When Lilacs Last in Dooryard Bloom'd," an elegy for Lincoln, another almost sacred word-skein that connects us. In it is the image of a train carrying Lincoln's body home across the prairie, and this landscape, too, suddenly seemed present in the village. I could see the train, I could hear the whistle.

Lilacs grow in the village, but for me Whitman's dooryard evokes my milder native landscape, near sand and water. The image of the lilacs worked in me like a medical tracing medium that showed up arteries to innermost feelings, all the while bringing American historical experience into relief, too. In forgetting that Memorial Day specifically commemorates the Civil War dead, even though I knew this well at one time, I repeated a public forgetting so insistent that, even as the Gettysburg Address, exhorting us not to forget, was memorized by American schoolchildren for a century, we forgot.

The story of a horror faced, and fought, at great cost, and then both horror and cost dropped into oblivion and replaced with charm in some ways induces a deeper despair than the horror of slavery, which incited the battle.

The holiday was first called Decoration Day; it was established in 1868 to honor the Union casualties in the war to end slavery, in May, when the battlefields were bursting with flowers. It was celebrated by northerners and black southerners, who participated enthusiastically. Most white southerners ignored Decoration Day, honoring the Confederate dead in autumn, mourning also the old ways of Southern life that had been undone by defeat. However, the North soon saw the need for postwar commercial ties to the white South, and a desire for interregional reconciliation became strong. In "Race and Reunion," historian David Blight has documented how the northern political and commercial establishment tactfully forgot that slavery had been the reason the war was fought. White southerners eased the lapse by pretending that they had never believed in slavery in the first place—that it had been on the way out in any event. Part of why this alternative interpretation of very recent history was possible was that many northerners, while horrified by slavery, were uneasy with the idea of racial equality. The historian Alan Brinkley wrote in "An Unfinished Nation" that it was "a pervasive belief among many of even the most liberal whites that African Americans were inherently inferior." The banner of social equality was carried by the abolitionists, a relatively small group. The intellectual historian Louis Menand has shown that many leading northern intellectuals of the day—Oliver Wendell Holmes among them—viewed the abolitionists as religious zealots while others actually embraced a belief in white superiority. Louis Agassiz, the eminent Harvard scientist, for example, was obsessed with proving it through measurements of black and white craniums. Slavery, and even suffrage, was one thing: social equality was another. Under these conditions, the quiet retirement of slavery as the leading cause of the war was not politically difficult to pull off in the North. Nor was there much northern resistance as Reconstruction was rolled back in the South, and white dominance reasserted through segregation and a system of sharecropping that, in many ways, replicated the conditions of slavery—arrangements that would remain unchallenged for a century.

To facilitate forgetting, Decoration Day was unofficially renamed Memorial Day in many places, North and South, beginning in 1882, and rededicated to commemorating the casualties on both sides. (The renaming did not become official until after World War II.) To honor both sides in a tragic divisive war seems, at first glance, a reasonable and reconciling change until one reads in *Race and Reunion* that, in the South, black people were asked not to attend Memorial Day celebrations. They were to be excluded because their presence would dishonor the Confederate dead. That fact jerks the entire reconciliation into a different focus, exposing piercingly what beliefs were served when we turned the Civil War into a romantic fratricidal tragedy brought on by obscure causes, which had been mercifully forgotten. Fields came into it. The most powerful image of reunion is a photograph by Mathew Brady of white veterans from the opposing sides—the blue and the gray, with the black nowhere in sight—shaking hands across a half-tumbled stone wall in one of those mid-Atlantic fields, lonely under the stars, gentle, innocent above all, where they had battled.

In both the North and South, the battlefields themselves went on being used as they always had been, with farmers turning up skulls now and then. Land was sold or altered as needed. Then, in the 1890s, a movement arose to preserve the fields as they had been at the time of battle. This was the first major effort at landscape preservation in the United States. Though preserving anything, let alone landscapes, was hard to argue for in a frontier nation, the movement was successful. In the last years of the nineteenth century, the major battlefields were acquired by various organizations and parties to be preserved for posterity. When, in 1916, the National Park Service was formed, first to save ancient native sites—our only true antiquity—and otherwise our spectacular wilderness landscapes, the battlefields passed into its care. Indeed, over time they became, arguably, our most tenderly moving national monuments.

Meanwhile the Park Service observed the spirit of reunion by leaving slavery out of all its curatorial material, on-site plaques, and ranger talks. The rationale—offered in the 1990s when the policy was finally challenged—was that the mandate of the service was to offer recreation and enjoyment, maybe some education, but not to upset people. The presentation should be patriotic, pleasurable, suitable for families. You wanted people to be comfortable, to have a good time. That ruled out what is probably still our most disturbing, divisive subject.

Curated in this tactful way, the battlefields, like the war overall, became mythical. Gettysburg especially is one of the most popular of our historical sites, a great destination for families. It and other seemingly remembering landscapes, so pent up with forgetting, over time took on a meaning that seems almost independent of their actual historical significance. Rather than conjuring scenes of horror, much less recalling for us the crack in our national foundation that was slavery, the battlefields somehow became touchstones of the American soul. They, not sites of Native American civilizations, or of colonial settlements, or of the Revolution, are the closest we come to a past about which we have mystical feelings. Does not the roll call of our Civil War battlefields—Manassas, Antietam, Bull Run, Chancellorville, Shiloh—trace directly into our complicated American place-love, mixing fate with noble heroism? It's as if the nobility of the cause of ending slavery and the heroism of the sacrifice of life to do that were lifted out of their circumstances and blended into an intoxicating mixture of tragedy and innocence extracted completely from its historical origins—and then the sites themselves became permeated with that peculiar delight.

As it happened, business took me to the city of Gettysburg just a few weeks after I attended the Memorial Day event in the village. There I visited the battlefield for the first time. Given the overlap of both landscape and one of our most sacred skeins of words, combined with actual military significance—at Gettysburg the war turned in favor of the North—not to mention the intoxicating mystical elixir in which the actual causes of the war were erased, to all of which I was not immune, the visit had about it an aura of pilgrimage. I took in the main battlefield, sitting on a boulder under an old oak on the high ground that had been held by the Union. It overlooked a series of wide, generous fields, golden with hay in that season, partitioned by wooden fences, that led successively to a faraway blue-gray ridge in the distance. In the fatal assault known as Pickett's Charge, Lee's Confederate infantry charged from the ridge across the fields toward the Union forces. Though it's a good long way, people like to follow in the footsteps of the Confederate soldiers. Sitting under the oak, I watched a group of boys approach, having evidently come the whole distance across, now panting as they struggled up the last stretch of hayfield, to collapse in laughter at my feet under the oak. It was all so lovely, and how moving to see the boys anointed into the national soul: something important would be carried on. The reproductions on sale in the gift shop were lovely: I bought a fetching satchel— graceful and honest; enchantingly quaint. On it the Confederate and Union flags were embossed, staves crossed.

The Battle of Gettysburg had been going on for more than two days before Pickett's Charge, with many skirmishes and engagements in sequestered meadow, under rock face, along intricate forest path, on secondary ridges, across tumbled walls under oaks: all dear scenes. I wandered around entranced—with the scenes themselves and with the confusing alloy of emotions they provoked. Only when felt as a landscape of avoided memories could the magnetic fascination of Gettysburg as a place be fully explained. There was the deflection of slavery and the forgetting of the cause for which the battle had been fought, both of which were layered into that landscape. But there was also the casualty count itself, which was in no way romantic. At Gettysburg, fifty thousand men died in three days; Lincoln spoke at a scene that was beyond words, but also a scene of shock. The kind of warfare that happened there had been seen a few years earlier in faraway Crimea: Europe was still struggling with the shock of that. But certainly nothing like it had been experienced on this continent until the Civil War. The war we later came to see as quaint was in fact horrifyingly modern, one of the first glimpses the world had of industrial-age warfare. A major improvement in weaponry was the rifling of gun bores, greatly accelerating the speed at which ammunition was fired. Rifled muskets were so powerful that shot bounced when it hit the ground. Gunners would "graze," aiming just in front of a line so that solid shot scattered into the enemy every which way, causing far more damage than direct hits. Rifled cannons sent canisters filled with shot over the enemy's head where they burst, raining down hot metal—what was later called shrapnel. Medical science had few resources with which to respond to wounds never before seen. The principal remedy was amputation. There has long been a myth about the Civil War—and Gettysburg in particular—that the North won because it had superior weapons created with Yankee know-how in Northern factories. In particular it has been believed that the Winchester repeater, an early semiautomatic rifle, won the day for the Union at Gettysburg. Actually the Northern generals rejected the repeater as newfangled: the few at Gettysburg were acquired privately. As for rifling weaponry, the historian Allen Guelzo has shown that both sides had rifled weaponry and both suffered from it. Casualties at Gettysburg were about equal: around 23,000 Union soldiers died, nearly half. The Civil War casualty count has been estimated at around 618,000, a threshold beyond which lay the World Wars of the twentieth century. At Hiroshima alone, 129,000 Japanese died, a bit more than double what Lincoln saw at Gettysburg eighty-two years before. The specter of nuclear war, to which industrial warfare led, is implicit in those lovely fields. How hard it is to see radical change as it's happening—and even a century and a half later! How falsely reductive old landscapes can be: how blinding. What is it we preserved when we made a national monument of those fields?

At Gettysburg, it occurred to me that our infatuation with the Civil War has masked an awareness of bottled-up pain, a need to know it and face it in all its complications—eventually. What else could explain our undying obsession with this piece of our history? I began to think that, for all its obscuring functions, our romance with the war ultimately served a wish to truly meet ourselves when we were ready. Seen that way, the romance of the Civil War is not, after all, an evasive fantasy but a preservative force in the most constructive sense. Is not knowing ourselves as fully as possible the sacred purpose of all kinds of preservation? Is not landscape itself—whether purposefully preserved or merely lasting beyond its time—also, ultimately, most precious to us not as an elegiac reminder of the past but as a mirror of ourselves, then and now, in all our complicated humanity? If we are not yet hungry for the knowledge a place holds, well, then, the place will let us preserve that gift in fantasies until we really need it.

Surely the usefulness of romantic salves has passed. We can thank it for helping preserve the battlefields, but now we must put these places to a more difficult use: a use that is their true treasure. The two aspects of American exceptionalism that really hold up are that we stand out among all modern democracies for having a foundation in slavery, and that we introduced the far extreme of modern weaponry to the world. That is the chord, the thrum of meaning in our Civil War battlefields. Blended into the chord is the human capacity for violence, but disguised as sweet music. One note has cloaked the violence of slavery in pastoral innocence, the other has wrapped industrial-scale massacre in a myth of a morally superior North's heroic know-how. But also in there, the third note in the chord, is the Gettysburg Address to which we have hitherto been so extraordinarily deaf. That is there too. The genius of landscape is that it can hold registers of meaning in relation to one another, no matter how contradictory they might seem to be when apart.

Now we can free the chord from what has become obscuring noise. I propose this not as a way of urging us to wallow in the evil embedded in our history but to understand ourselves in our full complexity: to have a knowledge of ourselves that is the equal of the predicaments we have created. This attitude toward the past is inherently forward-looking: is optimistic. It is different from the uncovering of hitherto hidden historical crimes, important as that is. This way of looking back is a first step in making the gift of the past we need now accessible. The fields at Gettysburg are an especially good place to begin to look for it, but the gift is everywhere around us, especially in our older landscapes; paradoxically those least changed: especially, I would say, in our fields.

Later, home again in the village, I began to see something of Gettysburg in the local fields. It came to me as an insight in some way long known that the powerful attraction of the common American field is in part drawn from the powerful deflection with which we made the Civil War romantic. The plainer, the lonelier, and the more innocent the eastern American field, the more charged it is likely to be with latent disturbance. We feel that our agrarian landscape expresses pure beginnings as yeoman farmers, but, in fact, the supreme feature and legacy of our agrarian history is slavery. We see our ordinary fields as a remembrance of simpler times, but in fact a goodly part of their inherent meaning is the most difficult part of our history. We see the field as a kind of solid footing in an honorable past that can help us as we struggle in contemporary societal mires, when actually those fields are meaningful to us precisely because they *are* the mire: beautifully so though they may often be.

After my visit to Gettysburg these hidden complications were there in the fields around the village, even the raggedy ones, like shoulders moving under the land, like a living interior terrain, revealed by the wind in full crops, by the corn stubble in snow, in the way golden hay takes the light, in those cryptic patterns made by cut hay lying flat, in the softly dark line between field and woods, so articulate of the delicate balance between effort and loss. Gettysburg had given me a new lens. What was revealed didn't erase other planes of meaning, not the triumph of settlement or transparency through that to prehistory, as we call it. All of our American country places, but fields especially, are little Gettysburgs, alive with this complicated attraction and aversion, horror and romance, shame and pride that reverberates through our societal life—forever occluding and revealing. This is our treasure.

Of course, the local fields were just fields, too. It's always important in reading landscape to let it return to just what it is, the ground we stand on, the underpinning. No one interpretation can supersede that. Still, when I allowed the Gettysburg complications into my experience of local fields, however faintly, they came fully alive. They no longer seemed pent up with unexpressed meaning, but rather had become eloquent and even at ease. This seemed important to me not just because I wanted to read them as well as possible but also because this deeper reading helps me approach the question of what fields mean today as we cross into a new era once again. Indeed the sudden freshness of the history of slavery in recent times may be a part of that new experience. Is it not just this crossing that has definitively invalidated the old pastoral romance?

That we have become doubly separated from agrarian times does not make the agrarian landscape less important to us. It is possible it has become more important. What is different is that the need for romance—the usefulness of romance—is over. What we really need from landscape now is truth. I don't want to spoil our everyday landscape pleasures by insisting on criminal associations. I pursue these avenues of landscape meaning because I think they can lead to a kind of moral sophistication that is profoundly aesthetic. Where our romantic deflection of the truth may have served some good purpose once—the glory of the romantic view of nature infused with transcendence, for example—it now seems to stupefy more than awaken. It now seems hackneyed. What we need now is as deep and complex a sense of our humanity as possible: to really know ourselves, because it is going to be out of that self-knowledge that an effective response to our latter-day predicaments will come.

After preservation of battlefields came preservation of wilderness, as if we were moving backward in time. It started with the Antiquities Act of 1906, promoted by President Theodore Roosevelt to preserve western sites of ancient native culture, such as Chaco Canyon, where a long extinct ancient Pueblo people had left artifacts, but also extraordinary landscape features such as Devils Tower, a topographical formation in Wyoming. It captures something of the meaning of wildernesses for us that the law that initiated saving them lumped them with ruins and artifacts: with "antiquities." For wilderness in a way is our antiquity, that blank page in place of the deep memory through which older cultures derive a sense of themselves. As the National Park Service, formed soon thereafter, began to acquire more and more sites of natural beauty, it found it necessary to erase signs of native occupation because they detracted from the "untouched" quality of the place. Yosemite Valley, for example, had long been populated by Native Americans; it was a landscape in the fully human sense, altered by cultivation, in fact: not a wilderness at all. As the environmental historian William Cronon has shown, the Service hustled natives out of the valley and erased the signs of their long presence there so that Yosemite could be presented as the iconic wilderness it wasn't. The question arises as to whether this policy was of a piece with the Service's curatorial omission of slavery at Civil War sites, in that the presence of natives in the valley would also unavoidably raise the disturbing history of their near erasure from the continent by European settlers. But a public conscience with regard to Native Americans as a living people at the time of European settlement—as opposed to extinct peoples who had left ruins—developed only later in the century.

Though we got around to preserving wildernesses only in the early twentieth century, the invention of wilderness as American myth goes back to the nineteenth. Indeed, wilderness served as a romantic symbol before the Civil War, developed to create a unified national identity in the hope of staving the war off. In the absence of antiquity, what else could transcend the long deflected contradiction between democracy and slavery? The founding fathers of this ingenious effort were painters: Thomas Cole, Albert Bierstadt, Frederic Church, Worthington Whittredge: a group that came to be known as the Hudson Valley School. The names may not be household terms, but the landscapes these painters created are so familiar that you barely have to look at them. One glance, and you are bored. Many of these paintings were very large, encased in heavy gilt frames. The scenes inside the frames were grand in what can seem to us today to be an overblown way, suggesting triumphant chorales in the sky. They were, in a sense, our first movies, though it was the audience that supplied the motion. Displayed in museums with red curtains surrounding them in theaterlike fashion, they were popular, crowds filing by.

We take these paintings literally—that's partly why they bore us—but the painters, and probably those early viewers, too, were well aware of complexity. Frederic Church even painted one, *Our Banner in the Sky*, in which the Stars and Stripes makes a ghostly appearance against a fiery sunset—it was painted in 1861 in response to the Confederate attack on Fort Sumter. His many paintings of Niagara show the falls as a great divide across the canvas, suggesting the catastrophic rift into which we were falling. A second level of tension in the paintings was between the glorification of virgin wilderness and the industrialization that was, in this period, despoiling wilderness. Both these counterpoint meanings were forgotten over time, which is why the paintings began to seem dishonest to a latter-day eye, or merely sentimental. Where they glorify natural splendor, we think, "What about mining?" Where they insist on innocence, we ask, "What about the genocide of natives?" That last thought, probably, was not in the consciousness of the painters, but both slavery and the depredations of industrialization most certainly were. If you look for that dark energy in the paintings, they change. They become anything but boring. They become complex images of a conflicted identity afraid of coming apart.

Some painters of this period were attracted to quieter, humble pastoral scenes, generally on smaller canvases: John Frederick Kensett, George Inness, and Albert Pinkham Ryder among them. These quiet cultivated landscapes were also very different from industrial actuality, and there is an implicit melancholy in them that acknowledges an end. This was the beginning of the elegy for agrarian times. Still, the quieter paintings also to my mind draw a charge from deflecting the immense reality of industrialization: from looking away. That desire to look away lasted long into the twentieth century. One could argue that nostalgia for preindustrial times still permeates how we see country landscapes today—what makes them "scenic" or soothing for us. Most of these paintings, even the ones of grand wildernesses, are northeastern, though some are of western scenes. None of this canon, however, portrays a southern landscape. This is a strange omission in one sense because the South was the one part of the country that was actually still principally agrarian. But how could a painter sensitive to the state of the country paint a southern scene without slavery pulsing in the brushstrokes?

George Inness was a master of the quiet melancholy scene, but an exception is *The Lackawanna Valley*, painted in 1855. Commissioned by a railroad company, it nonetheless defiantly portrays a train passing through pastoral countryside with a field of burned stumps in the foreground, a hellish landscape that railroads had wrought. An irony is that we have become so nostalgic about trains that a viewer can miss the raw statement of the stumps, seeing instead a tranquil scene with an old-fashioned locomotive as an integral part of the pastoral environment. It was the railroads that were the first and most obvious reconfiguring force of our industrial transformation. Post–Civil War paintings in the quieter style are inherently more harmonious in content, modest in particulars, expressing an accepting melancholy rather than protesting. I never find work of the quiet period sentimental. They are always mysterious to me, secretive, painful yet moving. In fact, when I first saw paintings in this style, as a very young person, I was taken aback by how closely these painters captured my own perceptions of the American landscape. That was before I understood myself to be managing a double reality in landscape beauty, personally but as an American, too.

Another effect as industrialism roared forward was that economic energy was drained from the rural world, which became marginal. The wistful quality in many of the quieter paintings could be attributed entirely to that. I had loved them first because I thought they captured the sweetness of the mid-Atlantic scene, and that the elegiac feeling even derived from a sense of impending disappearance and loss that is still true of our rural landscapes. But now I love them more for the complicated deflection of fear, and guilt, and the rumble of violence that is latently in play, to my mind, in even the quietest—or maybe it's just danger. Many were painted in a period in which the Civil War was the immediate past—indeed some say that the war gave us our first sense of a past—a period in which we were both diligently forgetting slavery and reeling from the scale of modern mechanized slaughter; caught. Meanwhile the same mechanical technology was reconfiguring the country not only physically but on every level of societal life. How effective these dreamy little paintings are, eclipsing the plantation and replacing it with lost innocence. For me these paintings are full of mourning mixed with a sense of vulnerability. Their power is an expression of longing for something that is inextricable from horror. It is as if they look both forward and backward with nowhere to go, so they go inward. In some of them the scene can almost seem to be disappearing. Quite a few are of a shore, but the meeting of beach and water in these seems to me healing rather than fissuring, less lonely than the gap between eras in which we were caught. Then, as now.

4

Natchez

W hat are the uses of the past in a nation committed to growth and inclusion, and how do they change as we move from one era to another? The fields of Gettysburg had given an answer: they help us to grasp the complexity of our nature, the predicaments it creates and their continuum from past to future. What about architecture? Natchez, famous for its antebellum mansions, was a place where the question could be put rather efficiently. I spent my first night at Monmouth, a planter's mansion in the grand neoclassical style, with big columns and a pediment and large social rooms, which had been turned into a luxurious inn. My room was in a former slave cabin on the grounds. The thread count in the sheets was high, and I could light the fire by flipping a switch by my bed.

The next day I began diligently making my rounds of the Natchezian mansions. The profusion, I learned, had to do with the fact that the plantations themselves, the cotton fields, had been across the Mississippi River, in Louisiana, where the land was low, flat, and rich, and the air was hot and humid. Planters had preferred to build their actual homes, their gargantuan extravaganzas, on the breezy cliffs on the Mississippi side around the small city of Natchez. The only surrounding land was for private parks. As a result, the mansions were relatively close together. Over time, the city grew up around them in a variety of styles—Victorian, Edwardian, twentieth-century bungalow—among which the white elephants soared out of scale, to topsy-turvy effect. This created a kind of architectural nuttiness that is a good antidote to the sanctimony of the heritage trade, the principal "industry" there. As for the mansions, there is something surreal about the sheer profusion, combined with a sameness in presentation: mint juleps, the theme from *Gone With the Wind*. Courtesy of Rhett and Scarlett, the antebellum mansion has become a kind of church of romantic love. The sites were, I learned, popular for weddings: a good business. Sometimes black couples made that choice, too. So heck! Who is complaining? Interior decoration was also a theme. Meals of many courses served in period style were a moneymaker. I was, on my first visit, almost perfectly confused as I pursued my inquiry into the meaning of the architectural landscape in the United States and how that changes over time.

For most of our history preservation of architecture has been a quixotic cause, the province of idealists bucking the mainstream in a forward-looking country. The very first efforts to preserve had to do with patriotic shrines—Independence Hall, Mount Vernon. The earliest movement to save buildings for their aesthetic value was fragmentary, largely on the part of daughters of planters hoping to save family mansions after the Civil War—a crusade amid ruin and defeat. An interest in the architecture of New England sprouted around the same time: indeed, some say the "idea" of New England was invented then. The next nationwide flurry of interest in preserving architecture for aesthetic reasons arose in the Depression, when the Works Progress Administration set unemployed architects to compiling an inventory of worthy American buildings. So a federal interest in preservation of architecture in the United States came largely after ancient ruins, battlefields, and wilderness. Antebellum mansions were a big feature of the WPA inventory. The National Trust for Historic Preservation, an offshoot of the WPA effort, was established after the Second World War. Its first purchase was Woodlawn, a Virginian plantation. You can't really say that federally sponsored preservation in the United States was fixated on the antebellum period. Yet it lists in that direction in a way that is perplexing. After all, this is our most controversial architecture. Why would a mind-set that seeks to admire the past be attracted to our least admirable period? Still, I have to admit that when I wanted to get to the bottom of the uses of architectural preservation in the United States I headed for Natchez.

One could say that preservation as we know it today started informally in Natchez, with roots in that first impulse after the Civil War to preserve a vanishing southern past, but much later and in a much different spirit. First a little history. Before the Civil War, Natchez had more millionaires per capita than any other city in the country, the fortunes made from growing cotton across the river. The period of postwar ruin, however, extended well into the twentieth century. This was a long stretch in an economic desert, broken by a few bursts of prosperity—oil in the 1920s, for example. But for most of its post–Civil War history Natchez was as if lost in time, and never more so than in the Depression. It was in that period that a group of establishment women, whose families were desperate for money, decided to open their mansions for a few weeks in spring, for a fee, widely advertising the event as the "Pilgrimage" and identifying Natchez as a place "Where the Old South Still Lives." That tagline was an inspiration—the "Old South" was not yet an established idea. The first Pilgrimage was moderately successful. Then *Gone With the Wind* was published, establishing the Old South in the American imagination. After that the Pilgrimage—a yearly event to this day—became a hit. NATCHEZ WHERE THE OLD SOUTH STILL LIVES was emblazoned on signs welcoming you to town.

In the novel *Gone With the Wind*, Margaret Mitchell's Tara is a planter's cottage. The vernacular form is, typically, an inherently modest, one-story structure, usually on stilts with a wide-pitched roof and a veranda running all around it, reflecting climate and blending naturally into the landscape. But David O. Selznick wanted a grand Tara in the mode of the antebellum mansions we now all associate with the "Old South." There is a very big difference. In Natchez, for example, before the cotton gin made mass production of cotton possible, most farmers grew indigo on small plantations hacked out of the woods on the irregular land around town, working in the fields alongside a few slaves, their homes modest planter's cottages, the slaves living close. The antebellum mansion, in contrast, is the architecture of industrial-scale agricultural operations, manned by armies of slaves picking cotton that was then deseeded in cotton gins for international trade, producing vast fortunes for planters who, in the case of Natchezian planters, in any event, lived far from the scene of production. The first way of life had its cruelties, to be sure, but it had an intermixing humanity completely missing in the second: a kind of shadow society of "darky balls" and "darky hunts"; a number of freedmen in town, including one who was a slave owner himself—Natchezians love to point that out; a weekly market in town at which slaves sold produce they had raised themselves; and, indeed, intimacy between the races, self-evident in the population. It's this relational way of life that the novel *Gone With the Wind* romanticizes, presenting its white characters as belonging to a benevolent, age-old aristocracy, in close, even loving relationships with the black people they enslave, a fantasy, yes, but nonetheless one derived from a social and economic reality that was entirely different from the fantasy represented by the grand architectural style of Tara in the movie. The first is like romanticizing the past at Howards End. The second is like roman-ticizing the Holocaust—perhaps not quite, but closer than not.

The people who built the mansions, far from local aristocracy, were mostly northern rascals, speculators, and adventurers who flocked to Natchez seeking to make their fortunes in cotton. Most passed over the irregular land around town for cheap, flat, rich swampy land across the Mississippi in Louisiana. They assembled armies of slaves to drain the land and then work it, some straight from Africa, brought upriver from the market in New Orleans, others "seasoned," meaning born in captivity, or at least having ex-perienced captivity and therefore familiar with the rules, and what was expected of them. Seasoned slaves were far preferable; many marched south from the big market in Alexandria, Virginia, along a route that came to be known as the Natchez Trace. The plantations in Louisiana were run by overseers enjoined to get the most out of slaves as possible: working them to death, literally, was not uncom-mon. The phrase "sold down the river" was coined in response to the disappearance of people into these plantations. What the Natchez story trenchantly demonstrates is that slavery in the United States got very much worse before it was abolished. This later version was the formative force that created Natchez as the mecca of our archi-tectural heritage that it became.

The first mansion of the lordly type—and it is said in Natchez to be the first in the South—was Auburn, built in 1812, in a mixture of Georgian and federal styles, by a carpenter who had left New York after standing trial for murder—he was acquitted but ostracized—taking with him his tools and standard architectural pattern books, which included the classical orders. It has big columns, a portico, and lovely tall windows almost to ground level. Then came Rosalie, Gloucester (acquired and expanded by the federalist governor of the Mississippi Territory, Winthrop Sargent, from Massachusetts), Lin-den, Mt. Repose, Holly Hedges, Arlington, and Glenburnie, all in variations on the federal or Georgian style. The next batch was built in the more austere Greek Revival style, symbolizing democracy and American independence from Britain. Natchez, a British colony into the first four years after the Revolution, was late in adopting this architectural fashion, but then it caught on big: Melrose, Choctaw, Magnolia Hall, Stanton Hall, Harper House, and Homewood were all in the Greek Revival style. But the cotton trade was a boom-and-bust affair. A lot of millionaires went bust, sometimes just a few years after moving into their mansions. It was a rags-to-riches time, but riches-to-rags, too. Then the war came and it was all over. Tricking ourselves into seeing these largely Yankee fortune hunters and their nouveau-riche extravaganzas as symbols of a timeless, tragic Southern nobility is, perhaps, one use of the past.

The heritage trade, catering to outsiders, may take a reverent tone in mansion presentation. But Natchez itself, though quite ready to trade on the currency of tragic aristocracy, is in its own culture much closer to the boom-and-bust mentality. A jaunty tone pervades, with piratical overtones, an attitude that resists easy stereotypes and loves stories that show people as wily and out for themselves. The tale of the founding of the Pilgrimage in particular is told, by the very founders and their descendants, with a touch of delight in a scam: How wrong the husbands were to think no one would come see a few shabby old houses in the depths of the Depression! And how they flocked! This trait holds for both races. Black Natchezians, like white, will give you a warning glance if you veer in the direction of piety, will talk of the mixed-race whorehouse that once existed or that black slaveholder who beat his slaves and also his mother. The races know each other well in Natchez. The population has stayed steady around 17,000 more or less, since the end of the Civil War, with most black Natchezians descended from slaves and much of the white establishment, as it was still constituted at the time of my visits, descended from slaveholders.

Under the charming, rascally insistence on the mercurial nature of human beings lies a violent history persisting well into the twentieth century. Natchez is, of course, a part of Mississippi, the scene of the racially motivated murders of Emmett Till, Medgar Evers, and James Chaney, Andrew Goodman, and Michael Schwerner, to mention some of the most famous atrocities. In Natchez itself, George Metcalf, a member of the NAACP who tried to integrate the local factories, died when a bomb went off in his truck. Wharlest Jackson, also a member of the NAACP, died by car bomb. The murderers were never found but the FBI and locals suspected the local permutation of the KKK called the Silver Dollar Group, which consisted largely of people who had come to Natchez for factory jobs and work in the paper mills in the 1950s. But older white Natchez, retiring into the culture of ambiguity, did nothing to resist the violence. Almost all Natchezians would start blocking, often with humor, if they thought you were about to say something simplistic about race in Natchez, but there was a signature sadness beneath the black version of Natchezian jauntiness that did not exist at all in the otherwise similar white air: not one bit. White insouciance, in contrast, was untroubled except in one regard. If you said the word "slavery" you could clear the room. One Pilgrimage founder literally ran when I posed a question with that word in it, arms outstretched before her, as in a farcical play.

Preservation became fully a part of official American life in the 1960s, with the passage of the National Preservation Act in 1966, the widespread establishment of municipal landmark commissions in cities, and the development of academic departments teaching the subject. The type of person attracted to the field changed, too. Instead of people of a socially conservative bent, many with family roots in the past, many women, toward the end of the '60s preservation not only had become a recognized profession but was germinating a subset of young idealists who wanted to use preservation to

But a few years before I came to Natchez, well into the Millers' tenure, Melrose, which had until then been privately owned, came on the market. Melrose was a fine example of Greek Revival surrounded by its original eighty acres, which had become very rare by this time, many owners having sold off much of their land, including slave cabins. It had been lovingly cared for by a couple who had operated the mansion as a bed-and-breakfast but in a way that preserved its authenticity. They had kept all the old furniture and interior decoration intact, as well as a functional punkah, a fanning mechanism with origins in India that had been common in Natchez, having made its way there from the West Indies. There was also a complete system of bell pulls and hidden passages to facilitate service without disruption. Its likely fate was to be bought by an entrepreneur who would compromise that authenticity with appeals to fantasies of Rhett and Scarlett. Then an inquiry was made to the Millers as to whether they knew of any fine Southern architecture worthy of preservation: they pointed out Melrose, as well as another site in Louisiana. It emerged that the inquirer was an emissary of William Mott, the head of the National Park Service, who had been approached by Lady Bird Johnson, who sat on the National Park Service Advisory Board, and felt that Southern architecture was underrepresented in the Park Service sites. Given the opportunity that presented here for first-class handling of this superb site, the Millers knew that it was time to step into the antebellum domain. They did so inventively, putting together a case for why the Service should purchase Melrose that, as Mimi put it to me, consisted of every narrative they could think of, including the obvious aesthetic qualities and intact land, but emphasizing—this, she knew, could be the winner—the opportunity to tell a part of the African American story, something not done at any of the other Service mansions. At that time the Service was dabbling in Martin Luther King Jr.'s residence and had honored George Washington

Carver and Booker T. Washington at the Tuskegee Institute National Historic Site in Alabama, but Melrose, as Mimi described it, "represented a clearly defined, very dramatic opportunity to tell the story of King Cotton and African enslavement in the antebellum South." The National Park Service bought Melrose. Then came the difficult question of how to fulfill this mandate in Natchez in its state of uneasy avoidance, its deep insecurity, its fearfulness where the subject of slavery was concerned.

This was the job of the Service, in particular rangers assigned to Melrose, some actually from Natchez. But Mimi was there to help in this difficult matter and suggested looking at the everyday life of slaves. This went forward under the curatorial supervision of Kathleen Jenkins, a Natchezian, and Bill Justice, a ranger from the Midwest, who devised, among other features, a Christmas pageant that would include the theme of slavery. On one of my visits to Natchez in the late 1990s, Mimi had come up with the observation that much of Melrose, including some of its finest craftsmanship, had actually been built by slaves and that this was something, surely, to be celebrated—to be admired. This did provide some more patter for guides, though I found the tour at Melrose to be tentative and a bit skimpy where the role of African Americans was concerned. As a special favor, Bill Justice took me out to a slave cabin—it was not on the tour. The cabin was totally renovated, its history lost: nevertheless, as we stood there, young Midwestern Justice began to whisper, as if he could hardly breathe.

By this time, the Melrose Christmas pageant had become a seasonal feature, though it included a part for only one slave in one scene, and that one silent: only one, because, I was told, only one black Natchezian could be found who was willing to play the role. It was at the time of this visit, close to Christmas, when a crisis was gripping the Park Service staff: the one willing candidate was too pregnant to play the part. It was a crisis because the fulfillment of the mandate to represent African American history was really important to the staff. At one point I saw, through an open door to a rather small office, staff members gathered in baroque formation, stock-still, fists to foreheads—desperately thinking.

The upshot was that Ora Frazier, a black Natchezian who was a guidance counselor at the high school, and Toby Jackson, an African American ranger at Mt. Locust, a Park Service antebellum site up the Natchez Trace, agreed to put on a scene, written by themselves, depicting a conversation between two slaves concerning their hope that the coming war would free them. This wasn't an easy decision for them. Toby Jackson told me he came round to it only after thinking about his ancestors and their fates whereupon he knew he had to do it. Though the rangers and the participants were anxious, the plan went forward. I had already gone home for Christmas, but learned that the scene was performed in an upstairs hallway by a window. By all accounts, the audience—which this first time was all white as always—fell absolutely still. A video of it was sent to me. It was dark and flickering. The words were difficult to make out. But I, too, felt the suspense, was rapt: the untrained voices reciting woodenly, the figures unsteady, as were the walls, the doorway, the windows as captured by a tentatively held camera.

There were in fact only two slave cabins at Melrose, both too renovated to hold the presence of those who had lived in them. In the course of my visits to Natchez, I learned that while slave quarters, on the whole, were as well built as the mansions, unless they were very close to the house—or unless they had become part of bed-and-breakfast amenities, as at Monmouth—they tended not to have been attentively maintained. Furthermore, most quarters lived in by slaves of Natchezian planters had been located across the river in Louisiana near the cotton fields. Most of these had become sharecroppers' cottages after the Civil War, but then had been abandoned once sharecropping was rendered obsolete by the mechanized cotton picker. In the natural course of events, even construction of good quality, if unmaintained, begins to seriously deteriorate at the point of a century and a half, give or take a decade. The quarters were now reaching a point of no return—indeed, were rapidly disappearing.

But there was, I had learned, a cotton plantation called Canebrake across the river in Concordia Parish that was in production, having been revived by a descendant of the original owner, a young man from Iowa, who had come south to try his hand at farming the ancestral land. He lived in what had been the overseer's cottage. Nearby, it was said, were some old quarters. Canebrake would bring me closer, I knew, but I didn't get over to the flatlands of Louisiana until my last visit to Natchez. I am not sure what stopped me— maybe the brute landscape of industrial slavery, no matter how far in the past, was more than I was ready for on any given day. On my last visit to Natchez, with time running out, I contacted the owner. He would be amenable to my coming over to see the cabins, he said. As it turned out, he couldn't be there on the day I was able to go.

Thus I finally crossed high over the river on the Natchez–Vidalia Bridge, from the highlands of Natchez, passing the mansion once owned by Jefferson Davis and a Ramada Inn, to the lowlands of Concordia Parish. There I found a disparate landscape of gun shops and hamlets. Eventually I located Canebrake. I knew from historical documents that there had originally been fourteen cabins at Canebrake, each having two ten-by-ten-foot square rooms, each with at least two windows and a fireplace, all raised well off the ground, with pine or cypress floors. As was typical, the quarters had been lined up facing one another across a space that was like a broad street, with the overseer's cottage at one end and a cotton field at the other. Slaves received a peck of cornmeal and three to five pounds of salt pork per adult per year, and beyond that were expected to forage for themselves. Cows and pigs that ran wild in the woods were considered fair game for slaves, who also supplemented their diets with catfish, wild turkey, and deer meat garnered after days in the fields.

The land was very flat; you could see for miles, but when I got to Canebrake I couldn't see any quarters, only the overseer's cottage, and a barking dog chained to a tree. There were some barns, some scraggly lawn that became rough cut as it extended away from the house, more field than lawn, with jungly islands of trees and vines interspersed here and there, oddly moundlike. And beyond that were the endless, flood-flat fields of cotton, boles bursting open. Snowy white in a summer scene is strange to a northerner's eye. Not seeing any cabins, I made my way toward the cotton. I had walked all the way past the jungly islands to the edge of the cotton field, when, looking back, I realized that there was a structure inside the last one. It was the corrugated sheets of the roof, sprung and flap-jacking, that gave it away—a wrecked ship about to go down amid dragonflies. Then I saw that inside the next mound there was another, again the telltale line of a roof peeling as if in a high wind, the vines frothing, and in the mound beyond that another, the whole cabin, in this case, leaning for support against a young tree into which it had crashed. As I came close to this one, my eyes adjusted: the door was open, I could see the floor inside, a floor that would hold no one, the chimney rising from the hearth, no wall behind the chimney. But the next one was almost intact. I clambered through the growth and went in.

It seemed that sharecroppers had been succeeded by youngsters. In that first room "the Bud Club" was crudely painted on a wall. Some bales of hay had served as seats; there was some red graffiti, an old Coke can, a fireplace, glassless windows. Brilliant spots of sun burned on the floor. The door of the cabin was ajar; I could look out from there, past the narrow porch and through the scrim of greenery to the other jungly mounds, long grasses around them blowing in waves, the forms of the cabins within still plowing through the land as they had for two centuries, the cotton field beyond a foaming ocean. It's always been the problem of architectural preservation that by restoring, or even just retarding deterioration, continuity is broken. The result is that the very depth we seek in the past disappears, because intervening history and, indeed, the passage of time as recorded by ravages have been erased. But then, if you don't restore and preserve, it simply disappears.

Still, there is no comparing the restored site to a ruin, a building that has been allowed to just sink into time, becoming almost lost, though not quite yet. I was uncannily comfortable in the Canebrake cabin. It wasn't horror I felt but commonality. I had stumbled into a sweet spot where an essence of life seemed to have pooled deep inside the predicament of history. Human presence: that is all, at home. My own mingling in. It was a simple feeling, and yet, the whole spectrum of experience seemed present in essence—in the old hearth, the sun spots on the floor.

5

Truth or Consequences

Because I didn't want to be guided by preconceptions, during the exploratory period of my place education, I at times allowed chance to have a hand in my itinerary. Perhaps my most purely random choice of destination was Truth or Consequences, New Mexico, a destination based almost entirely on the attraction of its odd name. In the course of getting to know this dusty desert town and its surroundings, I did my usual—pursued little stories, talked to people, got to know some of them, got up-to-date on local issues, and read old newspapers. The town had originally been called Hot Springs, for supposedly curative waters in which I soaked in a very plain hot-tub establishment, where the dour attendant handed me sandpaper towels. Tongue-in-groove partitions were painted a dull green, and daylight came in through high windows.

I also went to the Geronimo Springs Museum. There I learned about the Apaches who had lived nearby and used the springs, too, and that the town had been renamed in 1950 after a radio show, in the hope of sparking its dead economy. The show, *Truth or*

Consequences, was modeled on an English parlor game, called For-feits, that became popular on the frontier. A recurring phrase in Forfeits was "Heavy Heavy Hangs over Thy Head." Ralph Edwards, the radio show's founder, had learned Forfeits as a boy in Colorado and later took it to radio as *Truth or Consequences*, which it may also have been called in Colorado. In 1950, with the tenth anniversary of the show coming up, he made an offer: if a town changed its name to Truth or Consequences, he would broadcast the anniversary show from there. Hot Springs, in desperate economic shape, went for it. Six months later, Edwards took the show onto television. There were clips in the Geronimo Springs Museum. Contestants were asked a question of fact, and if they answered wrong there would be "consequences." In my favorite clip, a participant was asked what the average yearly rainfall in Colorado was. He gave the wrong answer—that is, didn't tell the "truth"—and as a consequence was handed the tail of a stuffed tiger. Then he was asked another, equally obscure statistical question, and he got that one wrong, too, whereupon he was handed the tail of a real tiger. Now that's good television! Ralph Edwards returned to the town renamed for his show yearly until the end of his life to participate in a monthlong festival in which he was lionized long after the show had faded into the past. Whether in the long run—or even the short run—the name change helped the town is hard to say.

In the course of my investigations, I interviewed an old rancher. It was fun for me, an easterner, to talk to this rangy old guy. I enjoyed his home, too, long and low, a true ranch house, not a suburban one, and the way in which older items having to do with the work of ranch-ing—I remember, in particular, an old, very beautiful western sad-dle—were around, as specific mementos as opposed to thematic décor. In recalling his life, the rancher told me that, when he was a young man, he had ranched in the foothills of the Fra Cristobal Mountains, just east of town. It just came along naturally in his recollections of those days that, without any warning, at 5:30 a.m. on July 16, 1945, he and others—ranchers got up early—saw a blinding flash behind the mountains, in the direction of the Jornada del Muerto desert. They later learned that the flash was the Trinity atomic test.

I had had no sense of the proximity of that momentous event. I had come across no mention of Trinity in the Geronimo Museum, or in chamber of commerce promotions. The place usually associated with Trinity was Alamogordo, which I knew to be far to the southeast. In fact, sometimes the test is simply called "Alamogordo." Nor was Trinity mentioned in stories about Truth or Consequences, though the town, struggling as ever, was pumping up every other available scrap of its history that might distinguish it, as well as creating an old-fashioned western Main Street that had never existed.

I asked the rancher where the Fra Cristobal ranch was, and went out there. Flat sagebrush extended into the foothills, terrain desiccated and monotonous at your feet but entrancing in the distance, especially in the direction of the mountains. This land had been ranched since the area was settled. Miles of range was needed to support a single steer. The long blue shadows of clouds on the foothills looked like bodies of water for sure—a cobalt gleam, the almost flagrant wetness of mirage. Though New Mexico was the site of several major events in the development of atomic weaponry, I had had no plans to visit those places, almost on principle. Many had made pilgrimages to such places, including writers, and to me there seemed to be a willful romanticism, even a pitiful desperation, in the hope that place could help us understand the release of a force that could swallow place as we have known it altogether. I got my map out of my car and then, as I stood there, began to understand that, in part, the absence of a sense of nearness to Trinity had to do with the separation the mountains created. On the map a dotted line indicated some sort of a road, but not one in present use, through the mountains into the Jornada del Muerto desert in the Tularosa Basin. Maybe it had been closed by the government as the Trinity test approached and never reopened. In any event, there was no other road across the mountains. To get to the site of Trinity from Truth or Consequences, you had to drive south about seventy miles to Las Cruces, get around the southern edge of the San Andres range, and then drive almost that distance northeast to the White Sands Missile Range, then north through the Tularosa Basin to Trinity. It was early evening, and the shadows were long. Jackrabbits loped off in their outrageously bare-bummed way. You can't adopt a random method of place selection and then ignore Trinity, if that is what turns up. Standing there, I knew that I would, after all, be joining my fellow place-pilgrims to the site of the first atomic explosion.

At the White Sands Missile Range base I was assigned a guide, who drove me the many miles up to Trinity in a big red SUV. She was irrepressibly chatty, spewing miscellaneous facts about the landscape around us: the presence of a rare breed of shrimp in the saline groundwater; the introduction of oryx, an African antelope that, having proliferated, is subject to a yearly hunting season; the "yield" of the Trinity bomb; how the site is open to the public on one day a year: pacifists to bomb enthusiasts attend. The route up through the basin had been called Jornada del Muerto by Spanish settlers. A small volcanic range up ahead was called the Oscura, for the skirts of black lava on its slopes. Evidently the government had dropped secrecy in favor of what seemed to be random running-off-at-the-mouth, a series of non sequiturs before which the mind of a listener soon blurred, and which was therefore almost as obscuring as secrecy in its effects. To me, my guide's jumble reflected our disorientation. It's as if we don't know what anything means anymore. Just a Dumpster of everything. I missed secrecy.

We drove straight to the Trinity site. It was fenced off, but we went in, and in the center was a monument that had been erected

in the 1960s, smack in the middle of the Cold War, at the height
of the arms race. It was a twelve-foot obelisk, squat looking in that
environment, made of black lava from the Oscuros. Black lava is a
horrid material, matte, soft looking even when hard, conveying a spill
even when shaped. It was to me ugly, subhuman seeming, a stunted
grunt, as from a prelingual layer of consciousness. Still, there was
surely a romance of place in this choice of a local element: a choice
that seemed to be imploring place to somehow endow this spot with
encompassing meaning. In this the government had abandoned its
usual façade of confidence, of having it all well in hand, so essential
to its posture where the Cold War was concerned.

White Sands had by then become a landing strip for space shuttles as well as a missile testing ground. Given that by the 1960s missiles were the "delivery system" for nuclear devices, maybe the artist's
idea was that lava, the stuff of the molten core of the Earth, was of
a piece with the sun, the exploding stars, that energy native to space
but not to our earthly nature—even though it's secreted away inside
it. Maybe the monument's maker wanted to convey with the lava that
earthly nature is bracketed by this energy in both outer and subatomic space from which it has spilled into our hitherto protected
in-between domain. The name Trinity was Robert Oppenheimer's
choice, but my guide didn't know why. Later I learned that it is said
to allude to a poem by the seventeenth-century poet John Donne
that begins "Batter my heart, three person'd God" and, a few lines
later "bend / Your force to break, blowe, burn, and make me new."
There is a sense in which this spiritual poem rises to an emotional
intensity that is the equal of the predicament created by the release
of atomic power, but I did not have it in hand on this trip. There was
instead a mildness, and the slight sadness of an abandoned site—
an old rusted-out furnace casing lying to one side of the gate. There
were wildflowers at Trinity and my guide knew their names: mallow,
alyssum. Elysium! The sand underfoot had been crystallized by the

explosion. My guide said it was illegal but if I wanted to take some home as a souvenir, I could. In a fit of high-minded dudgeon touched with hypochondria, I declined. Would I want radioactive glass on my desk among my little beach stones?

After that we went to the place where the "device" had been assembled. This was the McDonald Ranch House, which, my guide told me, was a sheep farmer's homestead built in the basin in 1913. The ranch house was small, simple; adobe, a single story with a sloping, four-sided roof. Two sheep-farming families lived there in succession, eking out a living in the desert until the federal government decided to use the basin as a bombing and gunnery range. The McDonald Ranch House was two miles from the Trinity site, and the explosion blew out its windows and bowed the roof inward. After the experiment was over, no one took care of it. Rain came in, and the wind got under the house and destabilized it, and sand blew up through the floorboards until 1984, when some preservation measures had been taken. The measures restored it to its pre-explosion state. I never oppose preservation, because there is no telling what we will need in the future, and once something is gone it's gone forever. But the very idea of preserving the venue at which the possible annihilation of everything was inaugurated had its own contradictions. The damage to this humble structure was hardly instructive as to the power of the atomic bomb. Still, I wished I could have seen McDonald Ranch House with its roof stove in and its interior sacked by sand and rain over the course of half a century. That would have offered a direct connection to the intrusion of the Trinity experiment, into the passage of time before and after. The McDonald Ranch House in that state would have conveyed the vulnerability, the humanity, and the animal time-boundedness of the physicists, the government, and indeed us all.

Inside the doorjambs were square cut and painted brown, the doors green, with lighter green panels. The latches were in small black boxes affixed to the doors, with brown glass doorknobs attached. The floors were of two-inch boards, brown, varnished, and worn. The walls were adobe, painted light blue, and had cracked, and fortunately not been repaired. The ceilings were twelve feet high, the guide told me. A naked bulb on a wire hung from the middle of the ceiling in every room. In one front room the moldings around the ceiling were a greenish blue and above them were faded alternating stencils of a daisy and a candle. An aesthetic touch to sweeten a lonely life on the desert range. The rooms were empty. Between rooms were wooden thresholds. One room, plainer than the others, was labeled the Plutonium Assembly Room, and there was a handwritten note attached to the doorjamb: PLEASE USE THE OTHER DOORS. KEEP THIS ROOM CLEAN.

The windows in the Plutonium Assembly Room were deeply inset in the adobe walls and through them I saw a stone wall and beyond it the range, flat as the ocean floor it had once been, bright desert, low mountains in the distance, and sky—a setting that puts one in mind of geological time. It looked as if you could just walk forever and then expire. The mountains at that moment were shadowed by clouds and I could hear the wind about the house.

It was only later that I got a few moments to myself, going out a back door just to see what was there. This evidently wasn't in my guide's guidebook: she had no interest in following. With relief I stepped onto a wooden porch. While I had been inside, a very light rain had fallen, and the smell of the desert was strong. Clustering near the farmhouse was a crumbled dwelling with a chimney, the ruins of sheepfolds, corrals, barns. They had been made of local stone and timber, neither plentiful here. The scale was scrimped, pre-picturesque, reflecting the brutal hard labor entailed in turning a wilderness to human purposes: extracting something out of nothing with mingy returns. Because the structures had not been preserved but had deteriorated naturally over time, the continuum was completely intact, and shocking. This little frontier sheep ranch had been built only thirty-two years before Trinity. Barely a generation and a half had passed since the building of the ranch house, and the way of life it represented had gone on more or less the same right up to the time of Trinity. You could sense the hardship of quite recent times, but there also remained a quality of established agrarian place that suggests there is no point in going anywhere else, in which you are here and here only while the rest of the world barely exists; the hominess of the tiny domesticated nook where cacti grew quietly and butterflies came out and fluttered whenever the wind momentarily stopped.

Mostly the wind blew, buffeting my ears. On one of the wooden window frames there was a loose piece of wood swinging on a nail, tappety-tap-tap-tapping in the wind. My notebook fluttered, and then the wind sounded as in pines, though no pines were around, and the sun warmed my back, and there were hawks in the sky, and then when the wind got still stronger there was a deeper sound in it. With the deeper sound, I noticed more clearly the scraggly bushes around the ruins, the shards of crockery on the ground, the crooked posts of what had once been a pen of some kind, become so wind-worn, so honed, that they had acquired a twisting grained expressiveness. A system of gutters on the house collected rainfall and deposited it in a cistern in which the physicists had taken swims, as I had seen them doing in a photo inside. The meaning of the site notwithstanding, I liked this place in the same way I had liked Canebrake: a pooling of time, an enlarging warmth, a sense of human presence past—sheep husbandry, the young men in the cistern.

In response to the situation that arose out of the test at Trinity, we have developed, perhaps, our fiercest, most diligent habit of deflection. While the Cold War was going on, we may have had no choice but to push this actuality away, to sanitize it in jargon and otherwise live as if it were not true. Who is to say that this choice was not the right one, especially after arsenals were built up to a possibly life-annihilating level? After all, we did muddle through intact. But muddling through does not necessarily lay a good foundation. Though the geopolitical situation and its terrors have receded, we go forward without an important part of our education: a fully felt and imagined response to a radically altered context—brought about by a new understanding of the physics of the world and the powers that knowledge had put in our hands—without a concomitant change in ourselves.

In other words, we might be missing an important piece of psychic development in never stopping to look back to understand this experience free of self-preserving deflection. In the 1990s, though the Cold War was over, part of an exhibition at the National Air and Space Museum in Washington that included the Enola Gay, the plane from which the bomb had been dropped on Hiroshima, was eliminated because of pressure from conservative legislators and veterans groups objecting to material that revealed disagreement among leaders as to whether to drop atom bombs on Japan, a well-known fact. As Kai Bird has pointed out in *Hiroshima's Shadow*, a collection of pieces about the controversy over the exhibition—as well as denial surrounding this subject—the controversial material did not represent that the choice to drop the bomb had been wrong, though it did not indicate that it was right, either. But, to some, to introduce choice at all was to question the brittle, good-versus-evil morality behind which we hid the enormous, unprecedented moral questions implicit in the Cold War. The best argument for using the bomb was that the war would be ended quickly, saving lives on both sides. The argument against it was that using the bomb would open the way to an atomic arms race and ultimately the possibility of a true Armageddon. I don't think our past leaders can be held responsible in retrospect for the scale of nuclear armament that eventually evolved. But I do think that we are now responsible for looking directly at where the course we chose led us, as well as where alternate courses might have taken us, and the stakes implicit in both. A consequence of the choice we did make, at which we have never dared to look directly, is that when the stakes became life on Earth, no human value was worth the risk—not democracy, not freedom: indeed, all beliefs fell before this risk. In this, there was a kind of moral annihilation, itself almost impossible to bear given there was no solution in sight, which we handled by going forward as if the stakes were no different from those of former confrontations with evildoers, such as Nazis— as if the main issue was democracy versus fascism or, as it had become, communism.

Oppenheimer, one of the physicists responsible for the device tested at Trinity, did understand the stakes. Famously, on the successful completion of the test, he said, "Now I am become Death, Destroyer of Worlds." He was quoting from the Bhagavad Gita. The speaker is a god. As it happened, during my first visit to Truth or Consequences, a series depicting the drama at Trinity was showing on PBS, with Sam Waterston playing the part of Oppenheimer. The ads for the series, on television but also radio—I heard them often in my car as I drove around—included a sound bite of Waterston speaking Oppenheimer's words: "Now I am become Death, Destroyer of Worlds." He delivered them in a way that expressed inconsolable sadness but nothing of the paradox contained therein. We could call it Oppenheimer's paradox: that though we had acquired this power, we were not gods and therefore did not have alternative worlds on which to stand while we destroyed the one we had. The tone in the isolated phrase suggested the allegorical wisdom of a much older civilization, as directed to the innocent young one that had gotten itself into this predicament of footing. Hearing the words over and over, spoken in exactly the same way, was grating, because the tone suggested that we had the needed wisdom, the depth of moral understanding to cope with this predicament when we didn't. Well, you can't get everything all at once. That the show was aired at all reflected a good change, surely. Indeed the restoration of the McDonald Ranch House by the government was in itself a good change in the direction of facing reality, although, judging from the fracas over the Air and Space Museum's exhibition, it seems possible that conservative legislators may not have noticed the plans for this preservation project. Then again, there was no curatorial material in the presentation of the ranch house that raised doubts as to our moral infallibility or capacity for true responsibility—the requisite depth and imagination—with respect to the weaponry inaugurated at Trinity.

Just three houses up from my Rensselaerville cottage, the village ends and a path leads into the woods, into the narrowing gorge along the stream, then up to the top of the falls, and beyond to a lake above. This is part of a preserve—a funny word for something wild, as if it were jam, something boiled down to intense sweetness on a stove in a kitchen. But, when I think about it, the word is just right for a protected wild place that has become intimately known through many revisitations, in multiple seasons, at all times of day, in rain and under the moon and in the extraterrestrial brilliance of a June summer morning. One walk that stands out took place many years after my visit to Truth or Consequences, on a day when the sky was lowering and the light in the space above the stream below the falls was green. The path up to the ledge at the top of the falls goes through hardwood forest with birch mixed in, and some of the birch was down: white slashes in forest floor. Farther along a gleam announced the lake ahead, and then the path led into the open, down along the shore, where mature oaks in long grass lean over the water on one side and, on the other, wooded land climbs steeply. On this particular walk, just as I came to the lakeshore, a light rain set in and a surge in the breeze indicated an imminent change in weather.

The oak boughs stretching over the path protected me from the rain, and then they didn't, so I moved into a deeper spot near the trunk. I could hear the patter of rain on the leaves, distinctive, almost assertive. I listened, and then, as the rain increased, a tiny rustle of rills coming down the slope behind me joined the patter, and the soughing of the wind became deeper, which reminded me of the McDonald Ranch House, and there I was: the sense of psychic largeness, warmth, the sense an agrarian place can convey that everything is where you are; that you need go no farther. The rain let up a bit, but a bottle of ink had been spilled in the sky above me, though the far end of the lake was already bright again. To escape heavier rain I hurried homeward and just as I got to the woods there was a big crack of thunder, and then torrents, so I took a shortcut to a road that pitches steeply into the heart of the village.

When I came to the crest of that pitch, I saw below me the rooftops of the cluster of houses. This was a sight I knew well. But rising behind them—what can I call it? Surely "rainbow" is too thin, a Crayola word. The prism broken out, and unembarrassedly Crayola it was, and gargantuan, and really bright, almost neon, powerfully upthrusting. It looked like the lower portion of an enormous column, except that you could just begin to see the curve before it disappeared into low clouds: a different architecture from ours. The village roofs huddling, the pot of gold down on the floodplain behind—the rainbow was a picture-book joke. The village does that every so often, testing our sense of humor—to see if we have become too grand, or too ironic for simple wonders. One day Santa will be on a roof. Well, the rainbow was funny, and it was cute, but I had just been listening to the wind behind the McDonald Ranch House,

so I was feeling more naïve than ironic, a stranger in a strange land
of enclosure, with which the rainbow was of a piece, outfolding, as
it did, the spectrum of bright colors hidden in seemingly ordinary
light, our rose window.

6

Flight

My partner and I are at the airport en route to Maine to visit friends. I have been looking forward to this trip, but right now I am in a bad mood, which has to do with finding myself in an airport. Everything about Terminal 2 rubs me the wrong way, starting with the word "terminal," moving on to how the structures around the concessions look more permanent than the terminal that contains them, then to the fact that even elderly people are wearing play clothes. Grow up! But the true source of my distress is that all this reminds me of the futility of travel. Of course there is lots to see, but it's also true that it doesn't really matter where you go, there really isn't such a thing as "getting away," and that, wherever you might go, an equally adventurous choice would be to stay home.

Trying to shift out of this dyspeptic attitude, I note the lack of hurry around me. If savored in the right way, an airport can put one in mind of a city park on a warm day. In an airport, everyone has all the time in the world, unbadgered by purpose. After a while I begin to notice beauty, even of the materials out of which the concessions with their branding décor are constructed—polished cherrywood with handsome brass to denote a bar, for example. I even begin to see beauty in people: for example, a group right now getting onto an elongated golf cart that serves as an internal transport vehicle. The scene is choreographic, an overall unity of motion in gorgeous tension with individual gestures, as in a baroque painting. An intent energy in each movement—leg shoving off from the floor, arm reaching forward for the back of a seat—gives the whole an arresting grace. Bare limbs as revealed by the play clothes enhances the effect. I am charmed by my observations. Just a moment ago I felt as if this environment were sucking up my life and now I am swimming in time deliciously. This kind of switchbacking mood is typical of my experience in airports.

My study of our landscape has been pursued in places where I am at home—the known place now offering a riskier adventure than the unknown place, because only when we know a place can we really begin to grasp how strange all place has become. But I have also traveled in the ordinary sense in my studies—gone places—often on short domestic flights. That is how I began to realize that airports themselves were perhaps more important in their way than my destinations, or at least in themselves were revelatory of the world in which we live, as was the plane itself and the experience of being airborne. It never ceases to amaze me how indifferent air passengers are to the view out the window. They read books or are absorbed in computer screens as if the world were not being laid out beneath them. In *Landscape into Art*, a history of landscape painting, the art historian Kenneth Clark notes that Petrarch, the Renaissance Italian poet, was the first person to record climbing a mountain in order to see the view. Petrarch also recorded that, after getting to the top and taking it all in for a few minutes, he opened the book he had brought with him. On planes I, too, but only eventually, open my book.

Domestic flights are of various altitudes, but there is a

classic height of around ten thousand feet, from which the scenes on the ground are unabstracted: trees, roads, houses—the human landscape—are the main thing. But as you get higher, all that begins to look superfluous, minor, a covering overlaid on geological formations that shift and ease themselves like a single giant who is careless of the thin blanket on his body as he tenses and relaxes according to his needs and whims. From the perspective of higher altitudes, geological time seems to be far more dramatic and important than human time. The creases in mountains, the river swings: it's these that are impressive while human endeavor seems oblivious of the drama in which it is set. Moving vehicles crawl blindly on roads. Towns look like a project left behind in a sandbox at the end of the day. Even the plane itself, floating effortlessly, can have a toylike quality. At lower levels, however, there is an only slightly sublimated sense of human struggle in the view. I am remembering watching the shadow of a plane in which I was sitting at a height of ten thousand feet: a small, thick cross haltingly creeping across the roughness of a harvested cornfield. Man-made textures from this height can be emotional.

If you are not looking out the window, the plane can seem to be not even crawling: to be in stasis, even when bumping about on air. When I notice this I usually think of the term "willing suspension of disbelief," which Coleridge coined for what we do when we enter into a fictional world in a book. What keeps this lumbering, obviously heavy thing in what feels like a shuddering, barely proceeding state aloft? I wonder: why doesn't it just drop out of the sky like a stone? This could be one reason people don't much look out plane windows. The manifest heaviness of the plane contrasts with the extreme dinkiness of most plane interiors. Over time, the synthetic materials of these interiors seem to have become vitiated, as if trying to be as close to nothing as possible. Those of us who fly coach have also noticed the gradual constriction of space to a point where it almost seems more symbolic than actual, or at best a token, as if under these conditions of flight the body itself has become a fiction: you suspend it. This internal contrast of heaviness to dinkiness in turn stands in contrast to the magisterial views. One is in steerage, just one notch above a stowaway, in an environment that is like nothing so much as throwaway packaging, but with a godlike perspective.

All air trips are both banal and fantastic: there is a sameness about them that causes them to merge in the mind. One of mine stands out, however. On a flight back from Japan, the entire population of the plane having fallen asleep as if on cue immediately after the meal, I was alone in my tiny pool of light, with all the time in the world to record my experiences of Japan in a notebook. I love to write on planes at night because, unless you have children with you, your life is completely suspended. There is nothing much likely to happen to interrupt your thoughts. It's a question whether being on a plane is really an experience—even when looking out the window it can be as if you don't quite exist. It's this lack of intervening experience that makes a plane the perfect place to try to draw real experiences together, for example, memories of the gardens of Kyoto, thoughts about the Japanese tea ceremony, reflections on Hiroshima, and to see if words will draw these subjects into relation to one another. We were very deep into the flight. All the little plastic lids had been drawn down over the portholes: there was no world other than the interior of the plane, from which I had disappeared into my notebook. But suddenly I was jostled back into my surroundings by a hushed hubbub toward the rear. It was time to stretch my legs anyway. Getting up, I saw a group of stewardesses clustered tightly around a porthole. What could possibly interest stewardesses in a view from a plane at thirty-six thousand feet over the Pacific at night? Two and three at a time, they took turns leaning down to the porthole, fannies pointing upward, then giving way to those eagerly waiting behind them.

I traversed toward this scene and immediately they made way for me, unable to tell me in English what for. In an excess of tidiness one of the stewardesses had slid the little plastic lid down behind her, and I would remember that lid later, so light, so inconsiderable, so of a piece with the artificiality of the interior of the plane. It moved up lightly at the touch of my finger, and there, below me—and not so very far below—were the snow-clad mountains of Alaska, crisply, solemnly visible under a full moon. Then it happened: irregular disco pulse, aurora borealis. Even now my heart stops a little when I think of it: the flagrancy. The mountains were dematerialized by the pulses, but in between the moonlight was so clear and the mountains so close that one could see into the snowy passes, could imagine having trekked into them, finally earning with risk and discomfort this spectacular intimate display of the world on its own. But looking at all this with my fanny up in the air was quickly uncomfortable. Anyway, in a sense I had seen it all in five seconds. Actually I think it was hard to look long: to occupy the perspective of being above not only the mountains, but even the northern lights. Turning away, I saw that the stewardesses had gone back to their duties. The banality of the plane was a relief. I reached out with my little finger and closed the lid.

The enclosure of sky roads is like a worldwide interstate, a superstructure that makes of the great outdoors an interior, in which all architecture, but an airport especially, because of its relation to the sky roads, is a room inside a room. Sometimes the spatial imagination of the agrarian age helps me understand our conditions today. The sameness of airports is like the sameness of Catholic churches the world over, manifesting a contiguous encompassing spiritual space in relation to which normal life in the landscape—streaming highways, flat-roofed factories, rooftops poking through trees—is secondary, only half real.

The first photograph in which the curve of the Earth could be seen was taken from a V-2 rocket fired during World War II from White Sands Missile Range, which went higher than any plane had gone at the time. The Germans had fired such a rocket first, but I found no evidence of photographs taken. With the development of the jet engine in the 1950s, test pilots and military pilots began to fly routinely at fifty thousand feet. Missiles, as they were developed, flew higher and higher, but with only cameras, not the human eye. The bomb that destroyed Hiroshima was dropped from a propeller plane at a height of thirty-two thousand feet. As thermonuclear weapons were developed, intercontinental ballistic missiles became the principal delivery system. Only test missiles were actually fired, but many missiles complete with warheads were kept in silos, in both the United States and the Soviet Union, and also in other countries, aimed and ready to fire worldwide on a few moments' notice. Those carefully planned trajectories, arcing from the ground, out of the atmosphere and back in, enclosed the ever elaborating sky roads, including the very high trajectories of test pilots, in a kind of phantom architecture beyond the atmosphere, establishing a new outer edge of our human landscape.

Within this enclosure of supersonic speeds there was still a relationship between distance and time, indeed several different layers, nestled within one another successively, until, down on the ground, at least for a person on foot, distance and time, and indeed place, seemed to be as they had always been. The missiles were no exception, but the speed at which nuclear war might break out seemed to nullify the continuum with time and distance as we experience it normally.

The gyroscope of sky roads continued to grow inside the missile-trajectory enclosure, thickening over time, its angled connections to Earth looping down in clusters in a formation that was repeated on a larger scale by the trajectories of missiles, with the points of arrival matching the most popular arrival destinations of airlines: the great cities of the world. But even as this outer enclosure was being completed, the carriers on the sky roads were propeller planes; and many travelers still crossed the ocean on ships. In 1957, Americans were shocked to learn that "the Russians," as we called the Soviets, had launched Sputnik, a satellite that went into orbit around the Earth, outside the missile trajectories. While satellite technology became a natural aid to nuclear warfare by missile, the launching of Sputnik inaugurated a welcome sublimation of the competition between the United States and the Soviet Union into the arena of space exploration.

Sputnik was the first piece of what is today our commonplace outermost enclosure—the exostructure of the information age, satellites with their basketry of signals that extend our eyes and ears, our voices and our proliferating messages and thoughts, enclosing our planet and all our doings on it. But it was actually the space race that geared up after Sputnik. In 1962, John Glenn, an actual human being, went into orbit around the Earth, upstaging Sputnik, mere artifact that it was. When he returned, a Senate committee, hungry to be amazed—perhaps to justify the cost—pressed him for details. But Glenn said that what he had seen was little different from the view of a test pilot at fifty thousand feet—in other words, earth orbit was really just a natural extension of the sky roads to someone familiar with the territory. Still, the horizon of the planet was different, Glenn said, for from orbit "the blackness of space contrasts vividly with the brightness of Earth," and the horizon was curved, though that was not so exciting to him, of course, even if more pronounced than what he had seen routinely as a pilot. It was other sights, ephemeral, aesthetic that amazed him. "The horizon itself is a brilliant blue," Glenn said, also telling of a kind of snow of particles of a greenish fireflylike color that would swarm about his spacecraft as he flew toward darkness, facing backward. At first he had thought he was looking at stars.

Apollo 8, which took off to orbit the moon in 1968, achieved the definitive leap out of the context of the Earth into the context of

space. On the way out, most of the windows of the spaceship became clouded and smeared by a sealing compound that had partially
decomposed in the vacuum of space. Two forward-looking windows
were clear, but the astronauts could not see the moon toward which
they were traveling at five thousand miles per hour through these
windows, because it was hidden in the glare of the sun. So were the
stars. This brightly lit environment was, paradoxically, black. When
the spaceship rolled, however, they could see the Earth momentarily: each time it was much smaller. At sixty-seven thousand miles,
astronaut Jim Lovell could stretch out his arm and cover the Earth
with his thumb. At this point, the brightness of the planet had faded
sufficiently that it could be captured on film and transmitted. But
because they were looking directly at Antarctica with Cape Horn
poking in, an unfamiliar perspective, they couldn't figure out what
they were seeing. When they got it, Bill Anders considerately took
the photo hanging upside down, so that Cape Horn came in from the
top, making the image more intelligible to earthlings. People were
now looking at the planet with a surrogate eye out in space, and you
could say that the planet was looking back at them. On televisions
in living rooms all over the world, the planet was looking at itself.
Indeed, it looked a lot like a blue-green eye.

Two days and twenty hours into the flight, the astronauts saw
a kind of shore of stars in the blackness. The stars were fixed, not
winking as they do when seen through the atmosphere. Lovell had
learned in the navy how to navigate by the stars. Should Apollo 8
lose contact with Earth it would be he, using the stars, who would
find the way home. It was at this moment that Lovell realized that
his points of reference had changed from what they had been even
on his orbits of the Earth on Gemini 7 and 12. Then he had been oriented to the landmasses and oceans beneath him. Earth, under those
circumstances, was the overwhelmingly dominant reference. Indeed,
there had been no other. Now, however, he had multiple references:

the sun; the moon ahead, which he could not see at that moment; the stars, which were meaningful to him as a navigator, but to which he had an entirely new relationship; and Earth itself, but as just another of the bodies among which the spaceship moved, in a continuously changing, centerless arrangement.

All around them were galaxies, unfiltered by atmosphere, unobscured by the sun's light, uncountable multitudes of stars of great brightness. When I think of this moment, a strange emotion stirs in me, a combination of inadequacy, dread, and tears of greeting combined with ferocious shrinking. This is the great moment in which we entered the cosmic environment, body and soul, leaving behind our Earth-centered orientation, however temporarily: understood that this is where we are now. It doesn't seem to me that we have gotten much farther than this. After his eyes had adjusted to the stars, Bill Anders noticed a large area in which there were no stars at all, a black area of nothing, rather large, with an edge. He could think of no explanation for this void until he realized that he was looking at the back of the moon. The hair stood up on the back of his neck, as it does on mine when I think of it: because something so big was right there and he hadn't seen it and because the spaceship was physically separated from the Earth by this mass. The moon now blocked contact with NASA in Houston. The astronauts were alone with the galaxies.

Every moment of the trip had been thought out in advance, including the points at which photographs were to be taken and of what. Indeed, the purpose of the trip was to photograph the surface of the moon as a way of scouting for possible landing sites. Anders was the photographer, and his camera was a Hasselblad that required some maneuvers in order to be set up for a shot. For forty-five minutes of the orbit, when they were behind the moon, it was lost in darkness. As Apollo 8 began to come around the other side toward sunlight, the radio kicked in, and space became once again starless, simultaneously black and sunlit. For the first time the surface of the moon appeared, though initially it looked to the astronauts as if oil were streaking across their windows. What they were seeing were the low rays of the sun raking mountains with no atmosphere to tone down the contrast of the shadows. "It looks like a big beach down there," said Anders to Houston. "The moon is essentially gray, no color. Looks like plaster of Paris," radioed Lovell. Earthly words performed poorly in this moment.

Frank Borman, the commander, was, in the meantime, intent on mechanical aspects of the journey and impatient. There would be ten lunar orbits, two hours each. He wanted the astronauts to save their sightseeing for later. Every shot had been thought out in advance, but at this point something happened that had not been foreseen. As they came farther around the moon, Earth slipped out from behind it, a little more than half in light, as we are used to in a gibbous moon. But the planet was blue-green and cloud-marbled. A photograph had to be in color, but the film in the Hasselblad, chosen for the moonscape, was black-and-white. It took moments to make the switch, which is why Anders's photograph shows Earth already risen, a little apart from the moon's horizon—actually a vertical, called a verizon—as they saw it from Apollo 8.

Though the photo of the full planet in space became the hallmark of the space age, Anders's photo of a rising, partially shadowed Earth is, to my mind, the image that captures our radically shifting consciousness during Apollo 8. The image of the whole Earth became the cliché, the Whole Earth Catalog logo, the airline logo—leaving this one fresh. The image of the planet in its freestanding entirety had long been imagined, even constructed in the form of globes as objects that had fit in comfortably for centuries amid the furniture in our living rooms. The gibbous Earth just barely apart from the moon that surprised the Apollo 8 astronauts on their first lunar orbit had not been imagined. Anders's photo inspires wonder but also is full of unresolved ambiguity. NASA named it *Earthrise* and published it showing the surface of the moon as horizontal, as in a normal sunrise, as if fearful that we might not be able to comprehend it otherwise—or maybe wanting to shield us from just how startling our new perspective was. But in the print that Anders hung on his own living room wall the surface of the moon is vertical, with the Earth moving away to the side.

Many remarked at the time that Apollo 8, rather than exciting us with the prospect of further adventures into space, drew us back "home," with those photos of Earth freestanding. NASA went on to put a person on the moon, but in a way that literal footing, while introducing the scale of the body, and the weight of the body, and the form of the body—an actual foot—into this vastly expanded frame, was still merely a follow-up to the big shift in orientation that had already happened.

It's commonly accepted that the view from the moon, showing us clearly the limitations of the planet, propelled the environmental movement into the political mainstream. But at this time there was little general awareness of the global aspects of environmental depredation. Even in the post-moon-shot period, environmental problems were considered piecemeal, as were their solutions, whether that was cleaning up a river or making a compost heap in your garden. Environmental problems were so much simpler, and seemingly more soluble, than the issues at play in the Cold War. Meanwhile the arms race continued in the background, behind the space race, solidifying into the policy known as MAD: mutual assured destruction. In contrast to MAD, environmental causes were downright delicious. The environment as "problem" offered multiple paths of address, some directly effective, and some even fun, such as the grand love affair with wilderness. Indeed, perhaps partly in recoil from the nuclear predicament, which was a planetary one too, the environmental movement in some ways leapt backward into a safer vision of the world, a romance with nature as a mystically grand force—a deflection even in the nineteenth century. Surely the lesson of the view from the moon was that our planet was a walled garden, of which we were custodians who also endangered it. Surely in seeing that we were surrounded by the utterly inhospitable true wilderness of the galaxies, the very concept of earthly wilderness came to an end. As I see it in retrospect, the environmental movement, however inspired by the revelation of the moonshots, in some ways offered a welcome escape from the planetary vulnerability that lay at the heart of that revelation.

We can hardly blame ourselves for failing to make the cultural leap into seeing ourselves as custodians of a frail environment on which we depend. But the romantic deflection hurt the movement, creating political division and holding back changes in our inherited ways of seeing the world. Because of the romance with nature, the movement came to be perceived as anti-people, engendering deep resistance, especially among people of modest means whose livings were affected by environmental laws—when the strongest argument was to save ourselves. At the same time, the movement used the high stakes to turn the cause into one that trumped all other causes, much as the nuclear predicament did. We have not yet really contended with this moral frontier, typical of our age as it appears to be. On a more mundane level, the elevation of wild nature, the utterly unpeopled terrain, the most nonurban landscape was reinforced by the long established structure of feeling among progressives, also going back to nineteenth-century romanticism, that cities were bad, that green places were wholesome, that a new kind of urban romanticism was just then getting under way, notwithstanding.

We can see clearly today that, from the point of view of the moon, the distinction between city and country of any kind, or even city and "wilderness," was meaningless: that it was all our "environment." But there was no alliance between urbanists and environmentalists back then. Nor did the small Ban the Bomb movement ally with environmentalists in any major way, despite the fact that the threats were related. All these advocates, for the most part, saw themselves as engaged in different causes. Urbanists were Woody Allens who couldn't stand the sound of crickets at night and didn't want to be too far from a café. Environmentalists fled the city at first opportunity and preferred no sign of civilization at all. To pacifists, environmentalists had their heads in the clouds. The walls between urbanism and environmentalism weakened both movements—powerful as they were—in the long run.

Something urbanists and environmentalists shared, however, was an antipathy for the suburbanized landscape. Environmentalists saw it as too degraded for redemption, when in fact the relationship between man and nature as loosely represented there ought to have been at the center of their concerns. As for urbanists, because suburbia drained energy from the city they saw it as the enemy. Had these two dynamic movements, each in its way remarkably successful within its own "territory," made common cause initially, we might have effective land-use powers at the federal level today. Instead of HUD and EPA as separate entities, we might have an agency that had scope that took in both together: in which responsibility for ourselves and for the environment was seen as the same cause. In later decades groups have emerged in which the two perspectives are combined, and that is a good thing, but the foundational split persists in our bureaucracy, our politics, and indeed our culture.

The view from the moon also subverted our sense of moral security, for it undercut all faiths, political and religious, in a way we have not yet been able to integrate. The astronauts of the various Apollo missions felt this to some extent; for instance, Anders, a devout Catholic, later revealed that his faith had been shaken by the evident inadequacy of any earthbound religion from the perspective of space. If the validity of religion falters, what happens to patriotism?

Frank Borman, superpatriot, never commented on how the perspective from space affected his values, but I wonder whether the fading of the American government's interest in manned space exploration after the Apollo missions—the end of manned flights to the moon and a significant reduction of the NASA budget—was really a recoil from unexpected radical effects of the perspective from the moon, effects that do not reinforce patriotism or traditional religion, or the geopolitical establishment least of all. We went to the moon to compete with the Soviets, but is that cause reinforced from the point of view of the moon? If one considers, as I do, that the Cold War, which generated world-annihilating weapons and a policy of standing ready to slaughter millions of people, compromised the authority of government deeply, then the view from the moon was only going to reinforce that subversive view. I find in the transcripts of the flight a subtle resistance on the part of Mission Control, as if they are insisting on the primacy of our old earthly perspective, undercutting the importance of their own accomplishment, by, for example, going on about the weather in Houston, "which is pretty clear around here. We've got high overcasts. But it is cold and good visibility, and it's beginning to feel like winter again." After the return Anders commented on the incongruity of this chat, which included football scores, with the experience the astronauts were having. There is no hint of tension in the transcript, however. Indeed, when asked to send a message back home the astronauts grabbed on to earthly tradition, reading from their spot in the heavens from Genesis: "In the beginning God created Heaven and Earth . . ." Like Oppenheimer, in order to capture a register of feeling that was the equal of the experience, they had to conjure a divine perspective as described in an ancient sacred book.

We have waited in Terminal 2 for almost two hours. It's now a half hour before departure. Prudently we approach the gate just to be extra ready. There we learn that the departure gate has been moved to Terminal 3. This was announced long ago, we are told. All the passengers—except for us—dutifully moved. A special kind of panic grips us. The person manning the PA system begins to call "Rover." I think this is a code of some kind, but gradually I realize that Rover is a transport vehicle. Then I realize that the scene of people embarking onto the elongated golf cart that I had admired as baroque was our fellow passengers getting onto Rover to be taken to the proper terminal and gate. As we wait anxiously, Rover does not appear and time, which was just moments ago so hurryless, develops a quality of urgency aggravated by helplessness special to airline travel.

The desk at the other terminal is called and told not to let the plane leave without us, but the conversation on our end seems altogether too casual. Another announcement calling for Rover is made, but Rover does not appear. We become outraged consumers, blamefully huffing, even though this is clearly our own fault. Rover does not appear. Ten minutes have passed. A stern announcement is made summoning Rover, and the woman behind the desk nods—this will do it, she says—and almost immediately Rover does indeed appear, driven by an African grandfather, who is shaking his head and huffing himself, saying "What a job!" in exactly the way I would if I had been caught out sneaking an illegal coffee break.

We zoom off, wind blowing our hair, up and down ramps and around curves, through a labyrinth of concessions. It's a long way, though we never see sky. There are obstacles: someone on a very tall ladder fixing a light; dawdling passengers. We huff some more. Our driver stops to pick up a Hispanic woman who looks to be a part of the lowest level of staff workers at the airport. She moves slowly—she is not young—and we huff more loudly, shouting that our plane is going to leave. "She needs help!" says the driver reproachfully. I know he is African from his accent but perhaps also because his attitudes seem unaligned with the importance of our catching our plane. The woman slumps in the seat in front of us, her exhaustion manifest. We are ashamed. But there is no way we can apologize, because we would have to lean forward and we are going at high speed, clutching a hand bar, and cannot safely move. Pedestrians, for whom the African grandfather seems to have little regard, dodge out of the way at the last minute. Acceleration suggests that even the African grandfather realizes that maybe time is very tight, and this, in its way, is more alarming. It is a long way, but we get there and without saying goodbye to the African grandfather rush through the gate and then onto a bus, an unforeseen leg of the journey—no one else is on the bus. Then we are in our airplane seats hearing about oxygen masks and safety belts, a message delivered as a bored old padre might say Mass in a Sicilian hill town, and then we are aloft in the static time and place of planes, the northeastern region of the United States pulling away beneath us, turning blue, and then we lose it as we enter the shelving clouds.

Whenever I approach the village after being away, especially if on a plane trip, there is a point about five miles out, a crest in a series of rising crests, after which I begin to feel the coming together of inner and outer topography, a pending completeness. Driving the hilly road, my body remembers. Through the medium of motion, there is in me a gathering sense of homecoming. I have experienced this many times. This time—the trip back from Maine—it was dusk: a white horse in a field up to its withers in hay, head down out of sight. Then, as I climbed a steep hill, a white cat crossed the road ahead, hurriedly, knowing something was wrong about its timing, and disappeared into another field of hay. The light was fading and the whiteness of the cat was grayed out a bit, making me unsure about what I had seen. But when I looked for it as I passed the spot, its whiteness, caught in a twilight gleam, was bright in the hay. That's how it was that particular time on the home stretch, a white horse in a field and a white cat crossing the road, and then the first glimpse of the steeple, and then, in the last bit of pasture before the village, another white horse, this one fully visible, swishing its tail, and then I was down the final hill and into the village, the houses close together, some windows lit, the church, and I look to see who is home, and is my friend's car there, and her kitchen is already lit in the early evening, but I don't see her in it, as I often do, and then I am past the center of the village and up the street toward the mill and the falls, and then, finally, I come to a stop in front of my cottage and turn off the motor. I feel a little excited and yet at the same time foolish in this, and then I get out of the car, foot to ground, and there it is, the sound of the falls, which I had forgotten. Something happening in the muscles of the back, and an opening of the lungs, a falling away of vibrations. Then normal life takes over—unpack the car.

7

The View from a Small Mountain

Summer is short in the village. In May growth bursts forth with what seems like pent-up force, and by August a fine but inexorable ratcheting down has begun, measured in small changes. The days still have their singularity, are as if forever, and yet implicit in them for me is a sense of uprooting to come. For I am just a bird of passage here, returning to city when summer is over, for work but also because that is home, too. This is a rhythm that has been established for years, and yet as the time to leave approaches I prepare for a wrench. It's a separation from that topographical alignment I felt on the return from Maine. Maybe it's an atavistic response, belonging to some former way of life. I have had many truly severe wrenches out of places in my life to which this leaving hardly compares. Still, the sense of approaching departure affects the character of my days.

When leavetaking is very near I might make a pilgrimage. One is to go to a high spot not far from the village that offers a 210-degree panorama. From here you can see the Catskills, motherly and close and today a kind of blue, like slate, straight across a wide valley. Fields in the foothills are splashes of emerald. The long, low ridgelines of the Berkshires, delicately interlacing, mark the other side of the Hudson. Just in front of me is the descending shoulder of a hayfield and then the land plummets out of sight. On the edge of the drop stands a white, capless silo held together by metal bands bleeding rust, and a wind-blasted shedlike building with half-paneless windows, tin roof peeling up into a shark's fin against the broad sky. I am sitting in a meadow a bit back from a road. Staggering along the road come telephone poles with stunted crossbars, no pole straight, one bent so far back that it gives the impression of a catapult ready to fire. Several poles clustering around the shed and the silo make a little Calvary: from there the parade lurches off into oblivion over the shoulder.

This meadow is of a local kind that doesn't look like much until you are in it. A famous motif of European tapestries made in the Middle Ages is *millefleur*, a thousand flowers: many small pretty blooms that create a crowded pattern against a dark hunter's green. In the tapestries the thousand flowers are either at the edges or under the hooves of horses bearing knights. If they are more central it's only because a unicorn sits in their midst. Here in America, however, where we have no unicorns, the meadow is itself the subject. The air, the aquifer: these are the unicorn here. In this American meadow there are some but not thousands of flowers: a few dandelions, some clover, another yellow flower I don't know, and a tiny magenta one. But really it's the grasses. Some grasses are bladed and blue, others are weighted with long, slightly purple seeds, bending over. Downward, a crosshatching draws me in.

The sky here is even wider than the landscape, and in it are different weathers: black clouds over the Berkshires, silvery ones ahead, blue sky to the right. Directly above, however, it's overcast: a low-contrast light. In this American place of abandoned hope I feel an expansive solitude. An easing takes place, a sense of safety, and yes, of alignment, though on a far larger scale than in the village. From here it's the Hudson River Valley with which the body aligns. I feel my levels of thought and feeling, from purely intellectual down to visceral, come into play, and I feel our collective American levels, too, for this desolate and glorious place in which promise and dashed hope coexist is insistently American. If there is an invitation here, the wrecked shed and bent poles make it one that is frank about the risks. If there is freedom here—and, for sure, there is lots of room—it's a freedom that knows grief. If there is prosperity—and, for sure, there is enormous wealth in the Hudson River Valley—it is mixed in with despair. Here the full spectrum of American possibility is in plain sight. The contradictions are unsettling. I have two conflicting agendas today: one to settle myself in that old cradle of providence—so capacious here, so that the part of me that always attaches to place and never wants to leave, wherever I am, can be reassured that all is well—and the other to climb over cradle's edge. Black wires sagging between telephone poles create a wobbly clef. Five birds like notes escape it, dipping in unison as they fly over the shoulder.

The habit of reading landscape as truly as possible has become almost too strong. Without choosing to do so, I start asking questions of the prospect: what are you now, what are you really? It has occurred to me that part of the problem we have in imagining the world in which we live has to do with the order in which it unfolded. The sequence was illogical. Big cars with fins on the interstate felt futuristic, but not during the Cuban missile crisis. Underground testing happened out of sight as the quiet prosperity of suburbia settled in. The industrial Midwest made us feel strong, yet was dwarfed by the siloed missiles. Of all the developments embedded in this panorama before me in unseen ways, the enclosure created by our subatomic capability is surely the most difficult to grasp. And yet it was the first of this series of spatial reconfigurations that radically altered our relationship to the physical world. This put us in the position of doing postdoctoral studies while we should have been in kindergarten.

Furthermore, the atomic predicament, the big assignment we faced in the very first stage of our education, was invisible, unless you traveled to Japan. Also, we had zero humanistic acknowledgment of the meaning and consequences of this technical feat for the human race—a responsibility that rested on American shoulders. Still reeling from the Nazis who had emerged from the heart of Western civilization and were even yet barely understood, we had no cultural underpinning, no orientation, to help us approach this other, very different, but atrociously advanced lesson.

Had the order of development been more logical—had we gotten used to the interstate and big cars, and then propeller flight, and then jet travel, and then the trip to the moon and the sight of the planet in space and the environmental movement it inspired, and then global communications and a daily experience of the netted world and, with it, an economy that dissolves national borders, and then, with those tools in hand, begun to grapple with worldwide climate change, and only after that faced the nuclear arms race; had we been able to move incrementally into that collapsed space typical of electronic communications, worldwide environmental dangers, and Cold War conditions, in that order, starting with its most peaceful aspect and moving incrementally toward its most dangerous—we would not have compartmentalized these challenges as we did, to the detriment of our understanding of them all. Certainly we would not have had to silo the nuclear predicament in the way that we did, turning it totally over to elites who tried to reassure us by pretending they had it in hand. Instead of arresting the development of a collective interior life in response to these worldwide conditions, we would have been able to build it, developing the morally imaginative grasp—the cultural maturity—necessary for effective political response going forward. Educated over generations in global enclosure, we would have learned gradually to accept the shift onto our shoulders of responsibility for our own physical survival—would have learned how to imagine the world, our relationship to it and to each other under these conditions.

One can ask, for example, had the view from the moon awoken us to the fragility of nature before we were numbed by the facts of the Cold War, might not the environmental movement have been less romantic? Had a more humanistic environmental movement, reinforced by the worldwide consciousness of the internet, cast itself as a movement to protect ourselves rather than nature at the expense of the poorest among us, might not a subsequent unleashing of annihilative atomic energy into a world quite used to seeing itself as singular and vulnerable have been received for what it really was: a grave threat to all mankind, to which the desire for an effective protective response would have been instinctive. With a foundation for the era of global enclosure already laid down, the political response to this panoramic danger would have been tailored to the actuality rather an improvisation based on out-of-date geopolitical legacies. In this revised order of development, people who wanted to eliminate the weapons would not have been seen as crackpot idealists who knew nothing of the real world. Would MAD, the policy of increasing the danger in order to hold it off, have been politically possible? Looking at our handling of biological weaponry much later, anthrax, for example, it's true that our government continued to invest in research on weaponized anthrax in the 1990s, for purposes of treating victims, work that required a supply of the actual agent, but in very small amounts, with extreme care taken to contain it, and secretly, because, were the public to get wind of it, political resistance would ensue, because of the obvious insanity of stockpiling any of this stuff at all. In the case of anthrax we have a deep active understanding of our vulnerability to our own advanced weapons: of how, though developed to protect us, they also expose us to their destructive powers. Though the nuclear predicament has, mercifully, receded to the point that the possibility of annihilation of life as we have known it no longer looms, though it has become merely a severe danger among other dangers, the memory of the full-fledged predicament in its prime can still serve as a classroom of a kind, in which we can catch up with ourselves.

The actual order in which developments unfolded is irreversible, of course, and, at least in part, laid down by the development of science itself. Still, the fantasy of rearranging it can make our present-day situation more comprehensible and maybe help us grow into it. A manageable order would have produced the interstate first, then we get air travel, then we develop the capacity to space travel to the moon, from which we see the planet as a single fragile entity. Then we learn how to unleash subatomic energy, at large in space but safely locked up in our fragile entity hitherto: how careful we would be with that! Momentarily, at least, the model seems almost settled. With this order of development in mind, our present, twenty-first-century situation can seem, sitting here in the meadow, to be almost natural—an unfolding of our nature.

The global enclosure before me, with its tensions between the visible and the invisible; between the old Newtonian world of human experience and the almost metaphysical nature of quantum physics; between proximity and distance as we know them in the human body and spatial relations that stretch between cosmic and subatomic scales, both far above and beneath the grasp of our senses; between the diurnal time of the body and the instantaneous time of collapsed space; all this begins to suggest a new spatial architecture that I might come to know as intimately as I have known the world I was born into. Oddly, it's medieval architecture that helps me with this. The Gothic cathedral is clearly a work of man's genius yet one that conveys a transcendent realm beyond our comprehension. But this enlarges rather than diminishes the tiny person kneeling in it, while at the same time engendering humility and awe. The grandeur of the global enclosure is also a product of man's genius, but to different effect. It presents the tiny person in the meadow with the problem that human beings have become so large there is nothing beyond us, leaving her grasping for humility and awe without success. With that she is diminished, even crushed. There is nothing to put this largeness in proportion: no measure outside it to help us learn to grow into it, to learn to occupy it well. While the medieval cathedral is all about presence, the global enclosure, however crowded, however lacking in escape, is all about absence. Not that I think the solution is to go back to the theology of medieval times. In the end, what an unfolding of the global enclosure in a logical sequence reveals is only a clearer vision of our predicament. But that is worth something. It's a space characterized by the paradox of our power and our helplessness, primarily over ourselves, the hallmark of this era, laying out the cultural, and the ultimately political, work before us. Not that I can hold this vision for long. If I allow my effort to slacken for a moment, the eerie architecture of the global enclosure vanishes, the panorama before me reverting to its old romantic self, becoming merely uplifting. How beautiful!

This mystical struggle gets me only so far. Soon the elemental question of work comes forward again. How does the hand of work contribute to the meaning of this landscape? To narrow the question, what does this landscape reveal of how we make our living on the planet and our relation to one another, not to mention to the planet, as we do so? Or, to turn the question around, how has the change in the defining tier of work, from industrial to mind-work, altered the meaning of this panorama? Immediately, of course, I know I am in the collapsed space of electronic communications: that was implicit in the cathedral as well. But in the sense of the work itself, of how we actually make our actual living, how strange it is to sit here, bottom on the ground, yet also taking in the truth of the ghostliness of contemporary work, its absence of expression in the landscape.

This landscape, whether directly or indirectly, derives its meaning from the electronically facilitated worldwide economy. This much I know beyond a shadow of a doubt from my travels: the new first order of work is panoramically and intimately infiltrative, without exception. It is grounded—if one can use that word—in the collapsed space of the small bright screen in which distance means nothing. But because of those bodies of ours, it is also, of necessity, in relation to place in the old sense in which nearness and distance do have meaning, though much more loosely, almost arbitrarily, than ever before. Still, the tether is there: the tether of the body. Though there are times when I would rather not know it, this half-pastoral, half-abandoned, half-wild scene is an extension of New York City. One of the paradoxes of our worldwide economy is that, while its formative energy is ferociously dispersive, it also requires a pattern of extreme centralization, points from which the vast dispersion is managed. As a result, while most cities are in danger of decline, a few exercise an extensive influence on the territory around them, far greater in range than that of the older, industrial city. This territory of influence is not consistently contiguous—especially toward the edges, which can become vague. In the case of New York, for example, much of Vermont, some of the seacoast of Maine, the prosperous parts of the city of Philadelphia and even Bethlehem, Pennsylvania, from which people actually commute to New York, belong to that geography. In fact, its outer limits extend to worldwide outposts, a kind of archipelago. In the end, the geography of a global city like New York extends outward in unmapped complexity, the terrain of a continent-hopping citizenry that could be seen as a class that is no longer really connected to a nation.

The Hudson River Valley is unified by worn old mountains, three ranges, all within sight from my meadow, and the streams running down them, successively enlarging, toward the river; by bear,

woodchuck, mink, otter, beaver, and bald eagles; by mixed hardwood conifer swamps, freshwater wetlands and fens where the
butterflies Dion skipper and black dash can be found; by the blue-
winged, cerulean, and blackburnian warblers; by eastern box, wood,
and spotted turtles; by fertile valleys, some wide, some narrow, in
which corn, buckwheat, hay, and vegetables are grown; by apple,
pear, and cherry orchards; by four pronouncedly different seasons;
as by its odd semifeudal history, an industrial moment, gentrification of some parts and economic abandonment of others, and
the architecture and culture—the landscape—arising out of that.
Within this container are the patterns created on the land by these
different layers of work, significant agriculture before the Erie Canal connected the Hudson to the Midwest, significant industry after that, much of it along the Hudson, some factories still, but that
age has passed. In our age, a new model of farming that feeds elites
has burgeoned. Entrepreneurship, some old, some inventively new,
is a part of the mix of contemporary work, though it must also be
said that for people whose families have lived here for generations,
reliably sustaining work has become sparse, leaving government,
in its various forms—road care, teaching, delivering the mail—as
probably the most steadfast employer and in many parts the biggest
one. Yet as we have moved into a new era, more and more people
from New York have settled here and they make livings that draw
on the energy of the city, a trend that, in my view, is what is changing the meaning of this landscape most profoundly. Distance—or
nearness—has a lot to do with this change: it matters that a person
can travel to the city in a few hours from much of the valley, too
long for the daily commute required by industrial-age office work,
but fine for the occasional visits to headquarters that is all that is required for much of the outsourced work that electronic technology
makes possible. The meaning of the panorama before me cannot be
separated from this distant nearness to the global city as a capitol

of the first tier of work in our enclosed world, work that is today the principal definer of landscape everywhere, if not much of a landscape shaper, given its ethereal nature, or at least not here in the Hudson River Valley.

And yet the character of the scene before me reveals nothing of what this top-level, landscape-defining work is, much less about how it is actually done. It has, rather, to do with pleasure. People chose to work here, rather than in the city itself, because they enjoy these surroundings and also because it is less expensive to live here. Its aesthetic features also make it a venue of second homes maintained for leisure time—vacations and weekends. But in recent years many people have actually moved into their vacation homes as they realize their work can be done from that proximate distance. So then: the primary economic value of this landscape lies in its aesthetic qualities: its value as an amenity. It's real estate of a special kind, new to the global age. The countrylike qualities of this bit or that determine price. Beauty, indeed, is the most reliable economic measure. Or you could say fantasy determines value: how closely a place conforms to our idea of "real country," which, of course, makes it not that at all. The real estate market knows aesthetic pricing in minute detail, far better than the banks that, being national now, get confused by "comparables," when properties not far from each other are actually vastly different in beauty/fantasy-determined value. For the geography of this kind of global country is an oil-and-water matter. One village is a part of the global archipelago, but another is back in the semiabandoned realm of the struggling agriculture of the late industrial age. Beauty is not the only determining factor in the oil-and-water map. Fashion and social prestige, and factors even more difficult to measure, play a part, too. There are very large swatches in the New York City sphere of influence—my friend Caroline's fashionable county across the river, for example—that have a social prestige that makes them consistently global. This side of the river is spottier. There are stretches of country where, if you mapped the real estate values in colors, you would get something that looks like camouflage.

I hate admitting this. Seeing my village and surroundings this way takes away from me my oldest place-pleasures. It certainly undoes a sense of security in the cradle of providence. I think this dismay goes back to the mysterious power of suburbophobia. What all this means is that my country is really suburbia of a new, worldwide kind. But these myth-shattering concepts in their own way are deflections of the true complexity of this scene. They comfort with an easy cynicism—it's all economics and status—that takes the heart out of the matter, when in fact the heart of the matter is much more interesting. For example, this scene immediately here, this seamless agrarian spot, so lonely, even desolate, with its abandoned shed and silo, all this belongs to M., who came up here in the early 1970s, when he was a photographer for the United Nations, to visit a friend who worked for *The New York Times*. The New York Power Authority was planning, at that time, to route major statewide power lines through the Durham Valley, as the valley between the Helderbergs and the Catskills, the valley immediately before me, is known. M.'s host and a couple of New York white-shoe lawyers who also had places up here were going to court to stop the march of pylons and cables through the bucolic valley and had asked M. to photograph the valley in order to supply them with convincing evidence of its beauty as part of their case. He did that, the suit was successful—the Sierra Club also supplied photos—and the power lines were routed elsewhere. With that, the meaning of the valley, and certainly the view from my meadow, was altered. Rather than the lonely spot expressing the deep slow withering of what had once been robust agriculture in this region, the scene was a cherished vista that had been fought for by city dwellers who valued the region for its beauty—and wanted to stop the natural course of development in order to preserve it. Four years later M. and his wife, L., bought the Hopperesque house near my meadow, as I call it—the meadow is theirs—from a local farmer whose family had been on the land for a long time and was ready to sell. Thirty acres came with the house, to which they have added over the years, including the hayfields going over the shoulder where the silo and shedlike barn stand. Thereafter M. and L. vigilantly increased their holdings whenever land came up for sale, designating it as a conservancy, in that way protecting the vista in its poignant loneliness for a very long time. They did this not for their own pleasure only, though that has been a part of it, but out of a desire to save this landscape as a collective inheritance from the depredations of development. If, as the global economy set in, the amenity market had been allowed to become the landscape maker here—had taken its natural course—the foreground of the view before me would, by now, have been filled with houses big and little, the owners drawn by the beauty of valley and mountains even as they "ruined" it by being there. I am sure I would not even see the valley before me because of a house perched on that auspicious shoulder. Indeed, many stretches of landscape around here are either pastoral or wild because they were quietly acquired by people who had means to do so, who also took on the sometimes onerous burden of husbanding them. (M. and L. allow a local farmer to hay their land for free, but others have more complicated arrangements.) This hardly makes the landscape a bastion of privilege, or if so only in a relatively minor and spotty way, but it must also be said that the wish to suppress development and "save" landscape, or even to just keep back reforestation, preserving the fields, tends on the whole to express the values of city people, of what is ever more a global gentry, thus unwittingly reinforcing a growing gap between those who belong to the global geography and those who do not.

This divide, which here replicates the national blue-red divide, can make local politics almost violent. The farmer who hopes to make some money off his land by developing it, working-class families who have seen employment shrink to nearly nothing but have been offered a meaningful sum by a fracking company—such people see landscape preservationists, like environmentalists, as the enemy. When I consider that divide, as I sit here, I feel I am getting close to the deep contradictions in the social and economic forces represented by this scene; and then I see that I myself am a part of that. I live on a writer's income, not lavish for sure; but the cottage is a second home, to which I retreat when my work does not require a physical presence in the city. I may be able to argue, weakly, that my cottage is old, so that in coming here I did not change the landscape. But I can't possibly escape the fact that I came here because I love the half-pastoral, half-wild surroundings. This puts me clearly on one side of a nearly unbridgeable divide. I am against fracking for environmental reasons, and glad New York State finally stepped in, but my gladness in part has to do with my wish to not, when I make my pilgrimage to the high meadow, see a fracking apparatus in my view.

The air of abandonment up here is beloved by many. The spot is so much photographed and painted, it's surprising it hasn't gone up in smoke for the attention lavished on it. There is nothing really lonely, much less empty, here at all. And yet, no matter how often I come here, I am always changed inside by the derelict structures, the heave of the land down, the way the wind touches, stillness. A guy in an SUV stops to ask what I am doing here—I have gotten permission from M., I tell him. Oh, that's fine, he says. He is a deputy sheriff; he farms his own land nearby and is also the guy who cuts the hay on M.'s land. A garbage truck pulls up; the driver is a friend of the deputy sheriff. You can't make a living farming around here, not even close, but these two men farm anyway, because . . . Well, it's hard to say why. They just do. Farming is an American religion. The garbage man and the sheriff are not citizens of the global geography.

And yet they do more than most to keep this place the way I like it, and they love it in much the same way as I do. Come to a conclusion about class and landscape, and it will be contradicted, maybe within minutes.

Dragging out the truth of landscape is exciting but exhausting. I do it, I think, out of faithfulness to place—and faith in place: if we ask it will tell. Yet doing this brings me a loss. Thinking about the truth of landscape nowadays unmasks and destroys old certainties, strips me, separates me, or can. Right now stray beams of sun are again illuminating fields in the foothills across the valley: emerald. I had a friend over there, a distinguished man in his nineties, who was distressed because that very farm turned emerald now is likely to be sold soon, because the farmer is old and his kids don't want to carry on with the farming. Likely, my friend said with disgust, it would be built up with ski chalets. That was as horrid to me as to him, but a musing on my part about how that change reflected global forces already defining the landscape more or less ended our friendship. Not in an argument but just in evaporation of closeness of feeling. These landscape matters go deep. This man had completely accepted, even applauded work I had done and decisions I had made that in general have appalled people of his generation. But even indirectly legitimizing—or forgiving—those ski chalets of the future was unacceptable. And yet trying to see through to the meaning of landscape now seems to me to be essential to connection, too. The effort will undo old bonds based on a common understanding of what the landscape once was, will unravel languages of place-love. But how are we to carry connection into the future unless we have a common idea of what our surroundings are; that is to say, what our new age, humanistically speaking, is.

Tired, I turn to the meadow immediately around me. I look down into the crosshatching of the stems and blades of grasses, into its porous yet guarded depths. A drop of rain spatters on my hand.

Startled, I realize that I am cold and hungry. Time to go. It's always like that here, in the end. I stay and stay, thinking that I can somehow get enough of this place, get to the bottom of it, possess and take its secrets. But it always outstays me.

Part Two

The Hollowed City

The Pumpkins of Bergen Street

In 1990 I moved to Brooklyn. It was still possible then to have lived a long life in Manhattan and hardly ever gone to Brooklyn. Moving to Bergen Street, I felt I had fallen backward through time into the arms of a city that was unself-consciously dreaming. Just as, decades ago, wandering into a Roman piazza one could feel oneself to have stumbled on Italians in their natural life, so I, on first getting to know my Brooklyn neighborhood, was entranced by what seemed to be the ordinary wonder of an intact civilization. But these were my own people and this was my own city, and while the particulars were new to me, I felt reinforced by something to which I belonged that was vastly larger and more enduring than myself. The fine-gridded streets were a trellis of accumulated idiosyncrasy: the root-heaved slab of slate, the rough bark of an old tree, a plaster Madonna to one side. In another front yard, Mr. Morales, triple-bypass scarecrow, saluted passersby from his aluminum chair with vigorous gallantry in almost all weathers. These were new to me yet part of a language of place I could read well. Classical cornice spoke through sycamore lattice. The faded formal façades gave the street a casual transparency. A garbage truck grinding in a cold rain was a groan from the gut of creation. Pigeons banking at the corner of Bergen and Hoyt, flashing white underwings, broke up the surface of the world, revealing understories of existence in myself too. The newly discovered native landscape can develop us in ways that in a foreign place takes years.

On Smith, the commercial street, the head of a pig wearing sunglasses regarded you from the butcher's window. On the far side of Smith, Bergen was wide for industry: an ironworks, a cheese factory. Hard-used vehicles were in style in this neighborhood: the rolling kitchen, the haircut truck, the low-slung Chevy wagon from which a Slavic man hawked shimmering bluefish caught off Brighton Beach that morning. I thought I had fallen into the work of a great undiscovered poet and that I had all the time in the world to get to know it, missing that this poetry was well-known and the bards long dead, this period of literature over: that I was living in an afterimage that in a certain way I already knew.

Signs that the world had, in its essence, changed floated in, but they were from afar and secondhand. My living room was on the second floor, high-ceilinged in the nineteenth-century style, making room for thought. One day in that room I was reading *The Ends of the Earth* by Robert Kaplan. This book is an antiromantic travelogue dedicated to shedding light on the grim contemporary reality of unvisited regions—shantytowns in Asia Minor, depressed cities in the former Soviet Union. Famous or beautiful sites are avoided, but one passage nevertheless described traveling by bus across a plateau in the Himalayas known as the Roof of the World. Even the jaundiced Kaplan was thrilled by this geographical drama, though the reader knows this only through his observation of three hippie kids who didn't look up from their paperbacks to take in the Roof of the World. In an unusual aside, Kaplan expresses disgust at the kids' indifference, in this becoming, in spite of himself, the old-fashioned traveler, agog at the mysteries of far-off places. I, Kaplan's reader, there in my lofty room, was shocked and angry along with him, but what really hurt was an intimation that maybe the Roof of the World had indeed somehow been drained of a meaning it once had; that the kids were just making a personal choice, as of one dish over another on a menu; that they were not, in other words, stupidly indifferent to something important. Later, in my struggle with the meaning of place, I would come to see this double take less as reflecting the reduction of the world to consumeristic travel—though that is a considerable effect of our time—and more as a stepping back of one layer of reality and a stepping forward of another. What was the difference, from the point of view of the moon, between reading a book or looking out the window, or, for that matter, dreaming?

Jarred, I looked up and saw the room subtly changed. Despite the settling proportions, the moldings, the plaster rosettes on the ceiling, the tall windows, the room, like the Roof of the World, no longer mattered in quite the same way that it had. I call this the Kaplan effect.

The Finnegan effect was akin. It, too, originated in a book, *Cold New World* by William Finnegan. In it he writes about a teenager in an L.A. gang who says to the author that there would be no point in going anywhere else—because it would be no different: he knew because he had hitchhiked all over California. The well-traveled Finnegan shivers at this closing in of the boy's horizons. I was with him in that but, again, also wondered if maybe the boy was right, and not just because he would probably find himself in gangland wherever he went, or facing the same absence of opportunity. Something had happened to the horizon for all of us that made moving from one place to another much less significant than it had been, maybe pointless.

The Umbria effect was related, too, and not from a book, but from Umbria itself, which I visited in this period. Long ago I had known Italy well. But this time in Umbria I did not quite feel that I was in Italy as I had known it. There were the vineyards, the olive groves, and the dog that somehow seemed to be barking in Italian and yet I had to keep saying to myself, "Here I am in Italy." Could it be the American-style supermarket? It seemed to me that the landscape was performing, and possibly for me. In this I was partly right: the E.U. subsidized old landscapes to bolster tourism. An elegant American at an alfresco lunch said with bored cleverness, "Rome is a theme park now, of course." I wanted to take her head off: church under church and under that a pagan temple, and beneath that a spring—this cannot be stolen. In the next instant I knew that in some sense she was probably right. But how? How could that be?

Back home in my neighborhood, the Kaplan, Finnegan, and Umbria effects came and went. The Umbria effect was, in a way, strongest. There were two regular manifestations. One would happen when I was writing down impressions of my neighborhood in my notebook and then would have the weird feeling that I was plagiarizing rather than actually describing what I had seen. The other would happen as I was walking down the street, observing familiar features—a certain doorway, the bar on the corner—and in a fleeting double take would "see" that the neighborhood, for all its apparent authenticity, just was not what it appeared to be. This effect reminded me of the movie *Invasion of the Body Snatchers*, in which aliens occupy the bodies of individuals without altering their appearance or mannerisms, allowing them to infiltrate a community in the guise of utterly familiar people.

Of course the neighborhood was changing, but wasn't New York always changing? Weren't the changes on Bergen Street of a piece with the city's ever moving texture—immigrant groups succeeding one another, decline of family town houses into shabby boarding-houses, an inner-city period, and then some young and middle-class people, attracted by low prices and good architecture, moving in? I took pleasure in details of what I took to be that classic movement, such as the fine social nuances of pumpkins. The best architecture was on Dean Street, one block away, and, as Halloween neared, jack-o'-lanterns made out of real pumpkins would appear on most stoops there. Indeed, the people who lived in the finest house, a very wide brownstone with beautiful windows, always set out on their stoop a big, homely, lopsided, gorgeous monstrosity of a pumpkin that, in its rural authenticity, was very high class. On my block you might see some ordinary-sized real pumpkins, as on my own stoop, but also lots of plastic ones, along with skeletons and artificial spiderwebs strewn about windows and doorways. These differences in Halloween décor expressed subtle gradations of background. If you had come to Brooklyn from Manhattan, then you set out real pumpkins, as I did, whereas if you were Brooklyn-bred your pumpkins were plastic. Did you grow up in Brooklyn and move to Manhattan, rising in the world there and then return? Then you set out real pumpkins, too. Did you grow up in Brooklyn and rise in the world but never leave the borough? Then you defiantly continued on with not only plastic pumpkins but maybe a gleeful overuse of skeletons and spiderwebs, too.

The bedrooms in my house were, in upside-down fashion, on the ground floor. Mine faced the street, and the windows were barred with handsome old ironwork. In summer, I kept them wide open behind interior wooden shutters. If I woke in the middle of the night, I would see white light from the street lamps slivered by the shutters against the wall of my room. After eleven, traffic was rare. Footsteps of passersby would sound crisply. Sometimes I would catch a whiff from the coffee factory to the southeast. The atmosphere of Bergen at night could be so deeply peaceful as to be almost pastoral. The experience of it could be a kind of sleep in itself. Sometimes, though, most often in summer, I would hear gunfire: a shot, or a series of shots, sometimes clear, sometimes muffled, in the night. This would be in the Gowanus Houses, a project, one finely calibrated block to the south, but not a part of the neighborhood as I ordinarily thought of it. Our street was not altogether safe, but people responded quickly at any sign of trouble. Yet when I heard gunfire just the one block away, there would be only a shadowy stirring of fear inside me, and concern, and perhaps a pang of abstract compassion. But the gunfire did not disturb the tranquil mood of the neighborhood or keep me from falling back to sleep, though it did disturb me that this was so, and not just for humanitarian reasons but also because such a divide between juxtaposed places seemed impossible. Why wasn't I scared or, at the very least, feeling for someone else nearby who might be? This was another of the ephemeral signs that something strange had happened—not only that the world was not what it seemed to be, not only that my experience of it was altered. Nearness didn't matter—necessarily.

I avoided the projects generally but not completely. I might be forced to search for a parking place there—always, if possible, choosing the north side of Wyckoff, where a block of classic architecture directly facing the projects would look after my car. Wyckoff had the feeling of a cliff edge. I had two dogs, Sadie and Rags, and for a while I walked them with a group that used a chain-link enclosure on the project grounds as a dog run. This was a little more like going into the project realm, though I still felt insulated in a bubble of pooches and treats.

All this bothered and intrigued me, so I began making the crossing consciously, without insulation. Doing so, I found I went into a little blackout, and experienced a popping sensation, a psychic version of what happens in one's ears when pressure changes in a plane, just at the crossing. Once on the other side I was simply there. I could sit on a bench and sun myself. I could watch a man from the city government overseeing six women sweeping a puddle of water: welfare to work. I could watch a crew of white guys doing renovations in the projects having lunch. Going back, I would have the same tiny blackout and popping sensation.

In the basement of a Methodist church that faced on the projects, I found a soup kitchen run by a skinny, hyperactive black woman in her sixties. Cauldrons of food out of large generic cans were on the stove. Tables covered with red-and-white-checked cloths had been set, and people sat at them quietly waiting for a meal. I was sorry to intrude on this peaceful moment. But the woman who ran the kitchen was glad to see me. She told me that it was hard to get financial support: the city contributed matching funds to what was raised, but the only people in the neighborhood who had ever contributed were two women for whom she worked as a housekeeper in Brooklyn Heights. Otherwise, she had no way of reaching people—the newer residents of Bergen Street, one block away, for example, who might have a few dollars to give. She lived in the projects with her grandson, who was in grade school. She told me that one August night when she had been sitting in her living room looking at television, a bullet had come through the window, barely missing her head.

Meanwhile, in this period I often visited a friend on Shelter Island. I noticed going there that though it was a trip of a hundred miles there was, compared with going to the projects, barely a transition. The two places were of a piece. It was almost as if Bergen and Shelter Island belonged to one geographic realm and the projects to another. Because I wanted to get inside the schism that broke Bergen and the projects apart, I decided to spend time right on the fault line at the corner of Hoyt and Wyckoff. The October day was so warm that I could take off my jacket. The weather reminded me of the previous weekend on Shelter Island, misty blue, sails moving in the outer waters. I sat on the stoop of a corner house. Immediately the owner opened the door to shoo me away, then instantly relented when she saw me, though slightly confused. From the stoop I could see directly into the area of the projects: what did I see? Many people there appeared to be battered by life—had something physically wrong: a limp, a squinting eye. Young men who should have been in school loitered. Nearby, a woman had laid down an old blanket on the sidewalk on which were displayed a few possessions for sale. With the woman was her ten-year-old son, who seemed to be made frantic by their situation: to be almost out of his mind. I thought I smelled human excrement; then I thought I had been hallucinating. I also saw a chic young woman with a portfolio case walking smartly toward Bergen and the subway, and another well-dressed woman in a blue silk shirt with two children, and a man in the distance with a miniature poodle who reminded me of a man I had seen on the beach on Shelter Island with a poodle also. Two Hispanic women, a mother and daughter probably, all dolled up, had heavily lipsticked mouths that looked like roses. I had been deeply wrong; there was no schism, just people, the same on one side as another. Still, there was something about sitting there that felt oddly forbidden. Directly opposite my perch was another town house, newly painted in sophisticated, historically accurate colors—rose with light blue trim. In the windows were real pumpkins.

Later that same day I drove out to Shelter Island, leaving the expressway for an old road that I knew well from long ago, turned blue in places reflecting the pale sky. Dessicated cornstalks, still standing, and there were apple and peach trees, much pruned, and vineyards. I knew I was alive and in good condition because the intensity of the vine forms, leafless and pointing upward crookedly, made my heart leap. Though the land already seemed to be going to sleep for winter, there was husbandry still, upheaval, also silly pumpkin festivals, and then, at last, pumpkins themselves, lying about, in the ruins of their fields. Where the road crossed a narrow sandy neck, the Long Island Sound on one side was Prussian blue, choppy, the air so clear that the far landmass was levitated and fragmented, the air become a bending lens.

Aside from my "effects," Kaplan, Finnegan, and Umbrian, I lived in those days without an intellectual superstructure with which to frame and name what was happening around me. I lived a compartmentalized life consequently: unnerved by an inexplicable falsification of place in the morning, and in the afternoon finding the lovely old world abundantly and poetically around me again. Looking back at those intimations of change, I see how complex and layered the faculty that reads place is, extending from intellect on down to somatic levels, and that this more instinctive registering leads the way in noticing. I cherish that touchstone of creaturely knowing as a reminder of the immensity of what we are going through, as of the consequences for us, even as it seems nothing much is happening, daily life going forward forgetfully, as always.

The architecture of my block was largely Victorian. In my parlor I was privy to the formality of those times, drinking in the restfulness and protection even while aware of the restrictions entailed and appreciative of being free. The tall front window suggested a matriarch looking out unseen at the theater of the street. I could see passersby, but they couldn't see me. A mirror hung between windows at the back. I might glimpse myself in my jeans and work shirt, a happy hermit crab, living in a nineteenth-century shell. I did not realize for a long time that, in the context of the world as it was becoming, I was more Victorian than not.

My garden in back was even more inward and protective. No hint of the street in the garden, or of the garden on the street. My dog Sadie was a preternaturally sensitive mixture of Lab and shepherd while Rags was an impulsive beagle. When I walked the dogs I usually came and went by the ground-floor door, under the stoop. Coming home on a nasty day I would unlock first the outer gate, then the inner door, the dogs crowding me. When I got it open Rags would rush up the stairs to see if there was something to eat in her bowl always. But in bad weather Sadie would rush straight to the back door begging to be let out into the garden, clearly assuming that the weather back there would be different. I knew what she meant exactly. The garden was an altogether other world.

The garden was a well of quiet: old cherry tree, ancient rose, teenaged Japanese maple in the middle of the postage-stamp lawn. In addition to the ground-floor entrance, an iron outdoor staircase led down from the parlor level. French doors opened onto the landing from which you could see across the tops of fences into the other shoe-box gardens. To one side was a house long owned by a Puerto Rican family, of whom only one, Luciano, spoke English. One spring day, I came home from work, looking forward to the quiet of my garden. Stepping out on the landing, I found that three women who lived next door had set up a TV in their garden. It was on at high volume. I tried to communicate a request to turn down the sound. When they finally understood they were clearly startled, as if the idea of not enjoying a loud TV in the garden was dumbfounding. Surprisingly, they were not annoyed once they got my message, but readily assented, as if I were the native and they were newcomers, eager to please. I went indoors to get something. When I returned I saw from the landing that everything in the next garden—tables, chairs, and television—was gone. In ways like this I was forced to understand myself as a part of the very change that seemed to be silently stealing the world.

I never saw the women in the garden again, but in the fall—having been away for a time—I saw from the landing that a crop of some kind had been planted there. Broad green leaves created a canopy; I thought they must be zucchinis. But the next time I looked a black-and-white cat was disturbing the canopy. I saw orange: pumpkins! Early in October I was startled to see that the vines had been cut right to the ground with slanting strokes as with a machete. Nothing remained but the barest bits of stalks and earth. The ruthlessness was alarming: was Luciano angry or was this just a sure stroke learned long ago on an island? I wondered where he had sold the crop. On Dean Street? Perhaps not a big enough market. Brooklyn Heights, where the dominance of natural-pumpkin-loving people had long been firmly secured? I hoped he had made a good profit.

The outward signs of gentrification were few and gentle: a brass knocker, a new Volvo on the street. And yet there was also a kind of forest fire in the roots, hidden but devastating. A building that had long before been broken up into apartments was sold to someone who wanted to make of it a single house, as it had been in Victorian times. However, the tenants in the top-floor apartment, African Americans, refused to leave. But instead of trying to ingratiate themselves they had loud parties late into the night and sometimes threw shoes out the window. They had never behaved that way before. I felt for the new owner, a kindly white man who wore flannel shirts as if he were in Vermont and smoked a pipe. But I felt relief in this bad behavior, too, of the kind that comes when something silent is made vocal. It was not just that poor residents were being driven out. Though I couldn't put my finger on why, I myself could feel loss, helplessness, dismay, a wish to defy, anger, and I was not even remotely in danger of being driven away. Displacement in situ was what was happening to me.

Just a few blocks away from my home, in a place that had become wasteland, there appeared a suburban-style mall, outsized, enclosed, a world unto itself, without reference to its surroundings. This was different from the divide between Bergen Street and the projects. The mall came up into the known world like a big mushroom. In its pure unrelatedness it was, in a way, harder to bridge to. I avoided it religiously, but then one day I needed something and I went. There were those strange, wide windowless corridors with stores off them we all know. But at the time the mall was still unfinished and few of its second-story spaces had been leased. A long corridor up there was entirely empty and at its end was a plate-glass window to which I was drawn. It looked out across a colossal excavated pit. Almost lost in the pit were railroad tracks that came to an end in the kind of scrappy vegetation that grows in bad soil. On the other side of the abyss was a large rectangular building made of white material and with no windows at all, just immense red letters attached to the blank façade, taking up much of one side: "JUST FEET." Beyond JUST FEET, exposed in a way that was never intended, was a row of brownstones and a church on the scale of my neighborhood. In this context they looked miniature and not quite real, as if they were in a photo. But the angle of the street, in this scene of demolition, seemed unnatural, like a broken bone, as if the old city had been stomped on by JUST FEET.

A bit later, right there by my tall parlor window, I got hooked up to the internet for the first time. The connection was dial-up, and took a while. A friend had warned me that waiting time between searches could feel dead and to have a book handy, which I did. But then my monitor flickered and there it was. A few random searches, reading in between, and I understood: the internet was the dumpster of everything: Shakespeare, medical information, maps, lies, advice, all unrelating. Junk and greatness cohabited cheek by jowl without speaking. Nothing like a library, even a disorganized one like mine, not even free associative in a private way, searchable only by often nonsensical keywords. Nothing at all like the trellis of accumulated idiosyncrasy, either. Still, this dumpsterish incoherence was strangely familiar, not unlike the illogic of dreams. The internet was a deeply distracted thing, but in that not new. One got used to it in almost an instant. "Okay. I got it," was the feeling. I was quickly bored—a deflective reaction, of course.

It was when I got off the net that I had my transitional shock. Looking out my window at the façades, the balustrades, the pediments, I now knew the truth. This steady-seeming scene was in fact perforated by the reality I had just entered through my screen. In a moment I understood—I am not sure how—that the global space compacted into such screens had swallowed place in its old sense and that what I was seeing with my eyes through the window was not solid at all but somehow secondary. The screen was a portal into a kind of collapsed space that had sucked the world into itself. I felt—rather than saw—that the block, even while gamely expressing Victorian confidence, was actually like Swiss cheese, perforated by holes that were portals to the collapsed yet world-containing space of the internet. In this our physical environment seemed to have somehow been turned inside out, with the seemingly containing houses actually inhabited by a kind of space that in its way was more encompassing— more "outside"—than even the great outdoors. As a result, the block itself was no longer entirely a "here" in the way it had once been. I know that I understood the reality of global collapsed space all at once because I remember how, that very day, encountering someone who had not yet been on the internet, I was acutely aware of what they didn't know—their innocence. I envied them and was frightened for them, because some of their most basic assumptions were delusions. I didn't know if it would be a favor to disabuse them or not, but in any event there was no way you could communicate this just by talking.

Even after my initiation into the internet, the old experience of place by some miracle sometimes still returned full-fledged. One January, a blizzard came to Brooklyn in the night. Climbing upstairs to the parlor in the morning, I found that snow had blown in under the rickety French doors that led to the garden stair. On the street side the blizzard had spattered the windows in a leopardy pattern. The wind whistled in the chimney, and it was cold. So I lit a fire and settled in beside it with a book. The book carried me away, while at the same time I felt supported by the solidity of the house. The scrape

2

The Market

I now live on Riverside Drive and 135th Street, high up, sight flying straight from my study window out over the Hudson River with hardly any mediation. Riverside is elevated here, on a viaduct connecting two hilltops, the West Side Highway angling out from under, Amtrak down there, too, with its woofing warble that I like to hear. A bit of industrial waterfront is visible and the river. Across are the Palisades, heroic geology, and, from the plateau behind them, planes rise and descend at Teterboro Airport. Apartment buildings set on top of the Palisades appear to be the same height as the cliffs and, in that, make nonsense of them. Upstream the George Washington Bridge plows into the Palisades from Manhattan, a bit below their top. Cars and trucks stream, or sometimes crawl, across the bridge, adding to the overall sense that I live in an environment of motion.

By the time I moved here, the struggle between seeing the city as I had known it and seeing it as what it was becoming was long behind me. As for the internet, I could go in and out of collapsed global space without blinking. I had come to understand intellectually, and a little less well emotionally, that the city I had known was a creation of the industrial age, and that that era had passed, leaving behind an intact fossil now occupied by a different time, the time of that collapsed global space—an era as yet without a satisfactory name, still incompletely unfolded and certainly far from maturity. It is an age that does not yet know itself, nor does the city know itself either anymore. I had gone from glimpsing the disappearance of the former world to looking for clues to the character of the emergent one, even while treasuring moments in which a human presence of time past fills the city as a wind fills a sail, then drops off—just a gust. These moments are precious, not only because of their sweetness but because they remind us of what living in a fully developed society, in its prime, can be.

The older city was punctuated by wells of stillness, of which homes themselves were the most common, but which were to be found in more public places also: a library, a church, a less visited part of a large museum, and sometimes even a busy corner. These spots, I find, still exist. You are hurrying in crowds and then there you are in a shaft of quiet from which you look out all around you in perfect calm. One spot where I find such a shaft is at the northwest corner of 125th Street and Lenox Avenue, just a bit above the intersection. The southwest corner of the sidewalk at Fifty-Seventh Street and Fifth Avenue, far busier, has, all my life, reliably contained such a well of stillness, despite the intensity of both car and people traffic. But the wells can appear temporarily almost anywhere. Without them, the ferocious energy of the city would become brutal. They provide outdoor counterpoints to a cyclonic energy, and in that are essential to livable existence in it. Especially in Manhattan, the simultaneous compacting and diffusing of energy would have no stability at all were it not pegged with multiple refuges of quiet.

But homes, in their normalcy and quotidian privacy, have long been the most permanent still points for New Yorkers, and the most necessary. For myself, until I moved to Riverside Drive, I had chosen homes that had an inward-turning, nested quality, physically positing stillness to the energy outside. They had a feeling of being way inside the city. That is not to say that a view is necessarily antithetical to the stillness of home. I lived for a long time with a view from lower Fifth Avenue across Greenwich Village, but that was in itself a stabilizing vista. The view from this new home on Riverside Drive is not. The building is old. Major elements in the view are old: the Drive, the river, the ancient Palisades. But overall the view with its enclosing motion thrusts me into the destabilized reality of collapsed global space, which had, in any event, whether I liked it or not, already invaded my home, in the form of the screen most obviously. Home itself, in other words, had already changed whatever its address. Still, even though I had been attracted to the apartment because of the out-flinging view, it gave me agoraphobia for a while.

As for this matter of New York having been an "industrial" city—that is to say, the creation of a manufacturing economy—one has to qualify that by saying that, over time, it became a center less of factories themselves than of corporate headquarters: of management. In this, it was the national apogee. It's not really natural for me to call New York an industrial city. Of course I have always known that it was that in an academic way, but to me, personally, it has been "New York," as distinct from any other city for most of my life. The economic interpretation of the man-made world is illuminating, but, to my way of seeing, it's also much too specialized and reductive to truly capture the layered complexity of a particular city like New York. Furthermore, one of the most blinding fallacies of our age is to see everything in terms of money. It is true that how money is made and how that has changed is a story that bridges the gap that has opened up between place as we have known it and what it is becoming. It's also true that in order to understand that gap as I experienced it in New York, I had to see the physical artifact as that of an "industrial city." When change of the kind we have been going through detaches so much of the physical world from the energy out of which it was created, so that it becomes a kind of fossil, the story of how money was made and how that has changed can show us how we got from there to here in a way no other story can. But I also distinguish between money, a sophisticated invention, and work, which is elemental, a part of both our nature—most of us want to be productive—and our condition: we have to work to live, whether money is in play or not. Work is embedded in our very existence in the sense of survival but also in our identity and desire for fulfillment as human beings, whereas money is our own creation. So even as I use the term "industrial city," and note how the way wealth was produced shaped the city, and do this because landscape itself taught me to do so, I also resist the tendency of an economic way of thinking to exclude so much else about life.

We can't really know what the city is today, much less what it is becoming. All we know for sure is that the metamorphosis has to do with work, and that electronic tools have a lot to do with how work has changed. For me, one of the most pervasive effects of those tools is a demotion of the physical world. It's this, above all, that has drained meaning from cities, as from all landscapes, often leaving the old, complex, expressive physical creation intact, but without its animating spirit. At the heart of my struggle with how to know cities under these new conditions is my belief that the genius of all landscapes lies in how, in addition to expressing a way of work, they serve as a substructure of our common interior life. To me, this symbiosis between physical and immaterial realms gets close to what civilization is. One of the most confusing aspects of this moment, in which the material world seems to have become altogether less important—people walking down the street on cell phones, the disappearance of the desk, the person in bed next to you vanished into the screen—is that we are left without the old fertile relationship between our interior and exterior realms. Carrying around with us, as we do, these tools that vastly extend our minds, we seem to have somehow floated free of the physical landscape, impossible as that seems. Where to get a footing, then?

Another result of the ascendance of the immaterial realm is that forms in the material one become fungible. In the industrial age, cities, however particular, whatever their previous histories, were generic, were The City. But as these fossils of an old way of work reinvent themselves in this new era—or fail to—the results are so various, their improvised characters so happenstantial that the question arises as to whether the city as long-evolving archetype, changing with the eras, is actually disappearing. Are our separately struggling old cities simply in metamorphosis, are they just overwriting themselves as landscape always does, puzzling us because we don't know how to read them in their new form, or are their various efforts at renewal like campsites among ruins? Sociologist Saskia Sassen has seen in New York, Tokyo, and London a new role for the city as command centers of the global economy, bringing an extreme centralization necessary to balance the extreme decentralization of work in an era in which locality is unimportant. She sees other candidates in play, such as Sydney and Frankfurt, but this is a role that only a few cities can assume. Are all the others then still kin as they once were in times past? Whatever New York, in its burgeoning prosperity, is becoming, we can say with some confidence that, with its deranging alloys of solidity and mirage, inheritance and disinheritance, continuity and severance, remembrance and oblivion, it is an epicenter of questions about the nature of the city in our new era.

There is an additional challenge to efforts to read all parts of our new landscape. Given that mind-work can slip quietly into the fossil of the old one, and given that the old one into which it slips is so well known to us as the expression of a fully evolved era, is so reverberative on multiple levels that our fluency in it will always override the stumbling discomfort of grappling with a new place-language, it's no wonder, given the power of the established archetype, and the deep imprint it has left on our imaginations, that most of the time we can happily overlook the fact that the world has changed at all. How, under these circumstances, are we to recognize an emerging world as such, much less learn how to read it with anything remotely approaching our understanding of the old one?

Though for me work is more elementally human than the abstractions of economic thinking, there is a strictly economic aspect of work in our present transformation that cannot be avoided, and which I have already referenced several times. It has to do with a kind of hierarchy of work. It has to do with what kind of work produces the most wealth in the wealthiest, most developed countries. In watching our transformation move forward in the city of New York, I cannot get away from the fact that when the first work of the world changes, just about everything else does, too, pulling the world as we have known it out from under like a rug. Other kinds of work—agrarian, industrial—go on, of necessity. But the first work of the prevailing economic powers is the dominant force that affects the meaning of all places and landscapes within its domain, whether they are directly the result of that work or not. Because, this time, the first work takes place in a worldwide arena, this time the change in place-meaning is worldwide, too. Because of the way our new electronic tools penetrate daily life, this transformation is not only panoramic but intimately infiltrative: inescapable. No place is excluded from this effect. New York, however, having become a kind of "command center" of the worldwide economy, has become a good spokes-landscape for our time.

One of the especially confusing aspects of the reign of this new world-shaping work, however, is that, though we know what the tools are, we can't say exactly what, of the many kinds of work that can be done with them, is the one that is recrafting the meaning of place. What work, exactly, is the hand of landscape design today? We are uncertain about the answer partly because the kind of work electronic tools can do is so different from any we have hitherto known. Specialists make guesses: the first work is "services"; the first work is inventing computer programs; the first work is managing the global economy with those computer programs. Of course, you must use money to measure which it might be, but it's important to try to think of these activities also as work in that sense of an age-old productive activity, rather than as defined by money. It is especially important for us to look at work as separate from money because it appears possible that money itself might be the actual field of our new first work—the creation of financial "instruments" and "devices" as made possible by our tools of extended mind, for example. If money itself is the real field of our new work, then we had better have a footing outside money from which to consider its actual use to us: its real productivity, its value, not to mention the way it shapes society and structures our common interior life.

One of the best views of Manhattan is from the Promenade in Brooklyn Heights, directly across the East River from Wall Street. One steps from the intimacy of old streets into a wide expanse of water and sky—the Statue of Liberty to the left, the Brooklyn Bridge to the right. This alone would be dramatic. But straight across, too close for comfort, the towers of Wall Street shoulder one another, ruthless and joyous, singing their "We win" aria. In my Brooklyn years I often walked there, but never failed to be shocked by the sight of Wall Street. The Promenade was, in itself, serene, but that serenity was no match for the blast from across the river. The intensity thrilled me, but it also brushed me with fear. Most of the coastline around the harbor is low-lying, though it is all urban artifact, spiky and boxy in silhouette, as opposed to the smooth lines of land; and in this you sense the extent of the industrial city, how it is in itself a terrain that envelops even the large harbor easily in its arms. In the shouldering towers you see vortical centralization, the primary spatial tension in the industrial city as a physical form.

When I was a very young woman, just coming to New York on my own, I worked for a spell on Wall Street, a touchstone experience of the city. This was in 1964. The job was in a top law firm: I was a page, which meant I carried mail and other documents around to the lawyers, and that was interesting, because of the Rembrandt-worldly faces, especially of the partners, full of irony and cleverness but also thought. Lawyering back then still had about it a certain grandeur, albeit tinged with Machiavellian sophistication. I remember wryness and ferocious intelligence leavened with humor. Sometimes I would proofread a document aloud with a lawyer, and that was interesting, because it was, usually, a contract for one the firm's big clients, household names—AT&T, Morgan, Westinghouse—a glimpse into the vast intricate word works behind entities so established in American life that they were a kind of terrain in themselves, kin to the Mississippi and the Rockies.

But the experience I took away as a touchstone was the atmosphere on Wall Street at noon. The public space—cow paths turned into canyoned streets by the crowding soaring towers—was intense and pressurized in a way I had never known in a place. The rush of crowds themselves, the mood generated by uncountable urgent enterprises in constant near collision, imprinted themselves on me. I had no friends there at first, so I would go out for lunch alone, a naïve little being, exposed without protection to the swirl. I think, looking back, that it was largely the low-level employees who were rushing—with messages, on errands, with lunch. Among them strode figures in suits with an air of princely leisure. Yet even that conspicuous privileged nonchalance somehow conveyed intensity. The rule of devil-take-the-hindmost was implicit. Wall Street at noon was deadly serious yet cumulatively lighthearted, too, like a high-flying circus. Everybody, from rabble to raja, was driven by purpose. The towers and canyons expressed and reinforced this intensity perfectly, but the source of the crazy energy of the place was the crouching classical Stock Exchange, sooty and ancient looking. If, in 1964, there was one place in the nation in which the energy of the mature industrial age produced its most perfect froth, that would be Wall Street on a weekday at noon.

Though in four years I would be on the ramparts protesting the corporate establishment, I liked the heady swirl. It wasn't that I had an attraction to the world of speculation, or even law, and certainly not the corporate life of the gray flannel suit. I think it would be safe to say that in me such aspirations were zero. My ambition was to be a poet and, as for money, I had given pitifully little thought to it. What I liked was how people seemed to be entirely themselves— too busy to pretend differently—as well as the feeling of unbounded pursuit combined with instinct, yet all shaped by the extraordinary form of the place. I liked the worldliness, I liked the human spectrum displayed, I liked the gutsiness, I liked the silliness, and I liked the head-spinning crisscrossing of intent that somehow seemed to all come together into a single engine. Wall Street then was a caste-stratified society, in which women especially were relegated to a lower order, but maybe because I had no Wall Street ambitions this didn't bother me. I was too busy taking in information about the world— about form, and feeling, and layers of feeling and the possibilities of being. The boisterous spirits of the lunchtime crowds that surged through the labyrinth seemed to set the towers topsy-turvy. When I think back to my first exposure to that voltage, the feeling that comes to me is of an ongoing earthquake of dizzying emancipation—a kind of cracking open, a sense of leaping possibility, a heart-seized, arrow-struck feeling of *you can do anything*. It was an invitation, of a particularly American flavor, I think. It turbo-charged the appetite for taking chances, for living—for poetry, even.

At the time, I interpreted the scene as entire in itself, but of course it was not. Behind the Wall Street of that time lay the Midwest, booming, belching, blasting. That is perhaps the most important factor that distinguishes Wall Street then from Wall Street now: that there was physical making behind it, and that it was secondary to that—drew energy from it. But there was something else, equally important to the timbre of the swirl and the invitation it seemed to issue. That was the array of countervailing forces that checked the raw energies of industrial society. Most important of these was the federal government that sought to tame the energies in ways consistent with civilized society. One can see the government as it was then as a grand contrapuntal invention, taking its shape in part from the very force it sought to regulate yet at the same time bringing intention—values other than sheer moneymaking—to the blast.

Nor was that all. While government to date remains the only power that can subordinate the primitive vitality of the market, in a mature society rings upon rings of other countervailing enterprises— all sorts of shapers and shelterers—exert their force to stabilize, balance, push back, distill, temper, and corral the primal energy in favor of purposes outside its scope. Many of these addressed government itself with critiques. Academia would be one. A lively, independent intelligentsia would be another. Newspaper journalism, which started in the late eighteenth century as harebrained sensationalism, over time had developed into a tradition proud of high standards of factual accuracy and of the role of counterforce to both government and business. A very large philanthropic establishment, a world of "nonprofits," was explicitly committed to values unrecognized by the market. A cultural establishment—the museums, the symphonies, in many cases themselves represented by monumental architecture, edifices that were the equal of government buildings—also saw itself explicitly as a realm that required protection from the barbarity of the market. The cultural establishment, in turn, had its own rings upon rings of counterresponses, of antiestablishment establishments, with their sovereigns and ragamuffins, their courtiers and hecklers, and around these were studios, back rooms, black-box theaters, cafés, bars where all sorts of experiments and explorations—what once was known as the avant-garde, because of the way it could upset establishment assumptions—flourished and failed but never doubted the importance of its mission. Supporting this, in turn, was an extensive artistic bohemia, an informal society of people who lived on little to pursue their art, and this collectively reinforced that choice, even elevated it. There was a sense back then that if a work of art sold well that suggested the artist had in some way "sold out."

But, even outside the arts, the structures of feeling that underlay our culture at the time did not derive from the values of the market. The enterprises that attracted the talented risk takers, in fact, were not those on Wall Street, but, rather those in the encircling rings of countervailing purpose. Indeed, in the culture of the educated young, to go to work at a corporate headquarters on Wall Street was a form of settling for the more ordinary thing—a better-paid version of the assembly line. The rings of countervailing purpose, meanwhile, far from the fragile will-o'-the-wisp it was later revealed to be, was in itself an establishment representing the full spectrum of the human spirit and as much a part of the landscape as the law firms and corporations, as inextricable from it as its very buildings. There is hardly a realm of life in which counterresponse was not manifested. Go back there and take up any perspective, professional or personal, and swing your telescope around: there is no end to it, fields upon fields, establishments and counterestablishment and counter-counterresponders, unfolding along an extended spectrum from the orthodox to the revolutionary, consciously counteractive and impulsive, systematic and improvisatory, institutional and ad hoc, conservative and rebellious, producing standards and their opposing standards, arguments and counterarguments, made by idealists and realists, crusaders and high priests, Good Samaritans, Quixotes, tsars, Rasputins, Goliaths and Davids, Philistines and Israelites: nations upon nations.

But much of this still exists, you might say, and there is certainly a sense in which that is true. Yet much of the countervailing world, if you look closely, has changed. The values of the market now infiltrate the most established cultural institutions. This is hard to pin down yet pervasive. Academia is one of our most formally designated cloisters, in the past vigilantly protected from market values, but less so today. University boards used to be made up of well-to-do alumni who saw their role as preserving those protective traditions from which they had benefited. Now boards act more like venture capitalists, of whom they are often composed, who understand success only in terms of growth, launching aggressive physical-expansion programs. As for the students in those universities, "business" is now the top career choice for so many of the best and the brightest of the young. On the side of social justice, a wide domain, once powerfully attractive to youth, the path is almost nonexistent today. How could it be otherwise when, for some time, the prevailing wisdom has characterized poor people as responsible for their condition? Therefore helping them is probably counterproductive, engendering dependency and keeping them from developing the competitive qualities they need to succeed. The assumption that the business sector offers the most interesting path in life is so pervasive that kids are confused if they find it unengaging: they must have some failing.

This mind-set penetrates fields that one might think were so far off the market chart as to be immune. You might choose to be an artist, for example, but for the choice to be valid in our current culture you must frame a "career"—that is to say, a path to market success. Indeed, your career likely determines the character of what you create—to do otherwise would be to choose insignificance. The idea that if an artist's work sold well he or she had sold out was pretentious; much of the old antimarket culture was flawed by vanity, arrogance, and snobbishness. We don't want that back. But the infiltration of all standards, all cloisters, and all countervailing establishments by market values ultimately compromises a society in substantive ways. Today even an idealistic kid assumes that if an artwork doesn't sell for a high price that probably means it's not good. How could he think differently, when the entire art world has become so entirely engulfed by the concept of art as investment? To be avant-garde now is to desperately experiment, not in order to upset bourgeois society or to critique the government, or even to shock the establishment critics, but in order to ride the next wave of market investment by plutocrats. It almost seems that a part of the art itself has become timing; the art of hitting that wave in just the right way and at just the right moment for market success. There is a playfulness in this that I like, quite different from the old superserious pursuit of greatness. But the totality of the market orientation is not fun. Meanwhile, it's the common sense of the time that a museum should set policy according to popularity—the blockbuster shows. And gift shops have expanded to the point of being major attractions. For a museum to do otherwise would make it a kind of "loser." Somewhere here a line has been crossed, putting us into a self-destructive mode. If you believe art is important, something to wake people up and alert them to possibilities beyond the obvious, this is, for all the fun, a crippling, self-truncating societal direction.

You can't escape this shift in values. Like other aspects of change in our time it wheedles its way into the soul. Even I, for example, though committed to challenging it, am overtaken by it often. The Carnegie Studios, on Fifty-Seventh Street in midtown Manhattan, is a city landmark, attached to Carnegie Hall, its commodious apartments long set aside by the Carnegie Hall Corporation for working artists. A few years ago the foundation, financially pressed, as most cultural institutions are, and with an aggressive market-values board, decided that it had to evict the artists and turn the tower into corporate offices. A documentary, *Lost Bohemia*, was made of this process, from a point of view partisan to the artists, but it was a good documentary, so it also revealed that many tower denizens were more eccentric than productive, some studios jammed with the results of pack-ratting lifetimes. Well, really, how can one blame the Corporation, I found myself thinking—the thought behind being that if the residents had been artistic geniuses then maybe the support would have been justified. Just think what that real estate is worth! Fifty-Seventh Street! Get real! Then a shudder at this shift in what had been my instinctive pattern of thought. The protection of a realm had become invalid to me because the individuals who were benefiting weren't "successful" (didn't make a lot of money or have fame). Since when did I measure the worthiness of a pursuit by particular performances, let alone financial success? In fact many stupendously successful artists had lived there at one time—Isadora Duncan, Marlon Brando, Leonard Bernstein, for example—but that was hardly the point: my reaction had been to the holdouts who on the whole were not well known, but there were exceptions: Bill Cunningham, for example, a fashion photographer for *The New York Times* who took fabulous photos of everyday people in their getups on the streets of New York for which he was celebrated. The worst of it was that most of the artists were old, and therefore in some cases not in their most productive years. Others were still going strong, which is what many artists do whatever their age. The residents of the Carnegie tower were, in fact, a small, lingering bohemia that I was just brushing away.

The reflexiveness of my "common sense" shocked me, violating some of my most deeply held beliefs about the artistic life, but the real lesson of the documentary was how hard it is to represent a bohemia of any kind as valid today. I have noticed, for example, that when the bohemias of former times show up in the movies now, or on TV, the people in them are almost always presented as drug-addicted impostors, weak individuals who, rather than doing something worthwhile, are avoiding the challenges of life. Their real agendas are nastily self-serving, usually having to do with bilking the productive people. That actual work went on in such realms, work of importance to which practitioners were justifiably committed, is no part of the plotlines on this subject that I have seen. I wonder if it would be possible today to represent any bohemian world, let alone a contemporary one, as convincingly admirable in a movie for mass consumption.

The world in which many countervailing rings surrounded Wall Street was far from perfect. Certainly the invitation was out of range of hearing for many. Harlem was about to explode right here in New York, as were inner cities all over the United States. Washington, fully fledged in its liberalism, was busy miring us in Vietnam. And yet today there is something missing that is so large that it can hardly be identified, like a vanished horizon that used to orient us all. It's the container in which those tragedies found their meaning. What is the tragedy of the Harlem riots without the theater of the industrial city within which they took place and as they affected it? The pressure that Vietnam put on us is hard to recall without the experience of a boundaried nationhood that went without question in industrial times. Can one even begin to make the argument that there is such a thing as an "establishment"—public, of long standing, respected, but also, on those grounds challengeable—now? A good part of the shock is how worlds vanish, even as they leave forms behind intact: traditions, architecture, institutional names—like part of an abandoned stage set. You can't get back in there, not really. You can't reanimate it. There is no play. The audience, the actors are long gone.

3

Youngstown

My first trip to Youngstown was in 1999. I drove from Brooklyn, across Pennsylvania, into Ohio. There the going got rough, and rougher still as I neared my destination: broken-down roads and buildings, a palette of rust stains and old concrete, bad directions from passersby: "Can you handle that?" Even the Pizza Hut waitress delivered her scripted graciousness in a way that let me know that I was on my own. My destination was a Ramada Inn just outside the city limits: I had been unable to find any lodging in Youngstown proper. The Ramada was a run-down establishment among boarded-up businesses with cracked concrete parking lots, tall weeds pushing up through them. I thought I was in the middle of nowhere. Waking at two in the morning, I heard a passionate male voice through the walls, declaiming in a theatrical way about "God" and "love," with a tremolo on those words: rehearsing a sermon, I gradually concluded. I had a sensation that occasionally overtook me in my travels—that I was at the heart of America: right here, right now.

Driving into Youngstown the next morning, I found a perfectly intact downtown, empty like a painting by de Chirico. The traffic lights at the clear, broad intersections faithfully but pointlessly signaled to no one but me. Youngstown was like a Playskool set, one of everything. But the opera house and the department store were shuttered, the single skyscraper occupied only by government offices, a bank, and the chamber of commerce. All around lay neighborhoods in apocalyptic desolation. Wooden houses with deep porches under mature trees had deteriorated past the point of rescue: a hanging gutter, a sagging porch, panes missing in a third-story window. Lawns had grown to unkempt hay; vines clambering over outbuildings, some crushed by trees downed by winds. The houses looked empty, but many were inhabited by the extreme poor, mostly black but by no means all. In a section locally known as the Gold Coast, mansions appeared to be occupied by squatters, the veranda of one packed with tidily bound collections of what looked like scavenged articles, the roof littered with the detritus of mature oaks.

Youngstown had been a steelmaking city, and some steel mills remained standing, improbably long in scale, weed-choked rails leading to them, square squat-roofed railroad towers still vigilant above engulfing vegetation. Some mills had been razed—sold as scrap, leaving behind open expanses of bare earth on which heaps of unsalable twisted metal artifacts remained. At one razed site a monstrosity listed, apparently too unwieldy to take apart or move— the remains of a blast furnace, I guessed. The physical reality of an abandoned twentieth-century American city is difficult to take in. You think war. But it's not war. It's a squandering. There is a problem with actually seeing it. You look and look. You photograph and photograph.

In *Reimagining Detroit*, author John Gallagher quotes a resident who observes that a person could hardly walk out the door without tripping over a journalist. Youngstowners didn't have that problem.

In my three trips to Youngstown I never saw a reporter—other than myself—who was not local. But while I can understand the frustration of being abandoned and pored over at the same time on the part of Detroiters, I can also understand why there were so many journalists there for so long. You know the explanation but still can't comprehend the scale of the waste: can't feel you have "covered it," no matter how long you stay or how many times you come back. "Ruin porn" is a phrase also quoted by Gallagher for the journalistic fascination with the deteriorating buildings of Detroit. It's true one feels these sights should not be seen, that there is something shameful about them that transfixes but from which one should look away. Yet that assumes the shame is someone else's. It's true that in reporting on these conditions there is a sense of an invasion of the privacy of those who live in them. And yes, the sights are shocking. But whose shame is it? Why is it that we can't stop looking and yet they are so hard to see?

It's true that in all the time I was in Youngstown, I always felt like an outsider from a safe and functioning world. No matter how hard I tried, I could not identify with this misfortune, this extreme vulnerability of an entire urban society. But this is my country. I was frightened by conditions in Youngstown, and unhappy there, but I also wanted to learn how to be there in full landscape-reading mode: to *be* there. It wasn't really so hard to learn the basic facts about the place. But my deepest thought and reason for returning was: "We may have squandered Youngstown, but this is a lesson, a truth about ourselves as a nation, that we cannot afford to squander, too." I wanted to find the emotional truth of Youngstown. That seemed like the only way to be certain that waste and social destruction on this scale never happen again.

The Museum of Labor and Industry had opened in 1992, well after the decline. There I learned that Youngstown, small as it was, had made 26 percent of the nation's steel. "Put all your eggs in one basket and then watch that basket," Andrew Carnegie had said, a quote etched on glass in one of the exhibitions at the museum. Youngstown had done just that. Old-timers remembered the mills going around the clock: the furnaces lit up the sky over the city at night. A beautiful little beaux arts confection of a museum, the Butler Institute of American Art, had been built by steel titan Joseph Butler in 1919. The principal collection consisted of nineteenth-century American landscapes, most of them of the quietly pastoral kind, long-ago fields in the dewy morning: romantic counterpoint to that furnace-lit sky.

I talked to people who remembered Youngstown in its heyday, the 1950s and '60s, and I also read about that time in the main branch of the public library, which was still open. Especially vivid was a personal memoir, *Steelworker Alley*, by Robert Bruno, a sociologist who was the son of a steelworker. Bruno describes communal, multigenerational neighborhoods of first-, second-, and third-generation immigrants, and families knit by marriage over time, children playing in adjoining yards, quieted when the night shift came home so the fathers could sleep. Josephine Chellis served cinnamon buns in her kitchen on Sundays for forty years. Church and union were the institutional underpinnings of this long established way of life, but at the center was the work. The men walked down paths to footbridges across the Mahoning River to the mills on the far shore. Bruno describes a core bond among them that developed through collaboration in often dangerous tasks on old equipment around and above molten steel. Breakdowns were frequent. To pass the time on those occasions, they played a gambling game called "the bug." The guys sometimes went on hunting expeditions in the Michigan woods. In one mill, a kitchen was set up in which venison was cooked with onions and garlic, the aroma filling the mill.

Foreign steel began to outstrip American companies in the late 1960s. But the first mill to actually go dark was Youngstown

Sheet and Tube, which closed down on September 19, 1977—a date Youngstowners know. It is said that the workers, on leaving the plant by bridge, dropped their safety boots into the river. Other closings followed. "We are not in the business of making steel. We are in the business of making money," said David Roderick, the chairman of U.S. Steel, when that corporation closed down its plants, in Youngstown and elsewhere, for a while changing its name to USX. The last fire to go out in Youngstown was Republic's Haselton's plant in 1981. There went the basket. Staughton Lynd, a labor lawyer, author, socialist, and resident of Youngstown at the time of the shutdowns— and at the time of my visits—had tried, along with some activists from mainstream religious denominations, to help the Youngstown Sheet and Tube workers buy the company and run it themselves. The plan was impracticable, Lynd told me, in part because, like most of the steel companies in Youngstown, Sheet and Tube had long before stopped investing in the plant. As in most companies, the workers had, for years, kept the mill going through ingenious, often dangerous, improvisation.

Many of the area's African Americans had come up from the South after World War II and, unable to get mortgages, had built their own homes on Youngstown's east side, which was less populated because it was downwind from the smokestacks. Some of them planted big gardens and used outhouses, as they had in the rural South. When I visited the east side in the late 1990s, it looked like country. But in the heyday years, some black families found their way into the more established neighborhoods. Every Youngstown story I heard during my visits had one such family in it. Pastor Gary Frost, who presided at a black evangelical church in inner Youngstown, described growing up with a bunch of white kids, all "little rascals" together. Robert Bruno's father recalled a black worker who was as close a member of his mill group as any. I have no reason to doubt these stories but as the plants closed, whites moved away—to Youngstown suburbs, or to places like Houston, where there was an oil boom—and black Youngstowners, excluded from the suburbs, remained in what became an ever more abandoned city. When Martin Luther King was assassinated in 1968, riots broke out in Youngstown, as elsewhere.

Meanwhile, as whites moved outward, the black population slowly moved into the older neighborhoods, further accelerating flight. But when the mills closed and the value of homes in all of Youngstown plummeted, white families left en masse. Unable to recoup the equity in their houses, most rented to those who could not leave, for whatever they could get, refusing, in bitterness, to maintain the properties, much less make improvements. It was this angry neglect that put the fine housing stock of Youngstown on the path to irreversible decline. Where other rust-belt cities gradually found ways to regenerate themselves—IT for Pittsburgh, a medical sector to build on in Cleveland—Youngstown had no alternative eggs in its basket. The only "industry" it could attract was prisons—four so far at the time of my visits, with the city government angling for more. The prisoners, as elsewhere, were disproportionately young black men. The prisons were new, corporate looking, with groomed grounds, by far the most prosperous-looking establishments in Youngstown. One prison was private, actually corporate in other words. Prison stocks were soaring on Wall Street at the time.

Of course the population of the prisons, one of which was federal, was not all from Youngstown. But it seemed nonetheless that Youngstown was surviving by cannibalizing itself. The withdrawal of industry had created conditions of deprivation that produced criminals: a kind of raw material out of which around 1,600 prison staff jobs, largely held by whites, had been created.

But black Youngstowners had no monopoly on crime in Youngstown. The city had long been famous for fraud and corruption of the Mafia variety; its old nickname, Murder City, had nothing to do with black crime. By the time of my first visit, the mob, having extracted payola from the unions for years, had turned to squeezing what it could out of the government, the last show in town with any money to squeeze. This sector was also providing fodder for prisons, in Youngstown and elsewhere. At the time of my first visit, two municipal court judges were scheduled to report to prison outside Youngstown, to start serving two-and-a-half-year sentences for extortion and attempting to influence a grand jury, and the city's former street superintendent had been sentenced to thirty days at the county jail for theft within his office. Within very recent memory, more than seventy convictions for bribery and extortion had made a dent, perhaps, in what *The New York Times* called "a resilient web of organized crime and political influence." Soon after my first visit, a reformist prosecutor was shot, though the attempt was botched: he was merely injured. Meanwhile, I learned that Charles O'Nesti, an aide to Youngstown's Democratic congressman James Traficant, had recently been convicted of making a deal with the Mafia chieftain Lenny Strollo, at the Captain's Table, the restaurant in my very own Ramada Inn. At the time of my visits, Traficant's poll ratings had not much suffered, though it must be added that Congress felt differently and, not long after, expelled him.

Desperate white poverty existed in Youngstown, too. I saw gangs of white boys in parts as neglected and nasty as any. I saw white homes with holes in the roof. The rot had extended beyond the city's borders to the contiguous municipalities into which whites had initially fled. A scene in the town of Hubbard became fixed in my mind: a pale blue house off which huge chips were peeling, a bedraggled white family sitting on its unsteady porch staring out into an overgrown gully. Just a few weeks earlier, six fugitives from the Northeast Ohio Correctional Center, five of them murderers, had been cornered in a "wedge shaped jumble of vines, trees and thistles," as the local newspaper, *The Vindicator*, described it, at an intersection close to that very house. Later I learned from a knowledgeable Youngstowner that the six prisoners had made a deal with one of the wardens, par for the course in Youngstown, who provided wire cutters to get through the fence but then welched on providing a getaway car, forcing the murderers to flee on foot.

Mainstream religious denominations were an important presence in Youngstown, focused on material conditions and providing services where they could. But the conditions were overwhelming, and the people staffing these efforts were so dejected they could hardly lift coffee cup to lips. Evangelicals were another story, especially the white evangelicals who were undiscouraged, even fired by a high-octane ardor. I eventually concluded that this was because they believed in the primacy of the Kingdom of God. The world in front of them was secondary. Their concern was saving souls, including mine. When I interviewed evangelicals, it was fairly obvious that they could not forget that I was likely going to hell unless I converted. Not that they proselytized but I could see them holding back: my hair had might as well have been on fire already.

As stoked as evangelicals were about helping Youngstown, their congregations had moved out of the city along with the majority of the white community, leaving behind church buildings that were, in many cases, taken over by black congregations. In some cases, relationships between the two congregations involved in this sequence had developed, and this had occasionally led to joint material projects—a charter school, some new housing, visits to young men in prison. There was a very high awareness among white evangelicals of the legions of young black men in the Youngstown prisons. A preacher exchange between black and white churches had also been established, though it must be said that only a few black inner-city churches participated. Several black preachers I met had had fathers who had been involved in the civil-rights movement. Following

Martin Luther King, they had rejected the belief that "love" was a force that alone could change the world and adopted the belief that "justice" also had to be pursued. One of these justice preachers would not speak to me, because of my race, though how that position derived from King was hard to grasp. Another son of the civil-rights tradition had rebelled against his father and gone back to "love"; he was one who openly participated in the black-white coalition, though he said he was regarded as an Oreo as a result. This was Gary Frost of the little rascals, and his church, though in the worst part of the city, was new and beautiful, with lots of blond wood and wide windows high up showing sky. He was a complex man. He told me his father had taught him how to handle black rage. At the end of our long talk he asked if he could pray over me. I said okay. We were both seated. Frost put his hands on my shoulders and with his head down ardently prayed. This felt enormously presumptuous on his part: I realized I should have said no. Another preacher was Dwight Dumas, a magnificent ex–football player with an anchorman's voice.

One weekday evening I went to a service in Struthers, another down-and-out municipality on the Youngstown border, white but battered and left for dead. As part of the preacher-exchange, Dwight Dumas was to give the sermon. The service took place in an annex of the church, in a small chapel. A scattering of white people attended, all broken-down-looking, in any old clothes—people scraping by in the forgotten ruins of a bygone world. The mood was desultory, participation seemed by rote. Some chewed gum through the service. Dumas, in contrast, seemed to be bursting with dynamic prosperity. Dressed in a beautiful midnight-blue suit and a dazzlingly white shirt, he spoke on the book of Job.

Job, Dumas explained, had been a rich man on whom a series of dreadful misfortunes had fallen, taking all from him—wealth, his children, and, finally, his health. Then he lost his reputation, too. This was because friends concluded that the only explanation for Job's misfortunes was that he had sinned in some terrible way, for which God was punishing him. Job insisted he was as virtuous as they were. But if this was true, then the friends were as vulnerable as Job to misfortune upon misfortune: they chose not to believe him. Job got very angry, but the friends didn't budge. Finally, Job just couldn't go on being angry and forgave them. But they did not accept his forgiveness, and this was the cruelest blow to Job. The theme of his sermon, Dumas said, was the pain of extending forgiveness that is not accepted.

Suddenly the church was electrified. It seemed obvious to me that Dumas was speaking about the relationship between African Americans and white Americans—about how many white people think black people have brought their misfortune on themselves. One person walked out in what seemed like a huff, but I couldn't tell how the rest of this down-at-heel white congregation was interpreting the tale as told by this fortunate-looking black guy. "Amen! Amen!" they said, as Dumas got really rolling on the pain of unaccepted forgiveness. Maybe they heard it as a story about human nature: about how, for another example, people who live in prosperous cities see the rust-belt reality as something apart from themselves and probably the fault of people there, in some way that would never pertain to them. Or maybe they were just elsewhere—in the Kingdom of God, as it were. This was, by a long shot, the best sermon I have ever heard. The fear of another's vulnerability and the pain of unaccepted forgiveness was such an unusual, complicated, human, daringly painful theme: I know I, for a while, felt no difference between myself and the Youngstowners.

When I came back to New York City, I realized that Youngstown was embedded here—revealed, for example, in the strange boundary between a gentrifying Bergen Street into which the energy of a new era was flowing, and the Gowanus Houses, a part of New York that was a dying industrial city, into which, as far as I could tell, no energy was flowing at all. As a way of pursuing that, I had, in the Brooklyn years, also gone into Manhattan to explore the more famous divide at Ninety-Sixth Street between the Upper East Side, the richest urban neighborhood in America, and Harlem, which was at that time the poorest. North of Ninety-Sixth Street I found enormous desolated areas, New York style: the stoopless brownstone, sky visible past a classical cornice where a roof should have been. Flanks of abandoned brownstones perforated by vacant lots, onetime private gardens in back turned into dumps. The population was sparse. Beleaguered families struggled among squatters and crack-house users. Whole blocks were razed, much like the sites of razed mills in Youngstown, though these had been residential neighborhoods. Eventually, I understood that under these circumstances a razed area represents maintenance. Still, they were extraordinarily bleak, these open sections of "urban prairie." They were the color of building rubble, primarily brick. They were surrounded by chain-link fences into which debris had blown and stuck. I remember seeing a woman on the far side of one pushing a baby carriage, no one else in sight, as if into a high wind. The subway, elevated here, was exposed at a distance. I remember it rumbling by and how surprising it was to see a sign of a functioning city. At the edge of the prairie, near the elevated, there were half-demolished buildings left with interior rooms exposed, semioccupied, protected by plastic sheets.

When, not many years later, I moved to Riverside Drive and 135th, I decided one day to go have a look at the Harlem neighborhood I had come to know back then. But when I got over there I was disoriented; in just a few years so much had changed. From block to block I had to recalibrate against memory; luxury condominiums where blasted brownstones had been, busy streets, populated by a mixture of middle-class and inner-city characters, some misbehaving in a territorial way but most immeasurably cheerful compared with what once had been—or so it seemed. The only elements dependably the same in the neighborhood were superblocks of 1950s brick public-housing high-rise towers—just too much for the bulldozers.

4

The Pendulum

In between Brooklyn and Riverside Drive, I spent three years in Washington and then returned to New York. This was in 2002. I thought it important that my partner, Noel, who had never lived in the city, experience Manhattan first. In that I betray my age, and a lot more, but Manhattan for me was the first city footing. We rented a place on the Upper West Side, very near where I had started out in the city. I remember looking out the window at a man crossing West End Avenue in the middle of the block in a motorized wheelchair while talking on a cell phone, glancing in both directions for oncoming traffic. I felt relief and affection. You wouldn't see that in Washington. Most people in the building paid low, stabilized rents. Some people in the building had been born there. We paid a high but manageable market-rate rent that went up a hundred dollars with each new lease, as had been my experience in New York. In a few years movie stars started moving into the neighborhood. Soon the forest fire of the roots that is nothing like past neighborhood change but the metamorphosis of a city into something else started burning our feet with a sudden 20 percent rent increase. Angry, panicked, we were propelled into buying—how else were we to feel secure? With prices going up and apartments selling on the day they were listed, we felt lucky to find a landing here on Riverside Drive. At the same time we had to be aware that, to many in the new building, we ourselves were the very forest fire we were fleeing. I had lived in a dangerous New York but never one so nakedly Darwinian. After that I never had the slightest illusion that I was living in the city as I had known it.

Though our new building was even older than the one we had left; though Riverside Drive, with its balustrades and broad sidewalks, separated in places from the street by gardens, expressed the aesthetic confidence of another era; and though we lived in the midst of a dense, stable immigrant community, the new location felt from the beginning like the churning ground of the new city. But by then I was ready. Indeed, the very same kind of changes I had disliked on Bergen Street, because they unraveled the meaning and continuity of place, here cheered me as reinforcing my investment.

Some years later, I was sitting at my desk early one summer morning, looking out at the river, when my niece called. She and a friend had been standing in line outside the Delacorte Theater in Central Park since four in the morning for tickets to *Hair*, the musical written in the 1960s about the 1960s. Plays at the Delacorte are free, but you have to stand in line: two tickets per person are given out at 11, at the earliest. If it rains at showtime, you are out of luck. It was 8 a.m.—hours to go. My niece wanted me to check the weather. I reported predictions of severe rainstorms, hail, maybe tornadoes. Planes might not be able to land: she had better go home.

As it turned out, she did not heed my auntly advice. At lunchtime she called to say she had a ticket for me. Improbably, the rain held off all day. As we approached the theater, the park was wrapped in mists, the ceiling so low as to put us nearly in a cloud. But no rain fell. As half the people in the audience had taken an improbable gamble, they were, almost by definition, young. They had also spent long hours in one another's company, as one could feel in the air of festive congeniality and common cause. The show was infectiously fresh, sweeping up the audience with its youthful charm, and I was no exception; it pulled me back into a time that had unfolded well before most of the people in the audience had been born. Yet because they were young, and I was not, it was as if the show belonged to them and I was an invisible onlooker. It was almost as if my presence was a little voyeuristic, not quite proper. There were other grayheads there, but we were isolated from one another.

Watching *Hair* took me back to my time at Columbia, in particular the student revolt in the spring of '68. Whenever I think of that protest, images of the physical campus come to mind first, as if it were not just background but a protagonist. The university sits high, the Hudson glistening through trees far below on one side and, on the other, one block from campus, dangerous, overgrown, cliff-like Morningside Park descending to the Harlem plain. But this dramatic topography is subordinated to the imperial classicism of the campus, with its broad, stepped promenades and terraces, its monumental buildings. Two massively colonnaded libraries face each other across an axis, one high, called Low, one low, called Butler, both so immovably grounded as to make a person feel like a feathery bit of flotsam. This is a perfectly coordinated and balanced environment that expresses unquestioned cultural confidence without one chink of self-doubt. The edge of Morningside Park is handsomely marked by stone balustrades. Back then, one looked over the balustrades, as from the deck of an ocean liner, over the unmaintained park, down into the then semiabandoned lawless zone of a Harlem decimated by riots.

The original Columbia protest was a gathering of several hundred at a sundial between the libraries to protest university plans to build a gym in Morningside Park, on the good ground that the park was public open space, one of Harlem's few, and in support of Harlem activists who called the project "Gym Crow." Student unease about the war in Vietnam, and the university's complicity, was a strong subcurrent, however. Columbia was allowing Dow Chemical, the makers of napalm for use in Vietnam, to recruit on campus and was also affiliated with the Institute for Defense Analysis, which did research on weapons for use in Vietnam: in fact the president of the university, Grayson Kirk, was on the IDA board. Kirk's office was located in Low Library, set high above the sundial and separated from it by two magnificently wide flights of steps.

At the protest, as planned, some raggedy students with a petition to the president in hand went up the long steps to the grand entrance to Low. But as they attempted to go in it became clear the door was locked. The president and his staff, it turned out, had all gone home to avoid receiving the students. Today it astonishes me how arrogant and yet fearful, how complacently overreactive, members of the "establishment" could be back then. How easy it would have been to courteously receive the petition! The locked door was an inflammatory rebuke, news of which spread rapidly. Soon additional protesters expanded the gathering at the sundial by many factors. Activist leaders were ready with speeches, but the gathering as it grew included many students of more moderate inclination— or at least they had been until now. Eventually the much enlarged large group marched to the gym site at Morningside Park. Over the course of a week, classroom buildings and Low Library itself, including the president's office, were "occupied" by students, shutting down classes. Eventually the authorities called in the police to breach lines of faculty, graduate students, and others that had formed around the occupied buildings in symbolic protection of the students inside—I was on one of those lines—and clear out the occupiers in a nighttime operation. This attracted huge numbers to the campus and made big news. The administration was stupid, but what strikes me looking back is what all of us who were involved in the protest at various levels took for granted: that a coherent argument could be made to a university that we assumed was ours to argue with, and that the last thing we needed to worry about was its own vulnerability. I think protesters against both the gym and Vietnam were right, but what that rather violent night brings back to me most vividly now, ironically, is how easily we took our institutions for granted back then. We saw no fragility in them.

Hair is more about the cultural liberation of the 1960s than about political activism, which is secondary in its plot. But it inevitably reminds one of the conviction so many of my generation had that ours was a time of beginning leading inevitably to a progressive future. We had no idea that we were in fact, historically speaking, positioned at an ending: no inkling we were situated on a cliff edge over which the entire culture was about to plunge, along with our visions of change. We thought we were "radical," or some variation thereof: at the very least progressive. Decades would pass before most of us—of any age—would begin to truly grasp the radicalism of the transition that all of American society was about to go through. For decades, the assumption that we were progressing on a continuum with the past—improving, reforming, carrying forward the causes of social and economic justice—would continue to animate us, though the actual lack of implementation, and indeed the political success of the right—Richard Nixon, for example—was a confusing contradiction.

There are various interpretations of when the era we are now in began, but my choice, in retrospect, would be the early '70s, when venture capital began to invest in manufacturing in the Third World. A major reason why this began to happen then, and not earlier, as I understand it, is that investors became confident that the World Bank would shore up shaky Third World economies, and hence their regimes, when they began to wobble. But with the emergence of electronic communications and the internet, and with them the capacity not only to manage manufacturing from afar, but to disperse it—with the parts of a single product made in several far-flung places—the exodus of industry from the developed world accelerated, the gains in low wages and taxes having become hard to resist. The outflow was swift: there were only four years between the first and the last blast furnace shutdown in Youngstown, for example. Meanwhile it wasn't clear what was replacing industry: what the first work of the United States or, indeed, of the developed world was becoming—exactly. Meanwhile, too, a devilishly confusing contradiction from which we have not yet recovered our political equilibrium became prominent: between an ever more worldwide market and national political systems.

Not only that, but our government, like that of most modern nations, had been actually formed in response to a growing industrial society. In the case of the United States, we were building from scratch—de novo. Our culture, too, had come into being largely in response to industrial forces, with its establishment of institutions and all the concentric circles of enterprises dedicated to shaping, critiquing, civilizing the powerful and ruthless market energies created as we shook off the colonial yoke and strove to catch up with the European nations. With the disappearance of industry, therefore, our federal government was a bit like a magnificent system of dikes with the ocean gone elsewhere. Much cultural tradition was stranded in that way, too. As what had been our primary order of work began to go out from under so, also, did the authority and effectiveness of governing philosophies that had been incubated and matured in a former era. But most of us didn't realize this. We couldn't understand why political debate became swamped and disoriented in the 1970s and '80s. Assuming debate would inevitably right itself, we went on with visions for the future that had also been formed in the disappearing era: for example, seeing environmental restrictions as inevitably ascendant within the old national frame; and becoming dumbfounded by evidence to the contrary, such as the landslide election of Ronald Reagan, who felt politically free to reverse much of it. The emergence of the Reagan Democrats, factory workers who had once been integral to the progressive base, now out of jobs or likely soon to lose them, was another headspinner. But many of us didn't realize that political continuity had been disrupted in an irreversible way. We noted the emergence of personal computers, and then the way electronic communications changed our way of life in small ways—bosses now had to learn to type!—but not, for the most part, grasping how the collapsed space of the screen was undoing the very warp and weft of our society. This obliviousness was possible because, unlike the early years of the industrial era, in which physical disruption was obvious, this new era infiltrated stealthily, without changing much of our tangible surroundings. The drastic effects were blatantly visible only in the calamitous abandonment of the industrial cities of the Midwest—but that was a special journalistic subject having little to do with the rest of us, living as we did in landscapes that looked much as they always had.

But another development occurred that further blinded us, while also adding to the velocity of change. This had to do with a long-standing alternating pattern in American political life, a pendulum swing between belief in the market as a creative force that is the source of all solutions to social problems, and a belief in government as a force needed to civilize the market with values outside its range. Both philosophies have weaknesses: the market can't regulate itself and eventually hurts itself and society with shortsighted excess, while government, undisciplined by competition, tends to get so big and inefficient it can't do its job well. We here in America are more open to the swing toward market values than Europe, where the weight of advantage has long lain with government, and where culture tends also to be more insulated against market values. Our swing is wider, therefore, and its terms possibly longer-lasting. As is often pointed out these days, Franklin Delano Roosevelt's New Deal was a response to the market excesses that led to the 1929 Crash, and it stood us well—until the 1970s, when the industrial society for which it was designed lost its industry.

What is confusing is that by the time the '70s rolled around, all else being equal, Big Government was due for a Big Critique. It had, in fact, become oversized, complacent, and bureaucratically sclerotic in some respects. Though my heart is with the protesting students, I can see from this perspective that, if we hadn't been in the midst of metamorphosis, a conservative challenge might have been salutary—much as progressives would have denied that at the time. But what happened instead is that the normal pendulum swing toward the market coincided with the penetrating, radical, irreversible movement into a new era. Our societies, and all the institutions developed to civilize them, including our governments, take their form from the principal ways of work at the time of their formation, from how people make their living on the planet. When, with the arrival of computing tools and digital communications, the top tier of work changed drastically, our American society, and all the institutions developed to civilize it, became untailored to the actual energies of the time. One can see it in government: in, say, the structure of bureaucracies that are much like those of the big manufacturing corporations. One can see it in welfare policy, for example, which mirrored the entitled security of working-class jobs, including stay-at-home mothers. But one can see it most easily in politics as politics tries to adjust—not that the answer is easy to provide. A great example is the way liberalism itself became discredited, not only in the normal way the right can challenge those ideals but because the society it sought to reform and refine was fast going out of existence. The very word "liberal" rather suddenly became defamatory—liberals themselves using it to castigate opponents: this happened way before Fox

News took up the campaign. The right used the defamation of liberals to promote the idea that government had become too powerful. This appealed to people like the Reagan Democrats, the working class that had lost its security, but I am convinced that to this day the real fear behind the rightward swing is not that government is too big and powerful, though that is what is said, but because it is weak—has become helpless before new conditions. Less frightening to go back to the days when it was merely too big. Meanwhile, then, as now, there was not even a glimmer of a vision on the progressive side of how to respond, politically, to the new society arising out of the new order of work, nor even much of an idea of what that society was—to this day the best progressives can come up with is the New Deal. But that was a vision for another world.

Throughout all this, conservatives, already with the wind at their back in the sense that the pendulum was tending toward government critique, haven't had to come up with a response to the radical reconfiguration of society that was going on, because of their basic premise that the market is the force that knows best. All they had to do is champion the market, and attack all efforts to control it, and that got easier and easier as the old controls, the old ideals, the once quite sophisticated Great Society of the mature New Deal became ever less attuned to actuality. As for the market itself, driven by greed, it adjusts instantly to new conditions, like water to a new topography. So the right, with its belief in the unregulated market as the force that finds solutions to problems, combined with a distrust in government, was much more convincing under these circumstances, much more at home in this new environment than the left. Lifted by the momentum of the normal swing toward market values, the elevation of the right wing was swift. Very quickly, the idea that market values could provide the best answer to all problems—poverty, how to run a university, what art is good—became not just a refreshing alternative approach, but the only approach that made sense. The effect was annihilative, of culture, but especially in the political realm, where coherent debate disappeared, with the right absolved of the burden of making sense as liberals backed off their core causes in confusion, offering, in their place, only technocratic, issue-by-issue policy recalibrations. We remain in this state to this day.

Hair was written and first produced in the late 1960s, when we were unknowingly beginning to move fast toward irreversible transition. It was a reportorial play: the phenomenon of "the sixties" was still unfolding. Sitting in that young audience at the Delacorte, looking back at the past from the vantage point of what we now know, I wondered if my generation had anything of value to hand on. It's a question each generation asks. In a society committed to growth and inclusion, the answer is never easy. But when the very armature of a society dissolves, the question of what can be let go and what must be carried forward becomes far more difficult to tackle. Sitting there, I was at a loss as to how even to create an arena of discussion in which such a question made sense. But one thing did come to me, though it certainly wasn't in the minds of we long-ago protesting students; a countervailing, civilizing response to powerful market forces is possible, was done, could be done again. The sequence of eras cannot be reversed but the pendulum of belief will, inevitably, swing back again toward faith in government instead of market forces. One question is: Will progressives be ready with a social vision suited to a new society when the pendulum swings back?

The performance of *Hair* that evening was shut down by rain only once, for a few minutes: indeed, a half-moon showed through the low rolling clouds several times, adding to a beneficent mood. At the end the audience jumped up onto the stage to dance with the cast, including us grayheads. After all, we knew how to be spontaneous, and did so with verve, not that our separateness from the young audience, or from one another, was really altered. The young loved breaking through the fourth wall, and I have to admit I did, too, though I knew it was planned—was part of the direction.

On brilliant days, the Hudson as seen from my window on Riverside is so glorious that the sliver of city between my window and the water all but disappears. But in an overcast, windless autumn dawn, the river is flat and very black, in a way that makes it almost not there. In such a light all I see are the man-made structures on either side of the river—not even the Palisades stand out. On the near side it's Riverside Drive, from under which, far down, cars stream in and out of the city on the Henry Hudson Parkway. The parkway can put me in mind of Robert Moses, under whose leadership it was constructed, and therefore of Jane Jacobs, who fought him in a struggle that has, over time, become a kind of passion play of urban-design values, with Jacobs the clear heroine, Moses the villain—though it's true some revision of this sacred doctrine cropped up after Jacobs's death in 2006.

Moses was an expert politician but also a trained urban planner whose ideas reflected the planning mind-set of the time; one impervious to aesthetics. The spirit of the City Beautiful movement of the late nineteenth century, which had produced lovely features along beaux arts lines, such as the Washington Square Arch, or Olmstedian inspirations like Central Park, was long forgotten as planning became a profession associated with engineering, both structural and social. The efficiency of the automobile was a dominant concern. Separating seedy parts of cities from forward-looking economic development sites was another. It was planners, not politicians, who routed early interstates into the hearts of cities across the nation. But to be fair you have to remember that from the nineteenth century onward—Olmsted's parks and then the City Beautiful movement notwithstanding—the structure of feeling of people of a humanist inclination deplored the gigantic industrial city as a social horror.

Though decline set in fairly early in the twentieth century, and was accelerating in the 1960s, the idea that cities were vulnerable, precious, and in need of curatorial attention just wasn't current. Get people out into the green country—in cars—that was the common sense of planning in Moses's time, had been for a long time, and, indeed, was the purpose of his parkways.

One of the most unquestionably deplorable aspects of cities, to people of progressive inclination, was slums. Moses razed slums, building in their place what he and other planners saw as utopian superblocks of high-rise public housing—the very same structures we now, in our turn, deplore. The idea was that the superblocks would break up the teeming grid, and, in place of tenements, provide apartments full of light and air with green space in between. Unlike postwar highways, which were a brand-new form, the public housing of this era had its origins in the socially idealistic modernist tradition—in the ideas of architects Frank Lloyd Wright and Le Corbusier. Indeed, public housing was one of the few realizations of their vision. Residential developers in the private sector, responding to market taste, did adopt a similar format in some urban projects, such as Manhattan's Lincoln Towers, but, the great arena of postwar residential development was the building of suburbia, and that, aesthetically speaking, took the dead opposite direction.

Jane Jacobs was a resident of Greenwich Village with no training in urban planning. In the late 1950s, based on observation and then some unconventional research, she concluded that urban planners were a dangerous pack of fools who were destroying not only what was pleasant about cities but also their economic viability. In 1961, she published *The Death and Life of Great American Cities*, in which she laid out, in vivid detail, the good that was destroyed by contemporary planning visions. So-called slums, she demonstrated, functioned as complex protective and connective social environments and were, in addition, entrepreneurial dynamos, in contrast to the isolation and sterility of the new housing projects. Using the yellow pages as one of her primary sources, she laid out the variety of enterprise in New York and the way the form of the city—sidewalks, stoops, windows on the street—supported business and social life. A case could be made that Jane Jacobs single-handedly changed the antiurban structure of feeling that went back to Thoreau. Her book made her a national figure. Is there a city lover alive today who is unaffected by her work?

But Jacobs also became very active in opposing specific urban projects in her home city of New York. Moses reigned there, so it was against him that she fought a number of legendary battles, starting with proposed changes to her own neighborhood, Greenwich Village, low-built, its narrow streets ungridded, an exemplar of a traditional urban charm to which the planners' mind-set was blind. The first Jacobs campaign was against Moses's plan to extend Fifth Avenue, destroying both the Washington Square Arch and the park around it: Jacobs won. Her tool was community organizing at which she was as brilliant as she was at writing. Next came Moses's plan for a cross-Manhattan highway that would have traversed SoHo and Little Italy, just below the Village. This would have entailed razing multiple blocks as well as putting high-rises in Greenwich Village. Jacobs's troops won that one, too. In 1968, Jacobs moved to Toronto to protect her sons from the Vietnam War draft. But she left behind a community well trained in resistance. In 1973, a truck fell through a portion of the old elevated West Side Highway, which ran along the river through Lower Manhattan up to the Henry Hudson at Fifty-Seventh Street, which it predated. With the highway shut down, a grand plan was put forward by the city, a plan in the Moses spirit, to replace the old highway with a state-of-the-art high-speed road with all sorts of ancillary development. This plan would have destroyed a wide swathe of the western edge of the Village. Community activists held off Westway, as the project was called, for over ten years and in the end prevailed. In fact, the power of community resistance to government plans that Jacobs tapped and developed has been a legacy so effective that some say it is destructive, making it close to impossible to implement large-scale urban plans, good or bad, in American cities to this day.

Jacobs was no romantic. But her ideas became romantic, and this, I think, had to do with the fact that her second book, *The Economy of Cities*, published in 1969, immediately preceded the moment in which cities began to definitively lose their role as dynamos of an industrial economy. Already in the early 1960s, the frailty of cities was becoming obvious—hastened by bad planning ideas, not to mention racial prejudice, that produced the socially abandoned inner cities in which the riots of the late '60s broke out. By then, Jacobs's vibrant slums, decimated by riots, were becoming half-deserted, dangerous places that had lost almost all their economic and social vitality. Then came the flight of industry from even the edges of the city, essentially making of the whole industrial city a mere husk of a former economy. Far from monstrous environments, cities overall were now vulnerable relics. A romance with urban architecture and "lifestyle" began to swell, and, with it, a pattern of gentrification engulfing the less damaged slums that had escaped destruction, an architecturally ingenious nineteenth-century city spared by neglect in an arrangement of blocks, stoops, sidewalks, in a variety of styles, the embodiment of the societal genius that Jacobs had detailed in her books.

Soon, all sorts of urban elements that had seemed ugly, like manufacturing buildings—always appreciated by artists—began to inspire tenderness in the ordinary city dweller and then to become the epitome of chic. Urban batteredness itself became beautiful, ennobled in high-fashion ads. The rise of this urban romance also coincided with the rise of the penetrating worldwide new era of mind-work that created a hunger for places of the former era, a hunger that actually, in itself, changed what the city was, even as it was driven by a yearning for what it had been. This very sensibility could lead one to assume that the city would last forever, as itself, as it always had: just more appreciated.

For twenty-five years starting in 1973, I lived on lower Fifth Avenue in Greenwich Village. The Arch and the Square were blessedly intact, and at first my walks took me that way. But then the cement truck fell through the elevated West Side Highway, which was then closed to cars. The old structure stood, now a quiet ruin on which New Yorkers could walk or bike, peering from the unfamiliar, midlevel height at the grungy half abandoned waterfront neighborhood, into tenements, or over the still-covered but unused piers on the Hudson River: parts of the city we never looked at from our speeding cars. One had a sense of freedom on the ruined highway, laced with a tinge of afterlife: there was no policing that I ever saw or safety measures—even the place where the truck fell through was barely blocked off.

One of the covered piers one saw during a walk on the highway was the Christopher Street Pier. It was completely windowless and shut up, except for a small entryway in one corner that appeared to have been torn open. It was well-known that an off-the-grid nighttime scene of gay sexual life took place inside, largely in darkness. In the '80s, the superstructure was taken down, perhaps in a censorious spirit, though one of the results was an open pier, also ruin-like, forgotten-seeming, free, like the highway. It was still a gay meeting place, and there was also a big chain-link barrier to it with a very small chain-link door, as if in remembrance of the earlier entry, but, at least in daytime, all went there, squeezing awkwardly through the narrow door with bikes and strollers. The pier extended far out into the Hudson, open to the sky. It was cursorily paved over, leaving open edges where enormous timbers were exposed: cracked and silvered, rust-streaked and fissured. The timbers had settled every which way, creating large, comfortable crooks: you could lie in their arms. The breeze was often spanking, and the surface of the widening river could have a wild feeling of the sea. But down in the timbers, the sun would be warm.

In 2009, after the old West Side Highway had been torn down, leaving drivers with a start-and-stop road with lights all the way to Fifty-Seventh Street, a stretch of long-abandoned elevated railway called the High Line, between Fourteenth and Thirty-Fourth Streets, once used for transport to and from manufacturing buildings, was, to great acclaim, turned into a linear park full of ornamental grasses and other features of postmodern landscape art. The midlevel height was similar to that of the old West Side Highway, giving older New Yorkers a sense of déjà vu in the still existing sooty tenements with laundry strung between fire escapes, all of which, by this time, seemed truly to be of another era. Making the High Line was a great idea, but it quickly became too celebrated, in a way that made more of it than it really was. People were so happy with the High Line that I wondered if we had lost our knack for exploring the city: it was as if people didn't know what to do, as if we were all somehow starved, but of what? Soon, fancy condos for young stockbrokers started to replace the tenements, whereupon the High Line has almost completely lost its midlevel perspective as from another footing in time, which had been its most interesting feature. The High Line also became so clogged with tourists, corralled by the linear form, that sometimes one could barely move in either direction. I pride myself on my ability to let go and move forward into whatever it is that the city is becoming today. There is no question that the High Line itself and the redeveloped waterfront are very positive changes. The relatively slow West Street instead of Westway, and the variety of relatively new architecture along it instead of homogenized high-rises, are a victory for humanistic urban values, in the Jacobian spirit. Still, on the High Line I can so miss the old free, forgotten-seeming

New York that I become a grouch. I don't like it when my urban experience is managed, "created." I want to find things in the city by accident. I want places that have evolved. There is no anonymity on the High Line, nothing hidden about it, no mystery, no poetry: ah, no transcendence. What is there to write about? Oh well, I guess what it comes down to is that I can't get romantic about the High Line. So there it is, the contradiction. Nothing could be clearer to me than the outdatedness of our old romances about place. And yet.

There is an oddness to looking back from a footing of accepted change to a moment when change was already happening but unsuspected. In some regards, I see myself as pitifully deluded back then on my habitual walks to the shut-down highway and the pier, both ruins, as in my romantic sense of Bergen Street, though that wasn't all wrong: it's just that I was tuned to the disappearing world, rather than to the emergent one. But some of these old experiences are lastingly revelatory in themselves: I can today, in memory, enter the stillness of the ruins, and the sense of being held by them, finding in that a footing from which I can pivot, looking back into the city's past and forward into what is still unfolding. It was not just romance. It was not just illusion. It was a period that was, where place was concerned, oddly stable, even while hovering on the edge of disappearance, for a very long time.

I see now, too, how the big changes unfolding over decades were obscured to me then by illogical sequences similar to those that befuddled our entry into the global enclosure made by man. The great canopy of the Cold War severely retarded my recognition of the immensity of the transition we were undergoing in the city—that in fact the industrial age was fading away, and, more to the point, the profundity of what that meant on every level of our collective lives. Something that is really confusing about the way the Cold War held back recognition of our transition between eras is that nuclear technology, arising out of the invisible world of quantum physics, was

actually our first, way-too-precocious experience of worldwide enclosure in collapsed space, the principal feature of the age to come. But
now that the Cold War is well over, we can see how it bridged the
transition in an obscuring way, reaching from the start of our mature period of industrial might, right over the flight of industry and
the consequent decimation of cities, onward over the '80s, in which
the pendulum in the cyclical grandfather clock, which had seemed
to be swinging toward a normal conservative correction, was carried
right off its hook as liberalism became disoriented. Not that I recognized any of this at the time. If the swing toward market values
seemed unbelievably reckless—the savings and loan scandal, junk
bonds—then, I reasoned, the pendulum would be swinging back
toward government, and a market-shaping philosophy soon. Meanwhile, electronic technology, though it seemed like just one more
invention, burrowed into the foundations of society as it perfected
collapsed global space. The Cold War, nearly half a century long,
becoming so familiar one hardly noticed it was there, was also conducted, politically speaking, as a mesmerizing high tea held by Met-
ternichian gentlemen in top hats, absorbing our attention—what
could be more important?—while thieves prowled the house, looting
our political, societal, and cultural heirlooms: liberals disavowing
their own flag, scandals breaking with no impact, universities jetti-
soning the humanities: one could go on. But there it was, the eerily
reassuring continuity of the Cold War high tea with the grandfather
clock with its well-attached pendulum ticking in the background.
True, our top-hatted diplomats were pouring mass annihilation into
porcelain teacups, then raising them to one another in a decorous
gesture of unclinking toasts to their own brilliance. One can make
the argument—and I do—that this charade in itself undermined
our society in the sense that the pretense of having this situation under control undermined all political authority. But there is also this
to confuse us: the high tea of the Cold War, so supremely important,

wasn't an economic matter. It was a geopolitical ideological contest
with the only alternative to capitalism, and this obscured the radical nature of changes in the world of work that were being wrought
by the same subatomic physics out of which nuclear weapons had
arisen. The existence of the enormous Soviet bloc, furthermore, together with China, held back the full worldwide range of the new
economy by keeping a significant portion of the globe out of play.

So when the Berlin Wall fell, in 1989, not only did we lose the
drama that had given us a role in the world as a nation since World
War II, but a major obstruction to the panoramic, infiltrative, electronically facilitated 24/7 worldwide economy was removed. Not that
any of us necessarily paid much attention. I was on Bergen Street at
this time, puzzling over why it was that the meaning of place, the
very soul of the city, seemed to have been pulled out from under. It
seemed impossible for that to happen. Surely the character of place
was eternal. How could it be?

The Cold War was akin to the age to come in that its weaponry
arose out of quantum physics, but also in that it was to meet war-
time conditions created by that weaponry that the internet was invented. The Pentagon wanted a communications system that could
survive nuclear attack. As Paul Baran, one of the originators put it,
the development of the internet arose not out of intellectual curiosity
but "in response to the most dangerous situation that ever existed."
The solution was a communications system in which information
(messages) could be broken into bits that could take multiple paths
to their destination where they would be reassembled by computer.
Bits encountering a hole in the system could reroute onto alternative paths to the destination. To work under the short time lines of
nuclear engagement, the system also had to be able to transmit very
large volumes of information very fast. There we have it: the internet
we know. Now that the danger that inspired it no longer overwhelms
us, we can, perhaps, see in this military origin how closely the two

forms of global enclosure, military and digital, really are. AT&T didn't like this phone-supplanting development at all and refused to let the RAND Corporation, where the research began, use their long-distance circuit maps. (RAND resorted to stealing the maps.) The actual inventors were scientists, of course. (Several, oddly, had started out in acoustical science, though they weren't very good at it. Others were attracted to gambling.) Much of the subsequent work was done at MIT. When it was discovered there that large files could be transferred by the system that eventually became email, that Stanford could share research with Harvard instantaneously, snobbish eastern universities couldn't see the benefit. Why on earth would they want to be doing that? Many of the uses of what became email were not intentionally developed. The scientists stumbled on the ways internet communications are superior to the telephone in daily life as well as nuclear war: on how their networks could facilitate group discussion, for example. At one point a group of scientists came down from MIT to Washington, D.C., to demonstrate a precursor of email to generals. Captains of industry were also invited to the demonstration. As an example of what their new marvel could do, the scientists sent a written message to Boston and got an answer right back. Welcome to the telegraph! The generals were not impressed. AT&T was uninterested. No one, not even the scientists who invented it, seems to have understood the world-reshaping capacity of this technology. How many other times in history has a civilization-changing invention been developed by people who had no idea of the significance of what they were doing. Fire?

A lot of people got on the net in the 1980s. But it wasn't until after the Cold War had ended that most of us found our lives altered—only in the mid-'90s that widespread internet use began to penetrate all domains, professional, domestic, and eventually even public, with the inexorable advance of the imperium of collapsed space, the bright hole into which the difference between this room and the next room,

From up there I could see over chain link topped with spiraling superbarbs, across Governors Island, with its brick neo-Georgian buildings among sere oaks, to overweening Wall Street rising behind. I painted against time, just going over the falls of the project pell-mell. If you think landscape painting is a peaceful occupation just because the product can be, you are mistaken. It's a hair-raising pursuit. Around three-thirty a young man showed up with a boom box and I thought, "Hmmnnn," because of Red Hook's old reputation, and there I was, a woman and the sun going down. But that was an old geography of danger speaking, and I wanted to finish my painting; and, anyway, something told me I was okay. It turned out he was there to wash the little school-bus shuttles that Snapple provided for employees between the factory and the subway. The music on the boom box was religious rap. We worked together.

To my eye, Governors Island and the skyscrapers of Wall Street behind it were different in scale in a way that needed puzzling out. That was why I had chosen the site. But what I hadn't foreseen and what emerged as a problem on the canvas was the relationship of the two towers of the World Trade Center, proportionally speaking, to old Wall Street. Even though they were on the far side of Manhattan, and thus diminished in size by distance, they were double the height of any other tower in my painting. While scouting, I just hadn't seen this. The reason, I think, was that I was so used to them, that even though they always seemed too big I'd learned not to notice how big. As tackled by brush in hand, they also seemed physically awkward, perhaps partially because of outrageous disproportion. But symbolic dissonance contributed. The towers were designed in the late 1960s and completed in 1970; by then, architectural height had not been of interest in New York since before World War II. Building higher than anyone else by then was the preoccupation of Third World countries—or Chicago, which built the Sears Tower, topping the WTC in 1973, as if it was the Empire State building topping the Chrysler in the 1930s. (Recovering its former first-city cool, New York did not take the bait.)

Other aspects of the World Trade Center were historically wrong. The location was outdated: "Wall Street" by the time the towers were built had more or less moved uptown. And the towers were out of step, too, in that together they provided 220 stories of office space in a period in which office space was going begging in the city. It was so hard to find tenants for the two towers, much less the international tenants engaged in world trade that had been envisioned, that New York State had to bail out the landlord by housing state bureaucracies there. This was not a glamorous substitute. But it's also true that the towers, in being too big for their time, were actually ahead of their time. We are still getting used to the jarringness of global scale, as in a liner that carries five thousand people dwarfing the pier where it has docked, or warehouse stores like Costco that reflect the realities of global trade volumes. But this was still the 1970s. We hadn't seen much of that.

New Yorkers got used to the World Trade Towers anyway, even though the towers never fit in, seeing them while in a way not seeing them, as I had not really seen them until I tried to paint them, becoming even affectionate at times, for the way they took the light in the morning, or shone in the sunset as you approached the city from New Jersey. For people in the neighborhood, they were experienced as a gargantuan double sundial.

But none of these thoughts helped with the fact that the towers had become a big, intractable problem on my canvas. What I like about painting is that sometimes the hand knows what to do in ways quite at odds with what you think it should do. But in this case my hand was stumped, laying down an unarticulated mass. By four-fifteen the light was fast fading. The towers had joined horribly on my canvas, but I had no choice but to accept what I had. I got down in a gingerly way from the high block. Trying not to look at it, I put

the wet painting carefully in the back of the car. On the way home, I
stopped at the butcher to order a Christmas roast, and by the time
I got home it was dark.

On a September morning, many years later, once again looking out
my Riverside Drive window while having my morning coffee, I saw
a small sailing ship with a high poop deck motoring upstream, a
replica of the *Half Moon*, in which Henry Hudson had made his
way upriver. The sky was clear, though the river was in shadow. In
some ways the scene—Palisades, sky, water—is not much changed
since 1609. The apartment buildings on top of the Palisades receded
in the sunless light, this time as if it was they who were of a lesser
order of reality and not some pushy new topography in their own
right. The long sharp bowsprit of the *Half Moon* measured progress
against the stone cliffs like the spike of a bow compass.

September has become memory-laden for New Yorkers on two
counts. First is the attack on and fall of the World Trade Center
seven years before the day I watched the *Half Moon* motoring upstream, the definitive end of the illusion that we were conveniently
separated from the rest of the world by oceans. Has ever the end of
an era been marked so succinctly? The attack has been memorialized
each year, though not for that reason. Seven years later, our economy
was on the verge of another kind of crash as Lehman Brothers, a
global financial-services firm, teetered, painfully exposing the flaws
in our strange new order of work in the money-fields. The teetering
was brought on by the "instrument" known as the subprime mortgage. Those who had constructed this instrument at first said it was
so complicated no one could understand it, but, as it turned out, the
cause of the problem was clear to most. Mortgages had been given
to people who couldn't afford them, the risk Cuisinarted into bits
that were then reassembled into composite securities, riddled with

hidden weaknesses—mortgage holders who were likely to default—but traded as sound. This is something that could be done only with the mind-extending powers of computers, which could keep track of the bits. But the risk was real—and, indeed, the computers were quite capable of interpreting the histories of actual mortgage payments or nonpayments, hidden as they were within the pixelated securities. As defaults were registered, the value of the securities decreased precipitously. A house of cards started to come down. But the houses so mortgaged were not of cards; they were real. The families now out on the street were real, too, though as a group they vanished into the interstices of society. But the houses didn't vanish. After the crash, as deficiencies of the subprime mortgage manifested in defaults, actual new though abandoned houses, fields upon fields of them, became a feature of our landscape. These scenes were kin to the abandoned neighborhoods of the rust belt. But no depth of time gave subprime McMansions the tragic complexity of Detroit. Rust-belt dwellings were inherently modest and in long use, conveying solvency and a kind of social solidity that one just can't square with their ruination. The subprime dwellings, in contrast, were spanking new and often lavish: the pediment, the Palladian window. These houses expressed overextension, on the part of the owners but also those who had devised the instrument, with fine print in which sudden jumps in mortgage payments were secreted. Nothing hard to understand about that strategy once the results started coming in. And there were the houses, a rare physical manifestation of our new mind-work, in this case the faulty mind-work that the subprime instrument was. Soon thieves began stripping foreclosed dwellings of valuable copper piping and other innards: just one more level of "ripping off"—why not?

But on that Saturday when I watched the *Half Moon* motoring upstream, Lehman had not yet fallen, nor had the true desolation of our landscapes—physical, financial, not to mention the landscape of promise—been fully revealed yet. In fact, on that very day the gurus of finance were sequestered in the Federal Reserve Bank of New York deciding whether or not to let Lehman Brothers fall. That was the phrase, should we "let it fall?" The gurus might have had only the weekend to decide, but, as it happened, Monday was a Japanese holiday. The world securities market would not pick up until Tuesday, giving them an extra day. In this atmosphere of bated breath I developed a hankering to go down to Wall Street and lay eyes on the Federal Reserve itself: just to be there.

I took the subway to Fourteenth Street, and walked from there along the river, past piers that were still seedy, and then through Battery Park City, a miragelike environment of mirroring glass built on landfill which can seem like a gated enclave escaped from San Diego. Then past the site where the World Trade towers had fallen. I remembered how, in earlier years, when most of the debris of the towers had been cleared away but the shock of the attack was still fresh, a platform had been improvised from which people could look into the still incompletely excavated site. The faces of Americans peering into that cavity had been open, querying, in learning mode—willing to endure uncertainty as the immensity of the shift of our country's place in world was absorbed. By the time of the pending economic crash, the cavity had become more utilitarian, a construction site of the vast, deep kind that is common in New York, only vaster and deeper. A touristic industry had sprung up around the site, but one that sentimentalized rather than probed. Undistilled meanings still floated in and above the cavity, but with the shock of the attack long behind us and even memory of the towers themselves receded, the impact of the site was of absence, the immensity of the space left behind having become the articulate feature.

I moved on downtown into the classic Wall Street section, where many of the towers had been turned into apartments. One Chase Manhattan Plaza, a then new tower where I had worked as a young woman was more venerable now but still a youngster surrounded by some fat old stone dowagers swanning and swirling in their ornamentation, as if they didn't know that the party had long ago moved on. One Chase was still a workplace. And there, right nearby, as always, was the Fed, noble, Florentine, fortresslike, with handsome iron grids over its immense windows set in a first story of massive blocks of rusticated stone: permanent. The only change was that it had been cleaned, and, possibly, the presence of a bronze plaque I didn't remember, maybe placed there later as preservation efforts took hold in the city:

LANDMARK OF NEW YORK
FEDERAL RESERVE BANK OF NEW YORK
INSPIRED BY FLORENTINE RENAISSANCE PALACES AND
COMPLETED IN 1924, THIS STRUCTURE OF INDIANA LIMESTONE
AND OHIO SANDSTONE WITH IRONWORK BY SAMUEL YELLIN
WAS DESIGNED BY YORK AND SAWYER AND BUILT BY MARC
EIDLITZ & SON, INC. FIVE STORIES ARE BELOW STREET
LEVEL WITH SUBTERRANEAN VAULTS RESTING ON BEDROCK.

The bedrock would be Manhattan schist. The vaults would be for gold. Of course, 1924 would be five years before 1929: so much for permanence. I thought of vaults of gold resting on the schist and then of the gurus sitting on them in the midst of this latter-day crisis. What did they eat? How was it served? Did they have cocktails, wine? Did they smoke cigars? All the while having déjà vu experiences of myself in a summer dress at nineteen. And yet I was also at the same time many decades older, and here was the Fed, as always, and yet not entirely, security itself having somehow moved on from the schist, from the vaults.

By Monday the gurus had decided to let Lehman fall. In the aftermath, I experienced the city as if returned to its former self. The relentless pressure on buyers in the housing market rapidly receded. The forest fire of the roots that had been driving people out of their homes became mere embers. Suddenly my neighbors weren't ghosts of a former era, but my neighbors. The neighborhood would be as it was, like it or not, for the foreseeable future. The older city was reinstated with a frank, improbable living beauty, sometimes in its least beautiful parts. Pumping gas one night at a station almost under the elevated subway not far from my home, I felt myself enveloped by the gorgeousness of the sooty steel structure on which a train rumbled over wooden ties far above. The backs of heads against the subway windows seemed momentarily to belong to people living in the long-ago city, complacent in its humdrum integrity, unaware of all that had happened since. I looked at the gas pump, thinking that it was no different than an older one, just drawing gas out of a tank in the ground and measuring it with a mechanism that turned the numbers. Then I remembered that it had already read my credit card and was drawing on a worldwide trove of information that had become, somehow, more real than my surroundings.

Meanwhile, our apartment was no longer worth what we had paid for it. To pay the mortgage now seemed like shelling out unconscionable bribes or capitulating to blackmail. But one would do it—fatalistically, as in corrupt countries where that is how life is lived. The gap between mortgage and value made our apartment un-solid-seeming in one light. Yet there had been so much fiction mixed into the crash that, in a way, our present housing finances seemed like just so much more fiction. Our apartment was where we lived. It kept out the rain and the wind. That was not fiction. Nor was it fiction that others were finding themselves out in the rain. The tension between the abstract nature of financial instruments and the concrete nature of their effect on life was strong in that period.

There was something very good about the moment, though I say that aware that for the many who could not keep their homes or who lost their savings it was unremittingly bad. Still, in my view, the restorative effect is worth recalling for what it revealed: how the collapse of a kind of market mania let us go back to living. The city was back, my neighbors were my neighbors, and all that, but there was something more, too. With the market's claim that it was the ultimate measure of value now brutally unmasked, other measures of value had a chance. Indeed, with the money value popped so suddenly, one was almost forced to reach for other measures of value. And yet there was no language for such measures handy. For we had by and large lost the culture that affirmed nonmarket values as a living, breathing way of life. There was only a very large empty space where such a language and such culture had once been, and where they could be in the future. The old city might have seemed restored, but old languages of value were not available. New ones were needed. This showed me how far we had moved on into a new era. Nevertheless, the empty space was at least revealed by the crash, even if we didn't know how to fill it: it was a kind of presence, and there was about that an almost sacred uncertainty.

As for the sense of New York as restored to itself as it was in a former era, the ultimate revelation in this was also that of something missing. For there was no Midwest behind the mirage of the older city: this was, in part, why Lehman fell. In place of Youngstown lighting up the sky at night with blast furnaces were the money-fields of Wall Street only. If inventing and proliferating securities based on the subprime mortgage was our new form of making, then Wall Street had produced the equivalent of very flawed steel. But the empty space left was also the equivalent of the space where the civilizing response to raw industrial energies had been. It was the space waiting for our cultural and, above all, political response to these new conditions. That is what was wonderful about those days after the crash—those weeks, those months. The tyranny of the reign of money as the supreme measure of value—its way of making other values ghostly—was momentarily over. We could feel what else we were and could become.

Meanwhile, New York pride was stung as prophets predicted that the "command center" of the global economy would move from New York to London. What would that make us? The Detroit of the money-fields? The same week that Lehman fell, Merrill Lynch was bought by Bank of America with its headquarters in Charlotte. Charlotte! And yet there was in the catastrophe, in its very rug-pulled-out-from-under feeling, a solidity that seemed better than what we had lost. Let Charlotte have it! We are on the threshold of invention! The moment passed, there was no invention, New York hung on as "command center," we went into a period of disillusion-ment and confusion, finding our well-being dependent still on the very financial gurus who had failed so catastrophically as our high priests—who else was there? This is the condition in which we still struggle. The water closed over our heads: to imagine anything dif-ferent became again naïve.

Three years after the crash, the tenth anniversary of 9/11 came along. By that time, the effects of the subprime collapse on the U.S. economy had settled in. The empty space that waited for the civiliz-ing response remained unfilled. We slogged onward, as in a kind of low-grade depression, capitulating to the reign of the very values that had brought about the disaster in the first place. What else was there? So it was, too, with our understanding of the assault on the World Trade Center. The yearly memorials had become empty and tedious. The moment of openness after 9/11 had been long-ago lost, the war in Iraq, into which we had leapt to dispel unbearable uncertainty about our place in the world, about our vulnerability, was dragging on still. A memorial monument for 9/11 had been much disputed. But the disputes had now been settled and the tenth anniversary, on which the new memorial would be unveiled, was approaching. The monu-ment would, as had been true of the annual memorial ceremonies all along, rely heavily on the casualties for its meaning. Obviously the meaning of the fall of the World Trade Center was far larger than the misfortune of those accidentally caught in it, but we had found no other way to articulate a collective response to the event than to turn the people who had the bad luck to be there into heroes. (The firemen who responded *were* heroes, of course, but not in a way that could help us understand what had happened.) We were still asking the dead to save us from any real thoughtfulness about what the attack could tell us about the collapsed worldwide space in which we now lived and our role in it. It was as if grief for them would relieve us of the responsibility of understanding the post-9/11 world. Still, the tenth anniversary seemed meaningful to me. I wanted to at least remember the uncertainty, the openness, and the pregnant absence of answers. I wanted a pilgrimage. But the unveiling didn't appeal to me—a good thing, really, in that thousands were going and you had to have tickets and they were all bought up.

For a while after the attack, in the period before the site had been cleared, what one saw as one approached the World Trade site was a mountain of smoking debris from the top of which a sheared-off I-beam, curved by heat, protruded like a scimitar raised aloft, in threat yet also beckoning out of chaos. The president of the Metropolitan Museum had passionately suggested in a *Times* op-ed that fragments of the towers, and particularly this remnant, be used as the centerpiece of a memorial. Now, that was an idea—in complexity and simplicity—that fit the measure of the situation: its ambiguity, its uncertainty, its hopes, its fears. The suggestion had been ignored, but what I remembered now was that all the WTC debris had been hauled away to a landfill site in Staten Island called Fresh Kills, which had actually been closed but was reopened temporarily for the purposes of receiving the ruins of the towers. This elevated it from a garbage dump to sacred ground. The idea was that it would be turned into a park. Over the years the Fresh Kills project had appeared in back-page articles. Somewhere I'd seen alluring images of a moorlike expanse by the sea. "Fresh Kills" is a Dutch name invoking the freshwater streams that ran through the original landscape. My pilgrimage would be Fresh Kills.

On Sunday of Labor Day weekend, I set out for Fresh Kills with my partner Noel by car from Rensselaerville, coming toward it through New Jersey, depending on our GPS to get us to the Goethals Bridge to Staten Island. In this period, a GPS was a separate device that one kept in one's car. The route was not direct, but GPS was already good at old infrastructure rendered incoherent over time by piecemeal additions and expansions—much better than maps. It got us to the bridge, but once over onto Staten Island it would not respond to the entry "Fresh Kills." In the kind of crazed absorption with the virtual world of devices to which we have become susceptible, overriding what the actual world might tell us, I switched to my Blackberry, which was the fashionable device at the time, where I called up Google. Google identified Fresh Kills as a park, but gave only Richmond Avenue as its location—no address on Richmond, nor were there any directions. We were at this point shooting along I-278, which would soon take us to the Verrazano Bridge and off Staten Island. The GPS at this point suddenly gave up and reverted to showing only a part of New Jersey from which it would not budge. So I entered a random number on Richmond into Google Maps, just to get us in the general direction of Fresh Kills. Immediately Google Maps directed us off I-278 and into grinding Sunday traffic on an old unidentified route through the impacted concatenation that is Staten Island. Soon the trip acquired a grueling quality. We became tired and hungry. Happily, the random address on Richmond I had given Google Maps turned out to be the location of an old-fashioned Greek diner. It was jammed, but, miraculously, a booth was free. I had a feta and spinach omelet. Noel had a chef salad, hold the roast beef.

Feeling much better, we proceeded south on Richmond, blindly, in the sense that Google Maps, while still showing a greenish entity called Fresh Kills Park, revealed no entrance to it. Then, improbably, a green terrain almost as vague as that on Google Maps appeared in the real world on our right. There it remained as we proceeded for a considerable distance. Surely this was Fresh Kills.

But there was no identifying sign, no entrance. Then we were past it, closed in again by Staten Island concatenation. Puttering on in stop-and-go traffic, we became discouraged. But along the way before we came on the vague green terrain I had spotted two joined trailers identified as NYPD. So we made an illegal U-turn and went back. The trailers were white, set in an L, with "NYPD" written on them in big blue lettering that did nothing to disguise the flimsiness of this law-enforcement headquarters. Inside, I found no one in the waiting room, or at a reception desk just down a narrow trailer hall. I called out, and a police officer, very young, dewy-eyed even, popped into the hall and in a flustered but official way ordered me to "back up" to the waiting room. Then, before I did, he inquired, with alarm, whether everything was all right. Over a radio I heard a deadpan voice describing a robbery. I said everything was fine. But could he tell me how to get to Fresh Kills? The officer applied himself to my inquiry with generous seriousness, bowing his head and then wagging it extravagantly from left to right, suggesting that this was a real mind-boggler. He had heard of Fresh Kills, of course, but a park? That was a concept somewhere far in the future. "If ever" was the implication. Well, could I go there? I asked. I just wanted to see the place, I said. He didn't think so but suggested I go down Richmond to the Sanitation Department—they might be able to help. After all, he said, it was supposed to be a park someday, but it had been a dump, and maybe still was, so maybe Sanitation still had authority over it. "You know—park, dump, park, dump," he said, making a gesture of weighing each in his palms.

The Department of Sanitation was far more majestically housed than the local NYPD. The building, monumental and of brick, had stylishly rounded corners and a lot of big bays for big vehicles. The parking lot was imperial. Circumambulating the building, I eventually found an entrance and inside, down a hall, an open door to an office area within which I heard voices. There I found a gathering of men, some in Sanitation Department uniforms, not dewy-eyed, some sitting on desks, all enjoying a fraternal confab on a holiday-weekend Sunday, and not in the least expecting me. None could at first speak.

So I asked my question, how could I get into Fresh Kills? This stumped them, too. Obviously our GPS and my Blackberry were not the only thinking mechanisms that had a problem with this destination. One of the men had about him something of being "brass." He was sitting behind a desk, and, addressing me, said, with gravitas, that if I went in there I would, for sure, be apprehended. Somehow it sounded as if I would be shot on sight, though of course he did not say that. It was just an impression. Still, the message was that going there was inadvisable. I would have to get permission from the Parks Department, he said, with authoritarian satisfaction, and the department would not be open until Tuesday. I replied that I didn't want to wait until Tuesday—getting even this far had not been easy. Was there no way to simply look at Fresh Kills without actually setting foot inside? "All I need is to see it." "Oh sure," he said, with a sudden collapse of resistance: "Left out the gate, right on Travis at the first light"—"the second light," said one of the men; "the third," said another—"left on Victory," he went on, ignoring them, "take the expressway, one exit to Muldoon," and there it would be. "You can't miss it," he said. "It's right in front of you, a big hill."

Though the way was a lot more complicated than he'd indicated—nothing in Staten Island is simple—and took us entirely away from the vague green terrain that my Blackberry told me was Fresh Kills, we found our way to the Muldoon exit, which delivered us into another Department of Sanitation domain, an expanse of cracked and patched pavement, a hard-used, somewhat haphazardly organized place of serried garbage trucks and huge snowplows. Straight ahead was a barricaded entrance with a checkpoint, unoccupied, and, beyond, an almost rural road that led across what looked like wetlands to a big plant with a smokestack quite far away and picturesque in the distance. Close-up was a methane purification plant, next to it a chain-linked semivacant space. In this space was a red pickup at the far end, and, to the left, a row of large white containers with "GUASCOR" written on them in navy blue letters. Beyond, both far and close, was the big hill. I was out of the car standing in litter, mostly of the "fast food" type, among weeds, up against the chain link, near a berry-bearing tree. Actually the big hill was more ridge-like, a long grassy cliff, the crest extending in both directions as far as one could see.

The slopes of the ridge were steep and covered with a variety of long grasses. As a landscape formation it was—like the towers—awkward. First of all, this was a flat marshy area, not in the least bit hilly—one could see that plainly in the direction of the smoke-stacked plant. This sudden towering ridge was so out of place as to incapacitate any native sense of landscape you might have. Still, if you managed not to think of that, if you just took it as a landscape in itself, the big hill had something of the look of places that are so far away from urban civilization that they haven't yet learned to be aware of themselves—the Falkland Islands, perhaps, or the steppes of Russia—the audibility of the expressway from which we had just descended notwithstanding. You felt lonely just looking at it, as if you hadn't spoken to another human being in months, years maybe. The grassland aspect was romantic in its way, though the grasses were of different kinds, in contrasting patches, creating a jagged, quiltlike pattern, probably reflecting a variety in soil composition. Overall the terrain was lumpy, in a suggestive, decidedly disturbing way. Pipes of some kind, possibly vents, arising from the ground sporadically, at irregularly canted angles, suggested old fence posts—a forgotten rural history lost in eons of agrarian toil. On the other hand, the lumpiness suggested something moving underneath. Rome might be a theme park, but Fresh Kills most decidedly was not.

I had no idea whether the World Trade Towers were here or elsewhere in the landfill, but in the vastness and heaping suggestiveness of the Fresh Kills terrain that didn't seem to matter. My journey as a pilgrim was complete. The sun had fallen behind the ridgeline, the lumpy grassy slopes were in shade—that darkness-in-daylight quality that comes near evening in faraway places, tantalizing and unnerving. Fresh Kills seemed innocent, but actually it was a perfectly uninnocent place. Still, there was something childlike about it, suggestive of a parent on the beach who has been mummified in sand by children. Everything about it had to do with ill-concealed hiddenness. In spots, trees, not full grown but well past the sapling stage, grew on the slope at odd intervals that perhaps reflected rare nodes of unusually nutritious footing. Though it was late summer, the trees seemed sparsely leaved, as if it were spring. Though they had probably been denuded by Hurricane Irene, which had hit New York hard just two weeks before, the seeming seasonal dissonance of leafless trees added to the disturbance of the place. A few trees on the ridgeline were silhouetted against the sky, which was bright with impending sunset.

I knew I could get to work on my Blackberry to find out whether the towers were here or not. Or Google Earth could have taken me to the top of the ridge and shown me the big hill in context far and wide. I knew that the fact I could do those things defined what this place was, but what I wanted here was something comprehended by the body, just as at graveside after a funeral—that this was an aboveground burial, and the corpse not convincingly deceased notwithstanding. It's something the human psyche, confronted with the passing of a person, needs, and so, too, perhaps, with an era. Even the identity of the corpse seemed to shift about—it was the industrial age, or the industrial city, or it was New York as we had known it, or it was just garbage, monumental waste, or it was the World Trade Center, in itself almost endlessly ambiguous—its awkward size and height, its misplacement in time as well as location, its symbolic illiteracy, its embarrassing and failed attempt to establish a continuum between one age and another. But so it is often at funerals, as seemingly mismatching parts of the deceased's life come together in one room. The big hill was nothing if not human. Sometimes at a funeral, but especially at graveside, you can suddenly get a sense of who the deceased was that you never had before, and in that can come a sense of what you yourself are and might be going forward, a new understanding of your own capacity, and with that a sense of freedom and possibility, while also realizing that the person for whom the funeral is being held will never know you in that new stage. You will never see the person again, it's only you now: it's over.

Part Three

The Absent Hand

The Corporation in the Woods

At the Sheraton

I know this hotel room well: the navy-pinstripe wallpaper, matching duvet cover, though changed lately to white with lacy trim. The picture on the wall of nature on steroids never changes, nor does the foundationless feeling. When I wake in the middle of the night and see that picture I lose hope of returning to what I think of as the normal world, when I am in fact deep in the normal world as it has become. For two weeks each year I come here on business. The room number is different, of course, but the room is the same. Indeed over time it has slipped into my psyche, in the way of well-known places, so that on arrival something in me fits. It's not a homecoming exactly, but not unlike that.

Yet almost everything about the room remains permanently strange. Housekeeping leaves the curtains pulled closed as if open they are like an unmade bed. The first time I entered my room, I immediately flung them open to see where I was. I looked across an extensive flat roof perforated by a green glass dome, cylindrical skylights, giant vents, a pickup truck right there on the roof, looking miniature. To the left, the slanting floors of a parking garage rose out of sight, sides open, occasional ascending and descending cars glinting in shadow. Vertical words in neon down the side toward a street I couldn't see: FRIDAYS, RAINFOREST CAFÉ.

Since then, I vary my strategy, sometimes opening the curtains and sometimes not—sometimes leaving them closed for days. A feeling can set in then, however, that the room is not a part of a larger building but more like a projected image, drifting. This place is not designed for such a long stay. Not the staff, not the businessmen, not the wedding parties stay as long as two weeks, I am sure. Part of the problem of leaving the curtains closed is that there is no night or day. But if I go online I am perfectly comfortable with that. After all, the internet, too, is neither diurnal nor located and, though full of so-called windows, actually without any at all. Actually, even with the curtains open I could be in Johannesburg, Hong Kong. I try different combinations, shifting around for comfort but also in an experimental mode. Sometimes, whether with curtains open or closed, I purposely don't go online in my room for days, because the room is so compatible with the nonlocated, nondiurnal nature of the internet. Not going online is choosing to live in the transition, with one foot in the old world.

The actual location of my Sheraton is Towson, Maryland, once a dignified county seat, now engulfed in elements that are compacted like a city but not in the least citylike: it's this that could be anywhere. To be in this environment is not entirely unlike being online: sure you know the name of the place and what continent it is on, but the idea of a larger context around it is irrelevant-seeming. Towson is right on I-695, which encircles Baltimore: if you step outside and cock your ears you can hear it. For some years the Baltimore telephone book was provided in my room. I am not quite sure when it disappeared, because I never used it. The hotel phone with the area code 410 on its dial is a clue, though used principally for intra-Sheraton communications: high billing discourages outside calls; we all use our cells. If you turn on the large flat-screen television that dominates the room, you will see local Baltimore news. But even the television, over the years, has acquired the slightly shameful, ghostly look of appliances that have outlived their time. It's too thingish for our ethereal age, too big: we like things to be as close to nothing as possible, to fit in our pocket and come with us. The air of the hotel is that it's new, but in fact it's rather old. A few years ago, while trying to maneuver a suitcase big enough to hold two weeks of clothes through the doorway, I bumped a protruding corner of the wall and a metal guard fell off, pulling plaster with it. The bathroom was just inside the door. I found the toilet handle hanging down on its cable. But the pillows were plentiful, the sheets rich, the bathroom floor cool marble.

The drifting quality the room acquires when the curtains are closed for days can give me the feeling that I am in a vast interior from which there is no exit, as in a dream. But sometimes I get that same impression when I venture out of the Sheraton into Towson. There is an outdoors, of course, but it exists in scraps, as if left over from another time. Over the years I have become numbed to this, but on my first venture into Towson the effect struck me forcefully. My purpose was to buy a book. Fortunately, I had a guide. We took an elevator down to the second floor of the hotel, walked through a mostly-cleaned-up party room to a heavy door with a crossbar of the sort that seems likely to set off an alarm. This kind of door, I would learn, is a signature feature of this kind of landscape. We pushed on to a footbridge over streaming traffic with the RAINFOREST CAFÉ sign to our right. The footbridge was a bit of outdoors but felt exposed; you wanted to get to the other side. There we found a similar door into the top level of the parking garage I had seen from my room. We descended the stairwell—four floors. At the bottom, pushing out through another barred door, we traversed a brief nondescript bit of ground under the sky and then, through yet another door, entered a windowless basement packed with islands of clothing, through which we maneuvered, not easily. Gaining an escalator we rose into a high, spacious atrium, with a domed skylight many floors above. I realized I was in a mall. Two more escalators took us to an upper floor, also close-packed with islands of clothing, that we traversed to another, very obscure-seeming barred door in the far corner, on the other side of which we found ourselves on the bottom level of a different parking garage that had been lumpily paved. We had been climbing a hill. We threaded our way through parked cars in this shadowy understory to a rough concrete staircase on the far side that led up to a burst of light that reminded me of Jack's beanstalk. At the top, we blinked on the edge of a fast-moving rotary. My guide pointed out a Barnes & Noble on the other side of one of the rotary exits and left me on my own.

Through the revolving door, surprisingly stiff, and into the realm of books. In their garish jackets, under bright lights, the books on display seemed a little ashamed, as if trying to hide their thingishness. I weighed one in my hand, as if in the dark, as it dawned on me that in their size, in their weight—that is to say, in their length—physical books are directly related to what the human hand can hold. What we assumed was an artistic choice of length is actually dictated by the body and likely to disappear as the weightless, edgeless electronic ocean closes in. That is what it was like for me in those early days in Towson. These were mundane experiences, but, because the environment was new to me, they had a metaphysical dimension. A feeling of no escape followed me wherever I went into Towson.

Accustomed to the strangeness, I no longer have these ingénue attacks. But it remains a fact that the difference between the older landscapes in which I forged a sense of myself and the contemporary environment is great, and no less because I have become inured. Back then, I could become downright hostile to such environments, feeling ungrounded and unseen in them. If there is no place for me in the world as it has become, then I do not like the world—that was my attitude. I avoided such places as much as possible, which is why Towson was strange to me. And yet it's that very same old sense of place that has pushed me to notice this environment more deeply than it asks to be noticed, however banal it might be, because, simply as a place, it has to have meaning. My old sense of place says the banality is a disguise. Sometimes I feel I am betraying my old self and the landscapes that formed me by even considering these placeless new places as comparable. At other times, and more truly, more enduringly, I feel that it is in this pursuit I most honor my former sense of place and all that it taught me.

Over the years, I have come to notice a peculiar vacuum in my Sheraton room. This comes on in the later part of a sojourn. It is different from the sanctuary of a hotel room in a city, different from the flimsy bleakness of a motel. I have always liked those paintings by Edward Hopper of old American hotel rooms—so plain. The emptiness here is nothing like that and yet it's related, almost as if in a reverse language. It's not just the latent Hopperesque qualities, like the seeping decrepitude underneath the luxury features. It seems to me to come more from a disappointment in luxury itself, indefinitely reproduced in the vast interior that is the world now. It's as if in such a room one is subjected to the withholding of something needed, putting me in mind of those experiments in which a person is swaddled in darkness with no sense stimuli. Waking at three in the morning, turning on the light, I catch the room in its true lack of allegiance to anything. As in a Hopperesque hotel room, I experience this quality as a condition of deprivation that is in its way revelatory, transformative: an exposure to the void. This is so unreal, I think, and yet it's the most real thing. Sometimes I embrace the stripping down of normal supports. When you stay so long in such a place, you begin to see through not to bones or to an underlying structure but to something more like the lack thereof. It's a feeling of no foundation. If I go on-line I can't feel it, not because it's gone but because I have entered the quintessentially foundationless realm.

In normal dreams, the mind creates seemingly nonsensical environments out of disparate elements from memory in which, some say, unacknowledged or dangerous feelings are expressed in a coded way. But whatever these secretive creations might mean, they are no longer real when you wake up. You might dream that you are trapped in an endless interior, but when you wake up you are delighted to discover that you are not trapped at all—the door is right there. You might probe the meaning of the dream, perhaps connect it to some form of psychic entrapment in your life, and that might be real enough, but you are still not physically entrapped, as you thought in the dream. In the case of the cryptically agglomerated and edgeless environment of Towson, it can be helpful to see it as derived from the aesthetic of dreams. But it is not something from which we wake up. It's something we wake to.

The Corporation in the Woods

I went to college in the early 1960s, some years before electronically facilitated globalism had begun to grip the world. My college was Manhattanville, in Purchase, New York, an old, wealthy Westchester suburb in which the pastoral illusion—stone walls, oaks, an impression of land—was diligently maintained. Not for one moment did I mistake this for country. However, the campus had formerly been the estate of a Gilded Age newspaper magnate and had extensive grounds, including a large section of woodland, long untended and off the map of the campus as normally conceived. I liked having a place to go that was beyond institutional sight. Broad paths were still passable. If I went too far in one direction I would come across the New York State Thruway. (Today, it's I-684). The Thruway sluiced through the landscape, disregarding terrain in a way that negated it. This may have been my first clue that landscape as I knew it was not holding. I learned to avoid the Thruway so I could enjoy the woods. The Hutchinson River Parkway, older, smaller-scaled, bounded another side of this tract. Once I encountered a hobo in the woods by his campfire. As my life went forward, I forgot this little escape. Yet an imprint was stored.

In the early 1980s, I found myself occasionally driving the Hutchinson River Parkway. As I passed the exit for Purchase, past my old woods, something that decidedly didn't belong flashed through the trees. It was not just that something had been built there—that would hardly surprise. Several passes later I began to put words to what was joltingly wrong in that flash: "marble and mirror: corporate, expensive." Corporate had no place in the carefully guarded aesthetic of Purchase. This got under my skin enough that finally one day when I was a bit ahead of time I decided to investigate.

Almost immediately off the exit was a long asphalt driveway flanked by the kind of funereal landscaping that looks more like a photo than a place you could step into. At the end was a formidable edifice of white stone and black reflective glass obviously of a very high architectural quality. It was most of all the quality of the building that baffled me. This was no office building for suburban dentists and accountants. It reminded me of the East Building of the National Gallery in Washington, designed by I. M. Pei. In fact, as I learned later, the edifice before me was designed by I. M. Pei, too, completed in 1980, two years after the East Building. Nestle was the first owner, though it was soon sold to IBM who was the likely owner when I encountered it. But I didn't know any of that at the time. All I knew was that an obviously "world-class" building had been set on a knoll in a patch of mild Westchester woods and that this made no sense landscape-wise. The building seemed to have been floated off its proper site elsewhere and carried to the knoll by a biblical high tide.

Of course I'd seen weird things before—high-rises in the middle of nowhere, boxy blue things in the scrub oak as seen from a train. But American growth patterns are so unconsidered and often nonsensical that you can't take everything seriously. This building, however, was nothing if not serious. Its aesthetic gravity forced me to see it was no fluke. Clearly authoritative, aesthetically grave, it was no mistake. Furthermore, it was located in carefully controlled Purchase, where architectural accidents don't happen. It would be a long time before I set out on my journey into the meaning of our contemporary landscape. But I see this encounter with the building in Purchase as the instigation. Struggling imaginatively to understand it, I remembered that IBM had moved out of New York to Armonk, also in Westchester—that had been in the *Times* years before. There was no sign identifying the owner of the building before me but maybe, I thought, it was associated with that. Yet this was an experiential rather than an intellectual moment. The voltage of the jolt, as I look back, recalls the innocence of a time before the radical upending of our assumptions had become routine. I was registering viscerally a massive decentering, an undoing of the archetypal form of the world—and because I knew in my bones that landscape means everything, it was not just landscape that was being undone before me. The disorientation was deep. I felt a kind of melting away of my interior.

My inclination was to circumnavigate the colossus. Treading tentatively across Kodacolor grass, I couldn't tell if I was trespassing. There were cars parked but no sign of anyone, though it was a normal workday. A portion of the building to the side was black mirror glass. It made me feel watched, but no one stopped me. I decided that the best thing to do was to walk around the building. In that way I'd get a handle on it. But this wasn't a building to walk around. The edges extended at odd angles, and on the far sides the land fell away precipitously. Around another wide-angled corner I would find only another long, blind stretch of building; on to a sharp-angled corner, then foresty humus gave way underfoot. Struggling, as if there were a shortage of air, I caught sight of my image in the black mirror glass, my body small, strangely faraway and vulnerable in its whiteness, stretched out as in a fun-house mirror, suspended and weightless looking.

King of Prussia

More than a decade passed before I set out to understand the change in landscape form and meaning and what it could tell us about ourselves as a society now. By that time many other clues of a deep shift had piled up. As I began my exploration, someone put a book in my hands, *Edge City* by Joel Garreau, which provided a context for the specific jolt I had experienced in Purchase. In the late 1980s, Garreau was a seasoned reporter for *The Washington Post* who had held positions in all the major sections and was ready to move on. Ever since Watergate, the *Post* had attracted ambitious young journalists, who all viewed national and international news, essentially Washington news, as the path to stardom. It was a configuration of ambition that reflected the age-old sense of the city as the theater of significant action. To such a young journalist an assignment to the Metro section—to subjects outside the Beltway—was a sentence to the Siberia of no-fame. Milt Coleman, the Metro editor, challenged Garreau to overturn this assumption by taking on the beat himself. Garreau had grown up in northern Virginia and had seen the rural landscape there transformed, not just by suburban development, but more lately, by clusters of high-rise office buildings, elements of the first tier of global big business far from its normal central-city home. He had seen this in Houston, but here it was in the East: he had wanted for some time to get to the bottom of these eruptions. He accepted Coleman's challenge, and the result, ultimately, was *Edge City*, a book that overturns basic assumptions about the composition of our landscape. It was published in 1991—though it did not come into my hands until 1997 when I was in the early days of my own landscape sleuthing. My impression from reading the book was that Garreau's edge cities were not, like the Purchase building, lone entities in an otherwise curated pastoral scene—although something I didn't discover until later was that the Pepsi Corporation had built headquarters designed by Edward Durrell Stone in Purchase in 1970, not far from the I. M. Pei building. But the standout characteristic of Garreau's edge cities was that they consisted of bunches of corporate buildings that had spawned a variety of secondary businesses around them: restaurants and office services and even residential buildings in some cases. What made Garreau's edge cities different from the movement of IBM to Armonk was that they consisted of clusters of corporate architecture surrounded by secondary businesses and even urban-style residential buildings, a splitting off of whole centers of gravity, challenging the hegemony of cities on many levels. In a way, this confirmed my early sense at the I.M. Pei building in Purchase— by the late 1990s owned by MasterCard, by the way—of an archetype coming apart. Edge cities were not just anomalies in an old landscape but were undoing deeply set patterns in a way that rendered old structures of feelings obsolete. I would have to go find them.

This wouldn't be easy because, as Garreau pointed out in his book, most edge cities don't have names, nor are they usually defined by zip codes or jurisdictional boundaries, which they routinely straddle. Maps are therefore of no use. But a number of specific edge cities were described in the book that were at least vaguely situated. Three were somewhere in the Meadowlands of New Jersey. I was living in Brooklyn at the time. With the book as my guide I set out.

The Meadowlands are a watery labyrinth, bounded on the west by mainland New Jersey, on the east by the Palisades. For centuries they were used as a garbage dump for the towns along the edges, as well as more macabre uses by the mob and other nefarious enterprises with disposal problems. Robert Pinsky, at one time our poet laureate, has compared the Meadowlands to Dante's inferno, a landscape of sin. Much of this off-the-grid domain is made up of reed meadows interlaced with passages of open water, of which the Hackensack River is one. But there is scattered solid ground, too, which over time became the site of sundry functions—a parking lot for school buses, for example, or a mom-and-pop factory. A very different element entered the scene in the early 1990s, when the Meadowlands became a national center of electronic transactions, or "postmodern money." By 1997, most ATM transactions in the United States were processed within a few square miles of one another in what became known as the Secaucus corridor—that is to say, the Meadowlands— though the exact locations were kept secret, lest sabotage shut down most U.S. shopping. A venture that in 1997 envisioned indoor wilderness adventures and, by 2005, had come to include indoor skiing and water surfing was a stalling mirage in the minds of developers (it is still in the offing as of 2018), but one that, like the movements of postmodern money, gave the Meadowlands, with its mild stench, its coffee-with-milk-colored waters, its eerily bucolic fields of reeds bending to the wind, and its bits of scenes from times gone by—a pathway, a shack, an old dock—a new albeit invisible dimension.

Garreau gave no exact addresses for the edge cities out there, however, and they eluded me. Most of the roads through the Meadowlands are highways on pylons. There isn't much opportunity to take a byway, or even to slow down and get out of the car. Occasionally I spotted spectral towers in the hazy distance, but they would vanish as I was carried elsewhere by the whizzing road. After some hours of this, running out of gas, I retreated to Union City, an old gritty place up on the Palisades—the kind of place that is full of tough, savvy guys who know exactly where they are and take pride in giving good directions. The problem with edge cities, though, is that one doesn't know how to describe them. "Some new office buildings near each other": I struck out in Union City. Eventually, by giving certain passages in Garreau's book an extremely close reading I noted that one of the edge cities I was looking for was near a mall. People knew of the mall; it was just south of the Meadowlands, they told me. I found it—called The Mills—but not the edge city. Coming across a Sheraton Hotel that seemed bizarrely placed, in that there was nothing around it, I decided to ask the concierge for help. He had never heard of whatever it was I was talking about, but, in case it might be helpful, he gave me a little map, put together by the hotel, that showed the location of nearby corporations. Looking at the map, I realized that I was actually in the edge city for which I was looking.

But this was not really helpful. Yes, there were some office towers but they were rather dispersed, hard to rope in visually. Driving around, I couldn't find a spot into which I could settle and get to know this new form. An edge city is a place on which there is no perspective, I concluded. Nor could I get "inside" it—not really. Check in at the Sheraton? I didn't think so. In this I was probably wrong; this was before my years in Towson. As an edge city beginner, I needed one that had a derivative connection to place as I had known it. Without that I found the new form so elusive that I couldn't actually experience it, even when found.

Not very long after this venture, I was trying to explain to a friend through a party din what I thought edge cities were and my difficulties in actually exploring them even when I found them. I can't imagine how he put it all together, but he mentioned King of Prussia, a name I had seen on the containers of prescription medicines.

He said something about a lot of corporations there and a contro-versy around saving an old inn. The inn was at a crossroads—now that was a place-syntax I could understand. A starting point. Plus the place had a name. What a name! Plus King of Prussia was iden-tified as an edge city in Joel Garreau's book. The hamlet of King of Prussia, as it was still known, was in the township of Upper Merion, in Montgomery County, west of Philadelphia, Pennsylvania, U.S.A., Earth, Milky Way, Universe, as we used to put it all together as kids.

This time I take off down the Jersey Turnpike with a sense of purpose and hope, continuing on the Pennsylvania Turnpike, and, just past the exits for Philadelphia there it is, KING OF PRUSSIA, spelled out clearly in standard white against green signage. The exit sluices me off the turnpike onto the Schuylkill Expressway, and then immediately there is another exit and I am down a ramp past an-other, smaller green-and-white sign to one side:

MALL

Next 4 Exits

only to be dumped onto a battered, clogged old highway that groans with grinding gears and clouds of exhaust. The mall itself, serene as a series of buttes, holds the middle distance. The "exits" are just turn-offs into mall parking lots, except for the one I choose, hoping to catch my breath and get oriented: it turns out to be a svelte, black, frictionless road called Mall Boulevard, which slides me through the mall, dividing it like the Red Sea, and to the back and then abruptly into an eight-lane toll plaza to the expressway from which I have just descended. Scuttling across lines of cars waiting to pay tolls, I escape through a cramped underpass, on the other side of which is a narrow, battered rural road through dusty brush. Then comes mirror glass across the supernaturally wide and groomed entrance to the King of Prussia Business Park.

Where the Meadowlands edge city almost didn't exist, King of Prussia, even to an American inured to decades of pell-mell growth, is landscape pandemonium: McMansions with horse paddocks attached near a garbage dump, a little Rube Goldberg chemical factory, huffing and puffing as in a cartoon. A persimmon pink apartment building—or is it a conference center?—dwarfing the hills. Fifties suburban development of small one-story houses with wary windows crowded by overgrown plantings. A working quarry. New housing in traditional styles, lightly placed like paper cutouts under beanpole trees. Preexisting landscapes lying about in pieces: serene eighteenth-century houses set back under ancient trees along a winding, narrow lane. Even a bit of Valley Forge is jumbled in, and there I finally take a moment to just sit. Inviolate meadows of full-headed grasses, through which the long lines of gentle hills register softly, wobble against the sky at the crests. Deep shadows in the folds of the land. Over there, along the edge of the woods, a person on horseback. But it's time to get back on unmatching roads: high-speed-fast-getaway-four-laner debouching into traffic-clogged two-laner, and then it's a back road with no shoulder, and then it's a swirling exurban-style road, decorously shaded by old overhanging trees. Some roads link up, some don't—most notably, a two-lane one that shoots upward through sumac and then summarily ends in midair. Another lonely country road leads up a steep hill past lowly dwellings with an aspect about them of faraway, country poverty. At the top, theatrically synchronized attached town houses block the view.

High over King of Prussia, the Schuylkill Expressway is an elevated river on pylons, imperiously carving the air. At its highest point it soars over an old church and its close-gathered graves. I have a map, of almost no use—there is something about this kind of landscape that does not lend itself to mapping. But the riverlike Expressway and the actual Schuylkill River show up clearly on it. Always looking for a topographical feature from which to orient myself, a familiar landscape feature, I want very much to get to the real river. But it is locked away on the other side of some major railroad tracks that also swirl through the hamlet. Eventually, I find an obscure, narrow bridge across the tracks, and then I am in an Eakins painting: brown stream, fading boathouses, ancient overhanging trees.

On the near shore is rusting earthmoving equipment, randomly abandoned in half-bulldozed terrain. Down a ways I spot a lone moving dozer that, on approach, turns out to be driven by an unenthusiastic African American man of some years, directed in what seems to be a futile earthmoving task by a rosy-cheeked, good-looking, not so young white man in a panama hat, who is eager to strike up a conversation. He tells me he rowed with Grace Kelly's brother in college, and has big plans for a development here on the river. Though presently out of funds, he was sure to make a fortune. He was also running for president. Listening to him I am suddenly awestruck, as in other unexpected moments in my explorations, with a sense that I am in the heart of America right here. Right now.

On that first visit I stayed the night with my beloved godmother, who lived in Chestnut Hill, an old Philadelphia suburb that had become a part of the city. She said that the landscape around King of Prussia used to be one of the most beautiful in the world and that she avoided it now because it broke her heart. I could sympathize with her aversion, of course. But I had on my coonskin cap: I could barely disguise my appetite for this consummate wilderness. My godmother lived in an old house that had been in her husband's family for some time, with a beautiful, mature garden, and I felt her to be whole and also wholly available to me. I loved encountering her there and felt the preciousness of our connection, and yet my interest in King of Prussia put me on the other side of a divide from her: she could not comprehend it. There was something upsettingly serious to her, as to me, about this difference of opinion. She was not, of course, the first person who revealed to me how deep landscape feeling runs, how disagreement about it can disrupt even loves. Not so, however, with her husband, Pete, a doctor who smoked a pipe and had a deadpan style. He told me that the King of Prussia Inn had been known in the old days as a romantic hideaway to which Philadelphia businessmen took their mistresses.

I wasn't able to find the inn on my first visit, or the next time, though I persisted in looking for it as for the link between the former world and the present. Along the way, I developed a bilingual vocabulary for what I found in King of Prussia as compared with the characteristics of the former world. Where the old landscape is relational, the new one is schizoid, with elements right next to one another that don't relate at all. Where older landscapes are defined by what is special about a given place, the new pieces of King of Prussia could be anywhere—were a part of ubiquity, as I was coming to call it. Our old landscape, formed by the logic of manufacturing, was coextensive. King of Prussia was a mixture of several archipelagoes, like the pieces of incomplete jigsaw puzzles thrown together into a box.

But the quality that I came to see as most profoundly different had to do with an inversion of scale, in which small containers attempted to hold elements far larger than themselves. Though King of Prussia was not technically a hamlet—it had no government of its own—it had an identity: there were maps of King of Prussia, and the address corporations used was King of Prussia. But actually the supercharged pandemonium that was this so-called hamlet was inside the political jurisdiction of the modest suburban township of Upper Merion. *Beowulf* helped me with this. Upper Merion was a sheep that had given birth to a Grendel: not the first mother to have had an experience like that. But the political reality was still dumbfounding. The corporations of King of Prussia were, many of them, international yet they were governed by the board of supervisors of the sheep of a township, who met in a room next to the public library, where mothers read murmuringly to their babies. Major pharmaceutical

corporations had plants in King of Prussia and the defense industry was there, too, as represented by Lockheed, which had revenues
many times larger than those of the State of Pennsylvania. The Lockheed plant was right there on Dekalb Pike, the broken-down highway onto which I had been debouched on my first visit, and which
was, I had figured out, part of the original crossroads. I couldn't find
the inn but how do you even begin to imagine Lockheed at a crossroads in a hamlet? For still another example of elements too large
for their containers, the King of Prussia Mall liked to call itself the
"downtown" of Upper Merion. But the mall was the second-largest
in America and proudly high-end: unlikely that the modest residents
of Upper Merion would be shopping at Tiffany and Brooks Brothers
on their daily round of errands. I found a variation on this theme of
outside-in, literally in this case, in a back issue of the King of Prussia paper. A local Girl Scout troop, in voting on a campout location,
had rejected traditional wildernesses nearby, in favor of the mall.
Residents were a little annoyed when I brought this up, as if I were
laughing at them. In fact, given that I was trying to see forward, given
that my explorations of all types of landscapes had pointed toward a
condition of living within a kind of man-made enclosure, I thought
that the Girl Scouts had been on the cutting edge.

There was something of a continuum to be found tracking back
through the story of the Lockheed plant; that it had formerly belonged to the Martin Marietta Corporation, which had, before that,
been General Electric. GE had bought the land, on which there was
an orchard, in the 1950s. When it finally built a plant there in the '60s,
it was informally called the Orchard by employees. King of Prussia
had been a true hamlet then, in the sense that it consisted of a cluster of dwellings around an inn by a crossroads surrounded by deep
country. Running this forward, I was helped imaginatively speaking:
the real orchard, later the GE Orchard and eventually Lockheed, was
not far from the crossroads where the inn I couldn't find still stood.

Another way I sought to get from there to here, from the landscape of the past to this present riddle, was by seeing what lay about me as related to early place-syntax by means of expansions of scale. The Schuylkill Expressway had superseded Gulph Road at the original crossroads, and the thousands of hotel rooms in King of Prussia were descendants of the old inn. I read in the library that a doctor had practiced next door to the inn and that a cobbler had had his shop nearby. One could then say that the pharmaceutical corporations had replaced the doctor and the mall, which had plenty of shoe stores, the cobbler.

However, there was something different at work here from an expansion of scale. That was a kind of haphazardness that denies there is any place-syntax at all. It was as if an explosion had happened, a breaking and flinging of shards of the old world that were now scattered and jumbled with bits of ubiquity which seemed innately incoherent to begin with. The almost violent disruptions of the old landscape seemed to be caused by a force coming up from underneath. This wasn't just an expansion of scale. This wasn't only evolution: there was an illogic. There was, between the two landscapes, a fundamental gap that I couldn't quite bridge with a development narrative. But that didn't mean I should stop trying.

Even before GE built the Orchard, a suburban development appeared in King of Prussia, the work of a local contractor. The first inhabitants commuted to work in Philadelphia by local roads. Then GE came in, and other developments were built, and then the interstate and, later, the Schuylkill Expressway eased the twenty-five-mile commute. Those who worked at GE, of course, had no commute at all: indeed, some GE people commuted to King of Prussia from elsewhere, the first sign of what Garreau later identified as an edge city pattern. Still, in the classic suburban way, most residents of early King of Prussia developments worked in Philadelphia. By the late 1990s, however, twenty-five thousand people commuted to King of Prussia for work, many *from* Philadelphia: Moscow going to Siberia. Meanwhile, Philadelphia, its economic energy draining outward, declined. That is the well-known urban story that finally rendered cities, once seen as monsters, into beloved wasting beauties.

From the head of the Rotary Club, Al Pascall, I learned that the inn had gone out of business in the 1950s, when a ramp off the expressway had cut it off from Dekalb Pike. It had been scheduled to be demolished, but when workers from the Pennsylvania Department of Transportation turned up to do the job, protesters stood in the way: one wielded a shotgun. However, by the late 1990s both the exit ramp and the Dekalb Pike had to be expanded, both encroaching on the inn's island, and traffic had become so heavy that there was no forestalling these improvements, so the inn was again threatened. But oh yes, it was still standing, said Al Pascall, who had made saving it a mission.

Also in the 1960s, Morris Kravitz, another local contractor, noticing that the country store did not serve all the desires of the new suburbanites in the hamlet, built a strip mall just a bit down the pike from the old crossroads. This was, in fact, still standing during the series of visits I made in the late 1990s: typical, one-storied, flat-roofed, with parking in front. Sometimes when I contemplated the physical history of King of Prussia, that little flat line of the strip mall roof became for me the beginning of the undoing of the settlement form there, first by moving the center away from the crossroads, a chiropractic jolt, but even more so by introducing ubiquity: that strip mall could be anywhere. It brought in an ephemeral, unplaced type of structure, on which signs are more important than anything else about it—TRAVEL, for example, in the period of my visits, with a big poster of an exotic beach in the window. I saw the flat line as a first slipped stitch in what, in the period in which the strip mall was built, was still a more or less intact tapestry of forests and meadows, orchards, quarries, quiet river, crossroads, inn. From one angle, I saw in that slipped stitch the gap in continuity that bedeviled my sense of the story of King of Prussia as a place—as a landscape.

When, in the late 1960s, far bigger strip malls anchored by urban-style department stores came into vogue, Kravco, as Kravitz's company was named, was quick off the mark. Ironically, in a way, the company moved back to the crossroads and there built a new-style mall, bracketed by Korvettes and Penney's, right across DeKalb from the Orchard. When, in the '70s, even larger, enclosed malls came into style, Kravco replaced the Korvettes and Penney's ensemble with the enclosed King of Prussia Plaza. Within a decade the company expanded the mall again, adding the King of Prussia Court right next to the Plaza, separated from it only by Mall Boulevard. That is a condensed version of how the King of Prussia Mall became the second largest in the country, outdone only by the Mall of America, outside Minneapolis.

Through all this, GE as a defense contractor, GE Aerospace, was involved in the manufacture of intercontinental ballistic missiles (ICBMs), including the nuclear warheads the missiles were built to carry. Well, that would do more to the syntax of place than a little flat roof. A bit of local history that caught my eye was that, in the late 1970s, protesters against the production of nuclear weapons started staging protest vigils at the GE entrance that faced the Mall, which gave the protesters a constant audience of mall-goers. Sometimes they poured blood at the entrance. Daniel and Philip Berrigan, brothers and priests who had been leaders of protests against nuclear armament, were sometimes among them. The vigils became a fixture at the GE entrance, the participants well known to employees, and friendly with both mall and GE guards, even though on occasion they were arrested.

Then one day in 1980, Philip Berrigan, with a small entourage that became known as the Plowshares Eight, breached security at the Orchard early in the morning. The protesters were armed with hammers with which to damage nose cones. According to the protesters later, two nose cones were hammered and Berrigan emptied a vial of his own blood on some blueprints. They were arrested, of course, but when they were tried at the old county courthouse in nearby Norristown they were found guilty only of burglary and conspiracy, and not of criminal trespass, disorderly conduct, or assault. No mention of damage to property, much less to a nuclear weapon. Was that because the good citizens of Montgomery County were sympathetic to a cause that, on the whole, never caught on widely? On the other hand, some retired GE engineers with whom I spoke said, with some righteousness, that warheads had never been made in King of Prussia: that had been done at the Chestnut Hill plant, undermining the protesters' story altogether—in a way. The engineers insisted that what had been made in King of Prussia were the computers to be placed inside the nose cones to guide the missiles. That seemed precise, to the point of nitpicky. That work could well have required the presence of unweaponized nose cones at the plant, confirming the protesters' story of having smashed two. And of course blueprints of the nose cones could well have been around, or of the computers, or of any number of things, for that matter. What struck me most about these contested details was a slipperiness that seemed a hallmark of Cold War space: it's not here, it's there, in your godmother's leafy neighborhood, as if that mattered—the idea of such a plant in that pleasantly prosperous neighborhood, seeming on the face of it absurd. Then, as if confirming slipperiness, I found no evidence that there had been a plant in Chestnut Hill at all. There was a Philadelphia plant but it was not in Chestnut Hill, which is a part of Philadelphia. Indeed Chestnut Hill old-timers tell me there never was such a thing nor was it likely that anything of the sort would ever have been located in those serene surroundings. I didn't pursue it further. After all, what did it matter? I had wanted to pin Armageddon down across the street from Tiffany—a new kind of crossroads. But the new geography had eluded me.

disappear into the lavish landscape of the day as into a shiny pack of cards. When I myself slipped into the deck, I found myself in a serene interior that did indeed seem churchlike. The athletic shoes spotlit and suspended in the window of Champs looked like birds of paradise. Music, something wide-ranging by Beethoven, close to overwhelmed me. I saw scripts of every kind, stern scripts, flirtatious scripts, plainspoken scripts, cursive, Roman, italics, but all of them, though spelling out English words, cryptically suggested that the words really didn't mean what they ordinarily did—if anything. Normally I get quickly claustrophobic in malls and need to get out. As an explorer, though, I was entranced. Looking down through a well from the second floor onto the first, I observed an overweight mother and small daughter, seated in chairs, eating soft ice cream, a potted palm between them. I was an anthropologist observing inscrutable customs.

Needing a bite myself, I stopped in Ruby's Diner. The booths and the stools at the soda fountain were done in a supernaturally red, shiny vinyl, the trim bright chrome, the floors and tabletops white. The staff, dressed in white and red, was young and comically hesitant—a sweet note. At either end of the room, mounted on platforms on a level with the top of the booths, were vintage 500-horsepower Triumph motorcycles, one black, one red. Above all this, near the ceiling, was a red plastic track on which a toy motorcycle traveled continuously from one end of the restaurant to the other, and on it was perched a Barbie doll, sidesaddle, with one leg raised high in the air and her arms outstretched in a gesture of either ecstasy or despair. In my exploratory state, I found in this an overt expression of feeling nearly as overwhelming as the Beethoven. It was freezing, but the only other customers, two mothers, with two toddlers sitting in high chairs, didn't seem to notice as they talked intensely, as mothers will when they can steal a few moments from their children. These toddlers were distracted by food, which they threw on the floor: the shiny white floor around their chairs was littered with tidbits. "Where's the lady on the motorcycle?" asked one of the toddlers. "Here she comes," said his mother, without breaking stride in her conversation with her friend. Neither of them noticed the real motorcyclist with a big belly and a dirty undershirt, with tattoos on his arms and a half-grown beard, coming through the door, though management eyed him warily.

Wandering some more in the mall after lunch I found the center of the plaza section, where, under a domed colored-glass skylight, a big clock, cartoonishly reminiscent of Big Ben, tolled the quarter hour softly near an elaborate two-tiered fountain in which water poured into a pool in four streams. Nearby also was a glass elevator to the upper level that was ever in use, going up and down with people in it. Sitting near Big Ben with my eyes closed, I heard a train whistle on the upper level, and the sound of water falling on water. I was on the prairie, I was in Rome. The atmosphere in the mall was supernal. Later, in another shoe-store window, I saw a sneaker, and my anthropological distance slipped, because I liked the sneaker and then remembered I needed sneakers, and that was the end of it. I couldn't hear the music anymore and soon I was eating soft ice cream sitting by a potted palm.

By the late 1990s, Morris Kravis, the contractor who had built the King of Prussia Mall in its various iterations, had been dead for a decade. But Kravco still managed the mall, so I went to speak to two of its principal officers. Like the GE engineers, they were cautious: why was I asking questions? At first, their replies were only promotional. But eventually they let me in on the worry that lurked beneath the supernal surface. One could hardly be vigilant enough, they told me. For new malls are forever trumping old ones, drawing away a fickle clientele with the allure of novelty and leaving the old ones to scrape by on discount stores and eventual abandonment, bringing down everything around them. If a shop doesn't produce a certain level of sales per square foot, it must be encouraged to leave before its lease is up, not because lower sales matter to the mall's bottom line, but because the company cannot afford to rent to "losers." That could lead to the entire mall's being perceived as a loser. Even stores that are booming can endanger a mall, I learned. For example, if Gap had a competitor that was No. 2, as Avis then was to Hertz, they could not afford to have even that good No. 2 in the mall. Though sales would be high, the presence of a No. 2 enterprise might give people the impression that the mall itself was in second place to something better. The big problem with this rule of thumb, they went on, was that the axiom itself created boredom. After all, everybody has eaten a Cinnabon, they pointed out, and yet if some smart new company produced a better snack they could not risk inviting it in. These guys were confiding. They were very pressured.

All mall managers, they told me, were in a state of fear over recent research that had shown that the average amount of time spent on a mall visit had dropped from eighty to seventy minutes, a sign that malls as a genre might be sliding down a slippery slope like dinosaurs. This was in 1998. Actually the problem of holding the interest of customers had vexed mall managers for years. A 1992 solution had been to introduce Disney-style rides. Most famously, the Mall of America had built a Snoopy theme park at its center. But then teenagers were attracted, eventually massing in packs of thousands. These packs roamed the mall on Friday and Saturday nights, alarming adult consumers while themselves spending very little. The problem became so severe that the Mall of America had had to ban everyone under eighteen who was unaccompanied by an adult. This ban made national news, which put the Mall of America in an unflattering light—a really bad bind from a manager's point of view.

Thus, while you would never want a bigger or a newer mall anywhere nearby, being No. 2 nationwide had advantages. You could, for example, avoid the trap into which the Mall of America had fallen.

A second generation of solutions had been that of bringing in entertaining stores like the Disney Store, in which the product was souvenirs of the store itself, or FAO Schwarz, a toy store that, at the time, was on the ascendancy in malls, trying out live clowns and interactive games for visitors. The feeling I got was of managers being on tenterhooks regarding keeping the mall-goer's interest all the time. As for daily maintenance, I learned that there must be nothing disturbing to the consumer in a mall, nothing to interfere with the impulse to buy. Unrelenting vigilance and diligence was required. If a soda was spilled, the cleanup crew must be there in minutes. Political activity was, of course, out of the question.

Back at Big Ben after my visit with the managers, my experience was different. I now was aware that the seemingly serene atmosphere of the mall was latent with tensions on small and large scales: the spilled soda that must be cleaned up immediately, the danger of a more up-to-date mall nearby or of people abandoning malls altogether because they are sick of Cinnabons. The global economy reinforces this kind of tension, garroting businesses. Competition in the worldwide arena does not leave much leeway for experiment or even for enjoying success. I had noticed that clothing was becoming ever more threadbare, literally, to reduce costs, as if the goal was textiles as close to nothing as possible. On such tensions was built the mighty edifice of the King of Prussia Mall. Sitting at the fountain near Big Ben, I visualized the threads in the clothing shops around me connecting this spot to the archipelago of sweatshops near and far all over the world, threads that were becoming ever more ethereal as costs were cut yet further, and ever more tightly strung to as close to the snapping point into nothing as cost counters could get them: in this I felt connected, there at Big Ben, to the world.

Not long after my first visit to King of Prussia, I went to Italy and one day, in the Basilica of St. Francis, in Assisi, I was contemplating a fresco in which an oversized St. Francis rides in a chariot behind an enormous horse that has stepped off the roof of a diminutive house into the air. It makes no sense in terms of Cartesian space, or the laws of physics, and yet it makes perfect sense in medieval space in which the Kingdom of God is the primary reality and our mundane environment, with its petty physical rules, is a far second. But what struck me, there in Assisi but fresh from King of Prussia, was that there was something contemporary about the image, too, prompting the first seed of a thought that medieval art could be a useful precedent in our struggles to comprehend our emergent world. In the Middle Ages the material realm took second place to a spiritual realm that was entirely beyond bodily perception. Now it's the digital enclosure that is becoming ever more primary and all-pervasive, and while there is nothing mystical about it, indeed the condition of enclosure to which it contributes undercuts our old relation to transcendence, the digital realm is essentially immaterial. To a very large extent, forces we can't see are configuring our world. In the Middle Ages it was the divine; now it's information, electronically stored and manipulated, that is claiming a similarly immense place in our lives, popping up constantly in the very grain of daily life.

In worlds in which material surroundings are unimportant, proportion and relations in landscape and architecture are also unimportant, just as people looking at cell phones are famously oblivious of their environments. In medieval art, a miraculous event, such as St. Francis appearing to reveal the realm of the heavens, so supersedes the importance of daily life in houses that it makes sense to render the architecture as unlivably cramped and dim. The vision of St. Francis and the heavens *must* be out of proportion to the earthly landscape. Similarly, a person on a computer in a room is in a realm which eclipses the room so completely that, in his consciousness, those surroundings barely exist. Of two people having breakfast together, one can be so engrossed in communications with someone on the other side of the world that, to him, the room and person in it and even scrambled eggs and sausages have vaporized. The kind of attention people give to their electronic devices could be compared to prayer, in the way it entrances with an invisible largeness while blotting out surroundings. There is, of course, immense silliness in the comparison. But there is a glimmer of truth in it that might help us, by comparison, begin to imagine more deeply the conditions in which we now live.

The mall managers told me something that changed my view of King of Prussia: that until the fall of the Berlin Wall, many of the businesses in the hamlet had been manufacturing concerns but they—all except for a diaper factory—had departed once the wall was down and the global economy accelerated, drawing industry toward cheap labor elsewhere. I hadn't thought of King of Prussia as industrial—I guess it was all the mirror glass. But once I thought about it, this underlayer was rather obvious. It was Pennsylvania, a famously industrial state, and there were gritty seams in which the former era showed, as in nearby Bridgeport. It was in the same period that GE Aerospace, including the Orchard plant, was bought by the Martin Marietta Corporation, which then, in the mid-1990s, was itself bought by Lockheed and then became Lockheed Martin. Lockheed wanted to close the Orchard, a disaster for King of Prussia. In the end, the corporation kept a third of the four thousand Marietta employees there, to work on a government contract to take a flaw out of GPS that had been put in to fool the Soviets. The mall managers claimed that the decision to renovate both sides of the big mall—the Plaza, the older side, and the newer Court—had heroically reversed decline in King of Prussia. They suggested that desperate landlords, seeing that the mall owners, by this time a consortium of investors, were willing to put money into King of Prussia—spending $200 million on the mall between '91 and '95—became heartened enough to slap mirror glass on their empty factories and hire some funereal landscapers. Somewhere along the way mirror glass was slapped on the old GE plant as well, perhaps by Lockheed. These cosmetic efforts were effective. I had picked up not one whiff of this time of difficulty, no sense at all that ashes had blown in the wind here so recently. But then forgetting is our habit. It was said in the late 1990s that, because of the wall coming down, the world was only ten years old. But news of this recent makeover made King of Prussia seem even younger than that. In the late 1990s, when I was visiting, the dot-com boom was in progress. Who remembered that just a few years earlier all of America had felt old and discouraged? Japan had been beating us in technology. The Midwest was in deep rust. Our schools were a disaster. We felt done. As for mirror glass, it offers an overnight new identity that almost deflects the reality of a building altogether, let alone what it might have been used for once. It is the perfect material of forgetfulness.

Eventually I found the King of Prussia Inn, hidden in untrimmed maples on a scrap of land between the exit ramp and Dekalb Pike. I had passed it many times as I whooshed off the expressway. I got there on foot, somewhat perilously crossing Dekalb. It was enclosed in chain link, to keep out vandals, but it was as if it were caged because it might itself be a danger or inclined to escape. Its windows were blank and dusty. Leaning against the chain link, I could make out the courses of stone that marked its gradual enlargement. Already both the exit ramp and Dekalb were scheduled for widening, which would mean that the inn would finally have to be moved. Al Pascall, of the Rotary Club, was advocating moving it to a bit of local government land where it could serve as a museum of King of Prussia. The campaign wasn't easy and dragged on after I left, but in 2000 the inn was moved to some land in King of Prussia owned by the PECO energy company, where in 2002 it became the offices of the Montgomery County Chamber of Commerce: a bit of a Trojan horse, you might say, bringing remembrance into the realm of forgetfulness, a tiny dislocated heart for the Grendel.

One day in the last of my late 1990s visits, I went to talk to a member of the Upper Merion board of supervisors in its meeting room just across the hall from the library. An aerial photo of King of Prussia had been mounted on one long wall, which I examined while I waited. Right in the middle was a large body of water. I had by this time driven all over King of Prussia many times. How could I have missed this prominent feature? When my interviewee came in, my first question was about the water. Oh, that's an old quarry, exhausted years ago, he said. But where was it? Oh it's fenced off, he said, puzzled as to why I was so interested but generously offering to take me there, if I liked.

We drove to a road on which there was a long stretch grown up with brush, which I had taken to be neglected land being held for development: the kind that just becomes a blank in the mind—you don't see it. Along the way he stopped and pointed into the brush. Through the brush I glimpsed a chain-link fence. That was the quarry, he said. He wasn't coming with me. I got out of the car and found my way through the undergrowth to the fence. Through it I could see only more brush. But as I moved my head around I glimpsed the sides of a huge pit, yellow hardpan, mechanically terraced, very steeply. Nothing grew in the hardpan. How far down the bottom was one couldn't know, nor was there any water in sight. I pressed my face against the fence, and leaned my weight into it, fingers interwoven and thus bowed it a little. There it was: jewel-like cobalt blue, completely surprising and out of place: the aquifer.

2

Atopia

Spreawlian

King of Prussia provided my basic education in contemporary landscape. Soon after it was completed, I moved to Washington, D.C. I settled in Georgetown, the capital's oldest neighborhood, formerly an eighteenth-century city in its own right, preexisting Washington, and in every way the opposite of the emerging landscape of our time. Its strong agrarian aura still suggested that the edge of town was near. Everything about it, even the little observatory at Georgetown University, suggested a settlement sheltered under the stars but not intruded on by them. Georgetown slopes down to the Potomac steeply. When getting to know the neighborhood on foot, I often went that way. Once on the shore, I naturally sought a bridge. That would be Key Bridge, an open gently arching span in the European style. I developed a habit of walking to the middle. Turning upstream, I'd see steep, wooded shores and rapids: Georgetown, once a port, was situated at the last navigable point on the river. This was a wilderness scene. Looking back across the bridge, I saw the neighborhood on its hill, crowned by the castlelike university—a storybook sight. Downstream lay the city of Washington, its buildings restricted in height to 110 feet at the beginning of the twentieth century, creating a quality of thoughtful restraint over which the Capitol Building reigns supreme. Washington is a symbolic city, our only one, of a piece in style. What was not of apiece lay on the other end of the bridge, disconcertingly near: high-rises, oversized yet lightweight, new yet already old, obstreperous yet weak, glassy but dusty, crowding and frontal, disrupting the proportional logic of the larger scene in a way that seemed less braggardly than ignorant. This was the gateway to my next schoolroom, a world akin to King of Prussia but much larger. Once I walked across Key Bridge and into Rosslyn, Virginia, on the immediate far side, a mishmash of industry, business, and residential buildings that began going up in the 1970s: a predecessor of the edge city or even an early version but, in any event, not built with pedestrians in mind. Thereafter I went into my new schoolroom by car.

That schoolroom encompassed the area around Washington, the very venue in which Joel Garreau had identified edge cities as a contemporary form—though his attention was on newer, more glamorous, and globally oriented excrescences farther out. What I wanted to learn to see was the larger picture of which edge cities were a part, the semicontinuous development that was once called suburban sprawl, then urban sprawl, and finally just sprawl. This seemed an insufficient designation. The word itself was problematic. I had noticed that when one spoke it, people almost invariably said, "What?" as if you had said, "Arrrrgghh!" And, once understood, it was almost always taken as a negative term. How was I to learn to read this landscape if I had only a negative name for it, first of all? And, secondly, how could I settle for a term that suggested subordination to cities?

A better term was "metropolitan area," though age-old and also implying subordination to a central city. The news of edge cities had been that they were not subordinate, radically skewing the old geography of city and surroundings. But then, the conception of edge cities that Garreau described as clusters was beginning to fray, because, as corporations of the first rank proliferated in what we called sprawl, they didn't always cluster. You could get a single shard of international corporate or a sprinkling of shards, in any pattern, with or without the city-like rings of secondary businesses that had been defining to Garreau. If there was a rule of thumb, it was "anything goes." Sometime later, I followed a Listserv in which urbanists, planners, and people interested in the political impact of changes in the metropolitan environment proposed new names for the proliferating edge city derivatives. "Edgeless cities" was one proposed by someone studying Florida. "Stealth cities" was my favorite, because of the way it captured an air these encampments can have, especially when in the woods, of having been erected overnight by Martians unfamiliar with our customs. "Scattered cities" was touching in its inherent desperation, since it didn't mean that cities were situated apart from one another, as they have always been, but that the pieces of this new kind of city were scattered. How we cling to the word "city," with its connotations of a citadel, a walled medieval town, at the very least a destination, something easy to find that you know you are in when you are there.

The term "metropolitan area" has been in use for quite a while. The concept of the larger area around a city as an extension of it is, in fact, an industrial-age notion that reflects the movement of economic and political power away from the agricultural country, and into the emergent, exponentially growing, manufacturing cities. Given that some central cities are now the hole in the doughnut of contemporary development, many "metros" have no "polis." Latter-day political life has not adapted, yet, to the shift of power away from the center into the intermediate zone around many cities, because power hangs on to the old jurisdictions that are its base. But changed as the meaning is, "metropolitan area" has the worked-in quality of long usage while also capturing present-day reality. It can seem boring in its Latinate vowelliness but, looked at closely, it is filled with complex, apt tension. "Metro" suggests the middle of something, which in the age of the disappearing city captures a dumbfounding paradox of landscape in our age, and "area" suggests a blur for a landscape of indeterminate boundaries that we don't yet know how to describe more precisely, and that is, in any event, constantly in the process of changing.

As a longtime believer in an etymological collective subconscious (now endangered by the disappearance of traditional spelling on the net), I am struck by the way the term "metropolitan area" also obscures reality. While acknowledging expansion, it quietly reassures us that the world is really as it always has been. It suggests that all that has really happened is that once again the city has become spatially enlarged: but it's still a city. It's not as if there is no truth to this. After all, no one truth, neither that of centralized forms, nor that of oceanic ones, clearly prevails. We live in an inside-out world in which the city, in many instances, is the empty place: but, then again, in many instances, it isn't. It's also true that except on the East Coast most metropolitan areas come to an end eventually and therefore are entities—can be seen as very big cities. A tolerance of ambiguity is essential to allowing our contemporary landscape to come into even vague focus.

But even then there is an amorphous quality—hard to pin down. One usage that has come to express just this elusiveness, as reflected in the contemporary metropolitan area, is double-barreled naming, as in Raleigh–Durham or Duluth–Superior, which creates a permanent but truthful locational dither, hemming and hawing and leaving us up in the air, trapped in ambivalence, imaginatively speaking. We even have trivalence, as in Albany–Troy–Schenectady or

Middlesex–Somerset–Hunterdon, each with a pace on it, metrically speaking. Brownsville–Harlingen–San Benito and Melbourne–Titusville–Palm Bay are particularly fine, both in sound and rhythm, but that is not to say that trivalence is always better. Killeen–Temple is first class, not to mention the superb Fargo–Moorhead, though none can touch Champaign–Urbana, which has by now been centering and decentering for some time.

Some of this ambi- and trivalent naming has been the formal work of the Office of Management and Budget, and used by the Census Bureau, which has embraced the idea of the metropolitan area for purposes of counting people. These federally named entities not only subsume cities but also counties, sometimes many—twenty-eight in the case of Metropolitan Atlanta, one of our largest official metropolitan areas, somewhat disguised by its singular, utterly undislocated traditional name. Sometimes in listing constituent counties the Census Bureau throws municipalities in with counties, like the venerable towns Falls Church and Manassas which, in one census document I saw, are left undistinguished from the eighteen counties in the description of the Washington–Arlington–Alexandria Metropolitan Division—another designation. To me this shows that even bureaucrats, and even in their home territory, get mentally wobbly when dealing with our contemporary landscape. But metropolitan areas get named by others, by chambers of commerce, by regional planning boards, by bodies that name airports. In this wider usage, the metropolitan area often doesn't respect state boundaries, though it has to be said that the Census Bureau has also recognized this tendency, crashing across state lines in defining its statistical divisions. In doing this it also added to their double- and triple-barreled names, little kite tails of grunts and sighs as in Davenport–Moline–Rock Island IA–IL or Boston–Worcester–Lawrence MA–NH–ME–CT. But sometimes metropolitan areas cross national boundaries, in which case they escape the purview of the Census Bureau: nevertheless, the kite tail usage has proved useful for those who strive to name national border crossing entities, as in San Diego–Tijuana US–MX or Detroit–Windsor US–CA.

In the end, the only name for this settlement pattern that is truly vernacular, that has in it the blood flow of real language as used, is "sprawl," which seems sloppy and slangy as well as hard to catch when spoken but which is nonetheless a real unbureaucratic, unmade-up word, even if it did originally appear as the designation of planners in the form of "urban sprawl." So as someone who believes in the etymological subconscious, I looked up the origins of "sprawl" before it was applied to landscape, learning, from the Oxford English Dictionary, that it is derived from the venerable "spreawlian," an Old English word, or OE. This is a bodily word, related to the verbs "to writhe" and "to spurt" but also to the ideas of strewing, sprinkling, springing forth, and spreading the limbs in a relaxed, awkward, or unnatural position. We still use it that way, as in "I sprawled on the sidewalk." This converted me, partly because the body remains one of the few measures that hasn't changed, and therefore one whereby we might be able to relate the emergent world to the one we have known. One way I am trying to understand our landscape is to see a "figure in a landscape" as it today is, truly. Something I grapple with in this effort is that, given the strange new custodianship we human beings now have of the world, the more apt term can seem to be "landscape in a figure." This is, I admit, esoteric. Could it be painted? But the final result of all this is that, while I have become entranced with the expressiveness of our ambi- and trivalent place-names—to the point that sometimes I can't stop saying them: Appleton–Oshkosh–Neenah WI, Fort Pierce–Port St. Lucie FL: so cryptically poetic, so rhythmic, so primal: WI!, MA!, OR? ME! ILL!—for me, privately—though I don't expect this to catch on—it's the bodily Spreawlian OE.

So off I went across Key Bridge into Baltimore–Washington

MD–D.C.–VA–WV. Immediately past Rosslyn I found myself in fierce King of Prussia–type close-packed jumble and heart-stopping pastoral country, too, as well as among Garreauvian edge cities, as well as multiple variations: tombstone processions, shards in the woods. Mixed in were confused old towns, blurred at their edges and even erstwhile country hamlets still dusty and faraway in feeling: the suspicious face in half-light behind the blackened bulging screen. The squat brick bungalows of Cold War suburban development, bright latter-day high-rise condos, a forest of grimly standardized apartment buildings, a five-point intersection of multi-laned roads. The place-syntax I had learned in King of Prussia stood me in good stead. Here it was blown out in scale with some new twists. You had the Pentagon, and you had the Pentagon City Mall. You had Little Saigon, a once large neighborhood that, pressured by gentrification, had devolved down to a single old strip mall where people smoked in the street and foreign-looking ducks hung plucked and whole in shop windows, with a gym patronized by white guys on the basement level. In a banal strip of shops on an overloaded route, an Ethiopian butcher. At a crossroads near a flatbed truck with squashed vehicles on it, Hispanic men massing your car in hopes of work. As I got deeper into the social patterns, massings rather than neighborhoods appeared: massings of black teenagers at a cineplex with no black-owned residences nearby, or massings of Koreans in a church but no Korean neighborhood. I came on a cute little old-fashioned street yet, at the end, it looked out on a colossal hodgepodge: turned out the cute street was a mall in the latest style. Fooled! In some parts, lawns were paved over for the cars of extended families, two, three, maybe four generations. I met a young Afghani woman from a mountainous redoubt who was confused because her American boyfriend took her to climb a mountain for fun. Millionaires in nearby neighborhoods were annoyed at households that slept in their beds in shifts. Much of this was Fairfax County. There were, at the time of my exploration, 165 languages spoken by students in the Fairfax County schools.

Of the nineteen counties in Baltimore–Washington, D.C.–MD–VA–WV, Loudoun County, Virginia, caught my attention because it had two clear personalities: a Martian realm in the east, in which AOL and WorldCom (as it was then) were at home and, with their ilk, had annihilated local terrain, and, in the west, horse country that looked not much different from what it was two centuries before, especially if you squinted over a few megamansions. Zoning that in some parts required fifty acres per parcel had kept it that way, but, as I learned, unsteadily; Loudoun's body politic was, at that time, stuck in an internal argument, voting in and voting out land-use-control candidates in a repetitive lurch between tranquillity and earthquake. At the time of my exploration around the turn of the millennium, tranquillity was prevailing, driving up real estate prices. If you weren't rich you had to look beyond Loudoun to WV, which was far too poor to preserve: it needed the earthquake. An odd experience was to take a drive, seemingly deeper and deeper into the pastoral landscape of western Loudoun, and then suddenly your country road becomes a four-lane highway amid condos and malls. In morning and evening, an almost unbroken stream of commuter traffic traveled the country roads of Loudoun, toward D.C. and the edge cities around it in the morning, and toward home in West Virginia in the evening.

The same leapfrogging pattern appeared to the north. Montgomery County, Maryland—twenty-five-acre zoning in places—was full of forgotten-seeming, sleepy country landscapes in which you were lucky to find even a country store. In fact, this landscape was protected by state as well as county laws, Maryland being one of the most progressive states in the country where land-use controls are concerned. ("Progressive" in land use usually means landscape preservation.) So, like western Loudoun, Montgomery was not naturally occurring country but, rather, a landscape that reflected politics and law on at least two levels. To avoid zoning restrictions, developers had leapfrogged over Montgomery to free-for-all territory in Pennsylvania, to the north—ensuring that PA would soon be added to the local kite: D.C.–Washington–Baltimore–Arlington MD–VA–WV–PA; a good addition, sonorically speaking. For those commuters from new Pennsylvania developments, there would be I-270—usually at six lanes, but, in some places, counting exits, twelve—right through pastoral Montgomery to our capital city. Beltways are a part of this geography, too. Did ever man build circular roads before—well, yes: racetracks.

The bundle of mismatched roads, like balled-up bits of saved string in your grandmother's drawer that I had found in King of Prussia, had evolved in the Baltimore–Washington Metropolitan Area, on a much larger scale. Such confusion of roads can make it difficult to explore a metropolitan area—to get a sense of being well traveled in it. I came upon a 1990 article in a scholarly journal by Robert Fishman, author of *Bourgeois Utopias* and student of spreawlian, in which he pointed out that people don't really share a common sense of geography in such places but, rather, experience them as individual customary routes. This helped me develop a working conclusion that it is in the very character of such places that you don't experience them as a common whole. (GPS has formalized this nearsightedness.) After a while I realized that probably only delivery people like FedEx or UPS employees really get to know a metropolitan area in the full way I was attempting to acquire, and maybe not even they if they use GPS. The mental map I was seeking to compile seemed ill suited to the very nature of this landscape that lent itself to the subjective approach, was anticontextual in a way that might be kin to how people experienced place before maps.

Sometimes a personal trip with no reportorial purpose at all was more revealing. A friend wants to go to a mall she has heard is upscale. For myself, I avoid malls unless in explorer mode, but I agree.

It's hard to find and takes much too long to get there—what is happening to my day!—and then, when we finally do, we find it in steep decline, many stores closed—a desolate situation. In the basement heaps of pawed-over clothing are tumbled together. Not only have I "lost" my day but I will never get out of here: that is my feeling. The idea of a landscape such as this robbing me of time reveals starkly my underlying, bred-in-the-bone aversion to spreawlian. In the fluorescent light a woman in a burka, her face not visible, is sorting through the goods swiftly, adeptly, as quick-fingered and sharp-eyed as an experienced forager gathering dinner in a wild field. Piercing my aversion, more forceful for the resistance, another of those experiences of having stumbled into the heart of America stills me with wonder, although this time it is accompanied by a sense of being in the very depths of the global enclosure of our time as well.

Death

One of the great comforts of older landscapes is that expressions of death, such as graveyards, are completely at home in them. This is less so in cities perhaps, but a funeral in a city is a completely compatible scene: one can even feel that the city was in part created to hold such scenes and give them meaning. For cities—even fast-paced New York—are nothing if not time rooms in which past people mingle with present. Trinity Church, with its ancient graves surrounding, is not only natural on Wall Street but a perfect counterpoint to the upsurging energy. I had noticed that out in spreawlian, however, the rituals of death seemed silly and out of place: a mistake. A funeral procession passing the International House of Pancakes belonged to another movie.

✦

Death came up on a trip I took in the period of my Balt–Wash education, but as part of a group interested in preservation. Traveling
in a bus, we visited the estate of a wealthy Maryland landowner, a
man of lineage, outgoing and elegant yet rather ordinary, too, as a
duke might be—a businessman in good, vaguely equestrian clothes.
He welcomed us to his eighteenth-century house—old brick, rosy
with memory—on a hill overlooking a rippled countryside of blues
and greens, of moving shadows and swatches of light. His forefa-
thers had built the house, and his family had farmed the land for
generations, and he wore house and land as easily as his clothes;
indeed, they seemed to be an extension of his very person. Though
his wife was brittle as glass, and intent on keeping herself formally
separate from us plebeians, this American duke's geniality could not
be faulted.

We had just previously visited another eighteenth-century house,
down in the valley, owned by people newly rich who reverentially presented the house as greater than themselves. This made the house
thingish and separate from normal life. It was strange to see people
relating to their actual home as curators—how could they relax?—
yet there was in their humility an offering of the house to us as on
an equal standing with them which was impressive. Now that my
fellow bus riders had met the duke, they were whispering disparag-
ingly about the first couple, saying that the duke was the "real thing."
I knew they were right, in a way, but it made me mad. I was instantly
on the side of the people in the valley.

After our tour of the house—fine proportions, intimate social
rooms, family portraits, a scene recently painted in a primitive style
of a foxhunting meet in front of the house—the duke showed us
around the grounds. Extending outward from the edge of his lawns
were soybean fields; by way of pointing them out, he squatted down
and snapped off a soybean sprig, fingering the beans while looking
at the sky in a way that conveyed an attractive, manly connection to

the earth. I did not believe for a moment that he did a lick of work on those soybeans.

Several times during our tour the duke mentioned his death in a jocular way, though he was a hale man in his sixties and seemingly in no way endangered. He mentioned it apropos of a family graveyard, where he told us he would be buried, and which he promised to show us before our visit was over. It was something to look forward to, a treat. I thought at first that this reference to death was an attempt to blur the social distinction between himself and us on the tour—death, after all, is the great leveler—and this made me warm to him. As it turned out, the graveyard only accentuated his elevated social station. It was small, but it went back far in time; the money had not been squandered among too many children; we could see that. It was on a high point, a crest overlooking the breathtaking Maryland land-scape. We stood there stupidly. Who among us had a private grave-yard on ancestral land? But it was not social inequality that bothered me. I don't really care if some people are rich if all have the necessities and the opportunity to rise if they choose. What provoked me was that he seemed to me to be expressing a kind of contextual comfort in the cradle of providence that has in fact vanished from the world, as if class could achieve that, a privilege conferred on superior souls.

Our host said—entirely without humor—that he looked forward to being buried there because of the view. I found myself in the grips of a paroxysm of hilarity for which I felt ashamed. I was going too far. He was hospitable; nothing obliged him to take time with us. I was just envious. Well, that was true. Looking out at the view, I knew it would be hard to find a countryside that more perfectly embodied my deepest attachments: the blues and the greens and the luscious dark clusters of woodland to the horizon, expressing harmony between God and man. The world is a paradise in which man—a man, this man—is safely encompassed in a web of connectedness and meaning. For a moment I seemed to be in a world altogether different from the one in which I normally lived. Then I remembered that we were, in fact, well inside Balt–Wash—by any definition.

I asked the duke how it had come to be that such a seamless pastoral prospect had remained intact in such a location, when the economics of farming had long ago been marginalized and the economics of real estate development were ascendant. He answered that the landscape was in fact preserved by the State of Maryland. How could I have forgotten that Maryland was in the forefront of containing contemporary development in the East? Preserving large sections of old countryside—calling them "hubs," formerly a word for cities and an example of inversion in contemporary landscape form—was a part of that effort. Here before me was a superlative outcome of Maryland policy. The illusion that this countryside extended indefinitely was perfect.

Certainly I would not have preferred to see a built-up landscape from the hilltop—though I was jarred, it's true, to learn that progressive land-use policy had ended up providing a proper view from the grave of a man such as the duke. When I later looked back at the scene in the little graveyard, and, in particular, at the duke's jocular attitude toward his death, his air of getting away with something began to make sense. I saw him as like the magician's assistant who emerges in one piece from a coffin after it has been sawed in two, though his actual trick was to get into his own coffin in one piece. Through a sleight of hand the duke would amazingly escape the universal robbery of the world, slipping into his stage-set graveyard in a stage-set landscape just as the curtain came down.

I was pretty sure at the time of our visit that the soybean fields around the duke's house were more exterior decoration than the source of his economic well-being. But saving old landscapes and architecture seems to me a good job for rich people. And, after all, I knew he did not actually have a more reassuring grave than the rest of us. My annoyance didn't last. Still, I was a little shocked when, later,

I learned that he had substantial interests in real estate development, despite his having implicitly presented himself to a busload of preservationists as embodying values opposed to exactly that. I decided to go have a look at a development in which he had been an investor.

To get there you drove down country lanes—part of the preserved landscape. Once you got to the development, it was easy to get lost—the layout seemed almost intentionally disorienting. The houses were capacious, in a medley of traditional designs, many of stone, rather close to one another, as has become the fashion, with large transplanted trees shading them, suggesting that they had been there a long time. On the whole, it was a tasteful development. The duke might even have conceived of it as a progressive experiment.

Whatever the case, this, not the soybeans, was his true plantation. This was where his grave should have been. Ah, but graveyards in a housing development in what was still essentially spreawlian? That would be as jarring as the hearse passing IHOP. Perhaps a solution is to be found in the work of Thomas Lynch, the poet-undertaker who has suggested that we solve the interment problem—there are too many of us—by having our bodies mixed into an alloy and shaped into hood ornaments for cars: a rather old-fashioned idea at this point, given that cars have receded in symbolic charisma and going places doesn't mean what it did. For the duke, I thought, a period brass knocker in his development would do nicely.

Extraordinary events in spreawlian can, at least momentarily, create a sense of shared geography in the otherwise subjective landscape of personal routes. Death had a part in one such extended moment. During a ten-day period in my Georgetown years, people were shot dead by a sniper at random spots throughout Balt–Wash. The sharpshooter picked off his victims as they went about ordinary metropolitan area routines—one was pumping gas, another walking across a Home Depot parking lot: places far separate from one another yet all in the "area." The precision contrasted with a quality of vagueness in this whole terrain, a feeling of nothing being fixed, as if locations had borrowed from traffic and were sliding around, too. The sniper, after picking off his quarry, easily disappeared into traffic. But the locations of the deaths created a constellation that pinned Balt–Wash down. Maps appeared in the newspaper. A context was created, something made up of more than just private routes. Edgeless as the entity was, these deaths of ordinary people in it became meaningful to all, just as the threat of random violence, affecting everyone, created common cause.

Divisions also appeared. Progressive people, who, on principle, love cities and despise spreawlian, made the point during the sniper terror that the perpetrator could not have vanished so easily in an urban street grid. It seemed an inopportune time to indulge in this piety. The police assumed in this period of fear that the shooter was male and also white. This inverted the usual prejudicial assumption that crimes are committed by black people, though it was equally revealing. Who but a white male could so elude the authorities, could hold a whole region in fear? As it turned out, there were two perpetrators, both black: a drifter and a teenage boy, who had done the actual shooting, directed by the older man. Evil incarnate. They were eventually apprehended at an I-70 rest stop, where they were sleeping in their car. That most unlocated of places also appeared on maps in the newspaper, not only in relation to the spots where shootings had taken place, but in the context of the Baltimore–Washington metropolitan region generally, including the two old cities and the interstates and beltways that were a part of it: Balt–Wash had, for a few weeks, become a landscape in its true role as the theater of life.

The nature of the District of Columbia distorts the truth of contemporary metropolitan form in that, because the federal government has not fled to Third World countries as industry has, the District has an intact centrality, greatly reinforced not only by Pierre-Charles L'Enfant's grand plan of radiating avenues but by the grandeur of the federal city—the Capitol, the Mall, the White House, and the mammoth classical temples that house government agencies. Though the industrial age may have retreated into history, it remains reflected in the organization of the government, especially the bureaucracies, as is eerily, yet concretely reflected in the physical federal city. To all this the surrounding metro area, however extensive, seems symbolically subordinate to the District, though in fact, over the decades, it has developed an economic life of its own—those edge cities—that may not have superseded but at least competes with the center of gravity created by the government. Meanwhile, the alternative presence of Baltimore, albeit so drastically abandoned by its population that vast sections of it have been razed, more and more, as the connective metro area thickens and spreads, throws the impression of the singularity and dominance of the District just a little more off-center.

Sometimes I experienced Washington as a traditional city, moments still vividly accessible to me in memory. Late one afternoon just before Christmas, I picked up my son Julian, who had come by train, at Union Station. Snow was falling. Washingtonians go right home at the slightest sign of snow. In a dusk fast turning to night, Pennsylvania Avenue was empty and soundless but for the crunch of our wheels. Around us the Parthenons of government disappeared upward. Enormous but perfectly proportioned wreaths of small lights had been placed on the gargantuan columns just at the point where snow merged with darkness. A warm, comfortable quiet enveloped us in the car. I felt myself to be in an intact society which was contained, knowable, endowed with all the qualities, good and bad, that comprise a civilized human nature, stabilized by institutions manifested in its architecture: a nation of modest size but deep culture, quietly living its life. The phrase came to my mind: "Washington in a time of peace." It was the year 2000. We have never been a quiet modest nation of deep culture but, as I look back, in a way I had it right. The moment on the threshold of 9/11 was close to the last in which we could experience ourselves, however retrogressively in fact, as, simply, a nation.

Disney

A few years before I arrived in Balt–Wash, there had been a battle that had also brought the metropolitan area into focus as a place for its citizenry—indeed, eventually, for citizens of the nation as well. Still lingering in the air when I settled in Georgetown was an attempt by Disney in the early 1990s to create a historical theme park to the south of Washington but within its gravitational range. The theme of this Disney creation was to be American history—right in the region in which so much of that history had actually played out. The prospective site was the village of Haymarket, in Prince William County, Virginia, an area thought of by many as "country." But I-66 went right by Haymarket, connecting it to Dulles Airport and points north, including the two beltways of Baltimore and Washington. At that time much of the county was indeed still rural and also poor. To the extent it had burgeoned on metro energy, it had done so unwisely, allowing a lot of cheap housing development without also attracting revenue-producing commercial enterprises to pay for schools, services, and roads. As a result, the local government was short of money—badly in need of a big fish, as the county supervisor put it. From Disney's point of view, this made the likelihood of getting local consent strong.

Prince William businessmen liked the idea, of course, as did local politicians. To rural people there, many struggling, the Disney prospect was a gift from heaven. It would bring much needed jobs

and property values would soar. But while Prince William itself was
in part hardscrabble, right next door was the luxuriant "hunt country" of Fauquier County. This was a land of dukes, of grand estates
and riding to hounds. The prospect that appalled the denizens of
Fauquier was not the theme park itself, which would be safely over in
Prince William—though that was hardly a pleasant prospect. But a
much more direct threat was the rings of claptrap that would grow
up fast around the new Disney encampment. This was projected
to extend to a radius of twenty miles, well into Fauquier's utopia: a
nightmare that had to be stopped.

Disney was probably lulled by the Republican cast of Fauquier,
forgetting that free marketeers will forget their antiregulation
principles in a trice in order to protect the nice places where they
live. Indeed, as soon as the Disney plan was announced, Fauquier
County residents mounted a formidable opposition. Wags rev-
eled in the bald-faced turnabout of piratical capitalists clamoring
for government intervention. Disney turned the uprising to its advantage, using Fauquier's opposition as an opportunity to pose as
the champion of the common man—who tends to enjoy Disney—
against rich snobs. This worked for a while. Disney also took the
position that it wasn't responsible for offshoots of the theme park
anyway. That hardly appeased the nobles of Fauquier. Perhaps the
factor that most favored Disney was the apathy of the general public. After decades of pell-mell development, residents of metro areas
can have outrage fatigue.

But, as it turned out, the sheer scale of the Disney project shocked
even the hardened population of one of the fastest-growing metropolitan areas in the country. The common man turned out to be
a sleeping giant Disney had not seen as it set its sights on obscure
Haymarket. The plans stressed Civil War history, including the
re-creation of a Civil War–era village, plenty of which could still
be found in Virginia, a restaging of the battle between the Monitor

and the Merrimac on a man-made lake (it had taken place on the nearby Chesapeake) and an underground railway on which visitors could "escape." There would also be a "family Farm," and a "State Fair," real ones still existing nearby—with Ellis Island, Indian Villages, and a Lewis and Clark raft trip thrown in. It's widely agreed that what lifted the anti-Disney crusade was the opposition by well-known historians such as David McCullough. Using their fame to reach a wide audience, they pointed out that many actual historical sites—Monticello, Mount Vernon, Bull Run—were nearby, but, even more important, the landscape in which much of our history had taken place, still fundamentally intact, would be destroyed by the theme park and the rings of development around it. How is one to really understand the Constitution without a grasp of the world in which it was written, a pastoral landscape of small towns and slightly larger cities, through which the fastest travel was by horse? How to sense the tragedy of the Civil War if the context has evaporated? "This part of Northern Virginia has soaked up more of the blood, sweat, and tears of American history than any other area of the country," said historian C. Vann Woodward. The sheer gall of the proposal to set up a fabricated version of our history right next door to the places where that history had actually occurred while at the same time destroying that history's context upset not just scholars and aesthetes but all kinds of people. Ordinary Americans, it turned out, felt there was a large difference between history as entertainment and history as something actual that had happened in particular places and they did not want that line blurred. In *Edge City*, Joel Garreau speculated that the only concern that can rouse Americans against development sufficiently to stop it is the destruction of Civil War sites. Founding Father history evidently had strong meaning to Americans as well.

In this way, not only did Balt–Wash become an entity in the public mind but the Virginia Piedmont in which it is set was revealed, both as the theater of action and as a protagonist in itself. It's one of the dislocating effects of metropolitan development that the natural landscape, even basic topography, recedes to a secondary level of reality, and even disappears—into the physically incoherent covering of pell-mell development, but also into the geography of personal routes and interests that tends to replace the sense of a common terrain. Cities usually have identities anchored in natural features of the landscape—the Potomac or Baltimore harbor, for example. Cities, in their relative compactness, are also small enough to be imagined in clear relation to these features. City natives always know where they are in relation to other parts of town, and rivers or hills can commonly play a big role in this orientation. Not so in the hundred-mile-plus radius of the prevaricating-proliferating metro areas of our time. But with the Disney fight, Balt–Wash became secondary to the Piedmont landscape in which it was situated. That older landscape—not the "metropolitan area" or any other built-world designation but rather that topographical entity—was now the container of the story, was the theater of life it had once been. With the historical argument gaining popular support, furthermore, the fight went national. The landscape of the Virginia Piedmont, birthplace of the country, became evident again, not only locally but nationwide.

To go ahead, Disney needed only the consent of county officials—that is how land use works in Virginia, as in much of the country. But the corporation was hypersensitive to publicity. An entertainment outfit can't afford a bad-guy reputation. And now, instead of being the champion of the common people against the snobs, Disney had become a greedy bully destroying an American legacy. To make things worse, Ken Burns's documentary series *The Civil War* was just then being rerun on television. Much of the Civil War took place in the Virginia Piedmont. Burns was another public voice opposed to Disney. Though the Prince William County planning board was on track to approve the plan, and an approval would be close to impossible to reverse, shortly before the vote Disney pulled out.

I was glad that Disney had been defeated. The argument for landscape as irreplaceable historical memory is a strong one for me. The Virginian countryside is, to my mind, one of the most beautiful in the world. But in the context of my education, the victory was not so clear-cut. Though unchanged, the pastoral parts of the Piedmont seemed eerily altered in meaning by the very struggle. The theme park had been routed, but somehow the contest in itself had turned the landscape into a theme park. Though the battle had been about preserving a continuum with the agrarian past, and had been won, somehow the continuum had been severed. Fauquier County, to take just one example, emerged from the fight having become "hunt country," as opposed to country in which people sometimes went fox-hunting. That in itself was not really new: county land-use laws had already done that, in a sense. What was totally new for me was that, somehow, the trashy secondary and tertiary development that would have been spawned by a Disney park seemed now more authentic in my mind than fiercely defended Fauquier—as did the projected Disney park itself. The now fiercely curated and defended agrarian parts of the Piedmont had become non-Disney—and, in that, perversely Disney-like.

All this was a bit elusive, and yet a powerful example for me of the eerie burglary of the world as we have known it. I still believed that any intentional intervention into "anything goes" American development was positive as a foray in the direction of responsibility for our surroundings. I certainly was still glad that the pastoral Piedmont still existed. But the loss in the process also seemed defining. It suggested that something much bigger than development issues was at work in the metropolitan landscape. Perhaps both because the battle had been national and because the Capitol was in the picture, I began to see the Disney aftermath as extending outward, edgelessly, maybe to everything—to all our landscapes. This was the invasively penetrating collapsed space of the enclosure I had already seen in a piecemeal way in my travels but now, because I actually lived in Balt–Wash, was experiencing firsthand. In the form of the Disney aftermath especially, the pervasiveness of the place-change in our time seemed to come up around me as if out of the ground.

I began to see why it was that all efforts to name the new landscape emerging from the change, by myself and by others, were in the end futile. For to name the new landscape as manifested in Balt–Wash, or the other dithering areas, would suggest that it was just one type of landscape among many, as different types of places have always laid themselves out in past times. But what I had been exploring was not just one kind of landscape. I had been studying the overt form of a new landscape that has subverted all places, whether visibly or not. It was the landscape of the collapsed global space in which we had encased ourselves sometimes, visibly manifesting as in spreawlian but often not. In this, it was fundamentally different in character from places as we have known them. For that reason I decided on the word "atopia" for the landscape that was really all-enveloping, though obvious only in areas where contemporary development, directly expressing contemporary times, was unrestrained. This change, this subversive opposite of place as we had known it, was everywhere, whether visibly or invisibly, whether brashly or in disguise—as in Georgetown, for example, which I was less and less able to maintain in my mind and heart as a sanctuary, or the Kentucky Bluegrass or, for that matter, Patagonia or the Arctic. Wherever I might go, I would deeply misunderstand my surroundings—would be choosing fantasy over reality—if I did not see them as belonging to the sphere of atopia.

A part of the Piedmont had been preserved, true, and its landscape freshly treasured, and all this was good. But the seemingly successful fight against Disney was showing me that we cannot escape this change. It was teaching me that even the most grounded-seeming landscapes were actually in the grips of an invisible ungroundedness, which separated them from their history, untied them from old layers of significance, stole their comforts. This aftershock affected my perception even of Washington itself, intact though it was. By no measure could the Disney venture be compared with Washington, and yet just the prospect of Disney out on the "edge" of what one still thought of as the skirts of the city was such a distortion of the landscape as we imagined it to be that even the gravitas of the capital was weakened by just the conception.

My entire journey, to this point and beyond, was a process of moving toward acceptance of the atopian landscape in which we now live wherever we are—and then recoiling. I could see it intellectually, but then I would go into emotional denial. When I did accept atopia emotionally, the most banal aspects of the world would light up with living significance. So, too, would those places seemingly most intact, though in a way entirely different from my previous experience of them. This was thrilling, but also unnerving. I would backslide, choosing the familiarity of a traditional sensibility—choosing calendar art. It's no mystery why I vacillated so. The losses in going from the world as we have imagined it for centuries into this emergent one are steep. So much of our sense of humanity is bound up in our older conception of landscape, from our creatureliness to our aspirational nature. Atopia in its overt form negates both our sense of dependence and of transcendence. It seems very hard to find a footing in it. It doesn't seem to be a context in the old sense, even for death. Above all it leaves us bereft of one of the most long-lasting armatures of our collective interior life. We will not have another until our new landscape, atopia, has been deeply, cumulatively imagined.

Art

Along the way I have looked to the arts for help in understanding the atopian landscape. Film in particular has, for a long time, seemed to me to pick up what is different about place in our time—not in its plots, which often strike me as off the mark as to what really concerns us, but in its cinematography, which for me sometimes tells the most powerful and relevant story behind the twists and turns of plots. Dubai rising out of the desert; creepily lavish office interiors in which you have no idea, geographically, of the location; the way an Italian hill town, though beautiful, has a dead feeling while a gym full of fitness machines is nonsensically vibrant. In a Southwestern setting, the strange unmooredness of strip malls in the desert, the odd, going-nowhere datedness of motion in cars, the strange smallness of the desert, even when it is vast, captures an essence of how hard it is for a person to find a footing in today's world—this in *No Country for Old Men* by the Coen brothers. The eye of the cinematographer, it appears to me, has been ahead of us all in searching out the condition of enclosure in which we live—the way it is everywhere, even in seemingly wild places, and is always the same, however different the surroundings. Sometimes the effect is sinister. But in other instances the contemporary landscape is filmed for comedy. One of my all-time favorites in this regard is the Angelina Jolie comedy *Mr. and Mrs. Smith*, in which a husband and wife, unbeknownst to each other, are engaged in opposed derring-do corporate-espionage operations, deceiving each other while living together in a McMansion. The McMansion is a major player in this story, in particular a high-tech kitchen fit for a large hotel, but in which food prepared elsewhere is heated, usually at the last minute, to deceive the other spouse into thinking their mate has been home cooking an elaborate meal instead of out murdering people. The end comes when the McMansion goes up in explosive flames. I saw *Mr. and Mrs. Smith* at a tottering drive-in near Rensselaerville, at which some people sat in air-conditioned SUVs while others had tailgate picnics and sat on folding chairs as dogs and children ran around. In the upper-left-hand corner of the screen there was a big hole. I perhaps would not have laughed so hard had I seen it in a state-of-the-art cineplex, in which it might all have seemed a bit too close to reality.

Literature, in my limited reading, lags with respect to plumbing the experience of atopia. I've probably missed some, but *Netherland*, by Joseph O'Neill, is the only novel I know of that explicitly probes for the emotional experience of atopian settings in personal life. One of the most vivid scenes is of the protagonist, on the other side of the ocean from his estranged wife and their child, gazing through Google Earth at the dormer of the room in which his child sleeps. Richard Ford's Frank Bascombe novels are set in elaborately described old suburbs of the latter-day edgeless metro of the Jersey shore. Bascombe is an aging but sensitive real estate agent, no stranger to grief where landscape as well as other life matters are concerned, but clear-eyed about all—especially the physical environment of which he is a knowing native. The books are full of the riddles of metro syntax. The style in which Ford wrote *The Lay of the Land* is itself a probe into the bewildering form of spreawlian, full of sudden switches in mood, choppy with unexpected juxtapositions, with a through rhythm of stops and starts, just like the traffic he describes. Chang-rae Lee is a younger writer who takes on metro territory with gusto in *Aloft*, set in overdeveloped Long Island. The novel is akin in hilarity to *Mr. and Mrs. Smith*, but without laugh lines. Lee just lets atopia appear deadpan through the eyes of residents who don't think anything of it, leaving the second takes to us.

I have long thought dance could be an art especially able to probe atopian reality, because the unchanging measure and expressiveness of the body might reveal what is altered in the meaning of our surroundings and our relation to them. There are certainly instances of explorations of this sort in the work of Trisha Brown, who took dance out of the theater and into the street long ago, and who later used industrial stage settings, and Pina Bausch, who brought mounds of earth and pools of water onto the stage. The widespread use of videos or stills of landscapes on the dance stage, often of nature and often enlarged, seems to me another way of taking the outdoors indoors. Athletes and daredevils can strike me as being dancers in the atopian arena, too—the aerialist Philippe Petit, who walked on a tightrope between the tops of the World Trade Center towers, or Felix Baumgartner, who was lofted by balloon to the edge of the atmosphere in a tiny compartment in which extreme claustrophobia had to be endured, then stepped out into a perspective from which the curve of the Earth was visible, and dove. In this he drew a line with his body from the edge of the atmosphere to Earth, delineating the full dimensions of the enclosure that is the theater of our existence. Fiascoes, too, can have revelatory power. That poor Italian captain who ran a global-scale cruise ship aground in the Mediterranean, because he wanted to get close enough to shore to wave to his girlfriend, was an unwitting artist of our physical world—it's all in the wave, combined with the spectacle of the toppled behemoth at a sickening angle in shallow waters off Tuscany, and the length of time that it remained there before experts were able to figure out how to remove it: a sculpture mixed with performance art and, one has to say, comedy, but there is something of dance, too, in the wave simultaneous with running aground in the deeply resistant material reality to which our bodies are native.

But the art that has most helped me make the transition between old ways of seeing place, so deep set that they seem basic to life, and atopian reality is Earth Art, a movement that emerged in the 1970s, just at that moment when we were creating a global economy. Earth Art is literally made out of landscape, in landscape—sometimes delicately as in the case of Andy Goldsworthy, who might carve a riverine shape in a sand flat and then film it as the tide comes in. Sometimes it's monumental, as in the case of Michael Heizer's bulldozed earthworks in the American desert. Sometimes it's in a museum, like Walter De Maria's *New York Earth Room*, literally a room in New York full of dirt, an exhibition sponsored by the Dia Art Foundation, which has subsequently put a wide variety of works of this sort on display in a vast erstwhile factory in Beacon, a town a bit up the Hudson from the city. It is all fundamentally unframed, insofar as I have known it, and this, too, seems to undo the basic orders of the world. The way much of it is made of landscape itself reverses the age-old relationship of art to context—a glowing Han vase standing out in the primeval forest. When landscape itself becomes art, the old composition, in which we and our works were figures in a context, is disturbed in a way that captures the disappearance of the ground under us.

Many Earth Artists are still working—Richard Serra, with his great bronze curving walls inserted into both cityscapes and pastoral scenes; James Turrell, whose Rodenbreter in the Painted Desert is a hollowed-out crater cone volcano with the vent rounded as cleanly as the oculus in the Pantheon, all to reveal light, this artist's true medium. The Rodenbreter was built to last millennia, like prehistoric sites, to which much of the work of these artists seems akin. We haven't cracked the code of all these prehistoric works, but we do know that many are in complex relation to the sun and the stars. Earth Art can seem cosmic in its reference, too—though possibly a part of that is from the way it reminds us of prehistoric works, in scale, in landscape engagement. Still, I feel in some Earth Art a warm companionship with these ancestors—a sense that, for all our sophistication, we are still struggling to combine the fact of our embeddedness with our capacity for aspiration.

One enormous difference between prehistoric works and our own Earth Art, however, is that the sheer difficulty of making the prehistoric works, still unexplained in some cases, is part of their expressiveness. We still don't know how the builders of Stonehenge did it, for example, given the tools available to them. Inherent to the magnificence of such works is the passion behind figuring out how to make them, possibly over generations: the sheer feat. This gives them a heroism that tops anything produced in historical times. Modern-day Earth Art, in contrast, is easy to do—the choice is in restraint. Some of it even seems to address the disconcerting easiness with which it is made, as in itself expressive of our predicament. We can do anything—but still we are embedded and dependent: how are we to understand that? The easiness creates uneasiness.

Sometimes difficulty is intruded, not in the making but in the viewing. An example is De Maria's *The Lightning Field*, an array of vertical steel poles set up in a stretch of southwestern desert. Their purpose is to attract lightning. Viewers therefore must not only travel to see the work but also spend the night there, in the slim hope that lightning will strike. These are extravagant requirements for art lovers used to centrally located museums with restaurants and gift stores. But the pilgrimage, and likely disappointment, is, perhaps, a part of the art—making up for too much easiness. You are forced into a humble relationship to the environment: lightning will not strike on order. Then you fly home.

Spiral Jetty, by Robert Smithson, is just what it sounds like: a jetty built out from the shore of the Great Salt Lake in a spiral. Made to be seen from above, the doodlelike jetty expresses an almost cavalier power. To anyone who loves marine landscapes, this inward-turning jetty in an inland lake is jarringly unromantic, telling us that, far from being free in a vast wild world, we are doodlers wound up in ourselves. Yet *Spiral Jetty* can seem to ask how we are to rise to the ambiguous role of partial custodians of the landscape in which we are also embedded. Embeddedness can also seem to be expressed by prehistoric earthworks like those of the ancient Mound Builders of North America who created lanscape-scaled mounds in grand symmetrical formations in which they buried their dead. Many contemporary works in this genre can seem to strive to assert a galactic range of reference—to somehow talk to the stars, and some are built specifically in relation to the movement of celestial bodies, as Stonehenge was. The work of both eras have, despite their monumentality, a prostrate quality—are both daring and prayerful, engaging, as they do, with the largest and therefore most humbling thing.

Much Earth Art has a reverent quality, but because it is usually the work of one artist, some can have a disturbing egotism lacking in prehistoric works. How dare you impress yourself in this grand way on the landscape we all share! The (comparative) easiness combined with the egotism can, in the large-scale works, seem more wasteful than expressive, more willful than precise—brilliant, yet offhanded. Where prehistoric works are powerful yet supplicant, supremely daring and yet humble, some of our works, in their easy egotism, remind us of a different vulnerability—our thoughtlessness and our endangerment of ourselves, of the gap between our powers and our understanding. In this, these works are the opposite of the works of prehistoric people, who went far beyond their normal powers to create a mode of expression that has to have closely matched what they felt and understood.

Our Earth Art and often our cinematography subliminally invoke the dawn of human time, which is always implicit in landscape, though usually it takes a while to get to that level. Yet where the builders of Stonehenge surely enlarged themselves through their efforts, we strive to find our smallness and vulnerability in the context of our runaway, outsized powers. As of now, we seem separated from one another by our powers, rather than connected through common effort. That is because we haven't fully imagined our situation on Earth now and so have no collective interior life to give it meaning, no interior footing from which to respond to it profoundly—culturally, but most important, politically: to discover how to govern ourselves under these circumstances. Earth Art can seem to me to begin this process. It tells me that, like our prehistoric ancestors, we see ourselves in a cosmic context even if we are far behind our predecessors in developing a sense of what our relationship to the cosmos is, imaginatively speaking. What other context is there for a species clearly marooned on a planet that stands out against the universe as distinctly as the Han vase in a forest? About Earth in space there is no ambiguity of figure and field, of foreground and background, of subject and context, at all.

The great gift of Earth Art, however, in my struggle to accept atopia was that gradually some features of Balt–Wash spontaneously began to seem like Earth Art to me. The first great breakthrough was the construction site at an intersection of I-495, I-395, and I-95, the Springfield Mixing Bowl, as it had been dubbed. The massively disturbed topography and the transparent incomplete structures in progress often seemed to me more revealing and expressive than completely built-out metropolitan scenes. With its enormous pylons, its soaring road ribbons clipped off in midair, its mountains of raw earth, and its mixture of chaos and intention, not to mention its vast scale, the half-built Springfield Mixing Bowl, at first an eyesore and an inconvenience, became colossally expressive to me. Because I was traveling around Balt–Wash a lot, I came to notice the way light fell across it, casting shadows even more powerfully cryptic than its actual shapes. It was a modern-day quangle-wangle sundial that somehow seemed to know in advance of ourselves what the civilization we would build in response to our new circumstances would be.

Soon much, then all of Balt–Wash appeared to me as Earth Art of a kind—as both illuminating our atopian condition, and pointing the way toward an effective expressive response. All present-day landscapes are atopian, by definition, but it is in our rambunctious contemporary settlement patterns—untethered, profligate, supplicating the galaxies yet also chthonic, helpless, catatonic, too powerful, wantonly incoherent, feckless, oracular, unframed, enigmatic, profound, beyond words—that our new era speaks to us directly.

I will never feel comfortable in it. Because of the time in which I was born, I will always feel stressed in our new era, will always long for and gravitate to our well-known older worlds, steeped in layers of inherited meaning, beloved classics full of old company, old tensions, old narratives, old tragedies almost enticingly unresolved, like a play cut off in the middle of the third act—even while knowing that atopia has engulfed them. I will always try to run away, but that is not because, as I once thought, our current landscape is meaningless: is really not a landscape but a destroyer of landscape. My first impulse will always be to flee the contemporary landscape because it's hard to engage with the tough new indispensable book of human life on Earth now. I don't always feel like being a beginner in a foreign language, continuously and mercilessly exposed to that special terror and despair, the deep inadequacy, that the unfamiliar syntax can engender.

In the midst of my Balt–Wash schooling, my father died. I had had a difficult relationship with him. Perhaps that was why at his funeral I was unable to feel grief. Instead, I was critical of everything— that the service took place in a hyperconservative Catholic church although he had been divorced, that the pallbearers were men though he had six daughters. And so on and so on. He was cremated a day or two later and then buried near the conservative church in a too-new cemetery: hardpan contained by chain link, cars whizzing by. But here I became collected, and present to my father's death. The mercilessly exposed quality of the location brought me close to him. I was sad to my marrow. But I was also impressed that he had had the guts to be buried in a place without any pretense as to the unprotectedness of our time—a place that offered no illusion of providential enchantment, that was undisguisedly atopian, bare to the traffic, a

car wash and a shopping mall down the road. I was awed by his un-
flinching embrace of the ordinariness of his disappearance, the mental and emotional fiber it took to refuse shelter in obsolete comforts.
Did I have that courage?

3

Whose Hand?

MAD Wonks in Toyland

While I was in Washington, I was given a fellowship at the Woodrow Wilson International Center for Scholars, on Pennsylvania Avenue, in the heart of the federal city. A perk was withdrawal privileges at the Library of Congress, also in the institutional heart of D.C. Generally speaking, only members of Congress and officials in the executive branch enjoyed that privilege, but I could ask for any book, and it would be on my desk the next morning. While, in the early years of learning to read our new physical world, I had purposely avoided the established fields of landscape interpretation in order to see freshly, the time had come to acquaint myself with the formal disciplines on this subject. But while the landscape fields were vast and numerous, and to know them fully would take a lifetime of reading—just the proliferation of specialized fields of geography would require a good part of that lifetime—it seemed possible to scan them from a desk in a central city with the help of this central library sufficiently to become confident that there was no part of this extensive territory that was unknown to me.

The Wilson Center had its own library, and a librarian who oversaw Library of Congress requests and therefore knew the wide spectrum of my interests. One day in spring of 2002, she drew my attention to an item far afield, strictly speaking, from my topic, which she had come across and thought might interest me. I mention this because of the serendipity—of proximity: two minds, two physical library collections, a far-ranging subject. We forget, perhaps, the value of limitations in our limitless world: the footing closeness can provide for leaps of intuition. The item in question was an article in the January issue of *Cold War History*, not a journal that I was likely to look into, titled "The Reduction of Urban Vulnerability: Revisiting 1950s American Suburbanization as Civil Defense." In it, the historian Kathleen Tobin shows how, beginning in the 1940s, the fear of atomic attack drove federal policy makers to try to find ways to disperse the population out of cities—for defense purposes. If there was one area of land-use history I knew fairly well before embarking on my explorations, it was the history of suburbia, and yet I had never come across this key fact. It had been, I surmised, more or less forgotten until Tobin resurrected the story. The chance intersection of the librarian's work with mine and the hand-off of the physical journal containing Tobin's article, as if between people momentarily moored in the same cove, was, in its own way, an experience of a disappearing landscape.

My commute to the Wilson Center from home entailed walking diagonally across and down through Georgetown to Foggy Bottom, the next neighborhood, where I could catch the Metro. Georgetown had been laid out on a small-bore grid that offered many routes. The textures, materials, styles, features, and details of the architecture, intertwined with botanical elements—topiary, unruly roses, ancient

trees—were so richly varied that I never ran out of surprises: a strik-
ing window pediment, an old weather vane, an odd dormer, a slate
roof, a blossoming tree overhanging a garden wall. These garden
walls, some with high wooden gates or doors set into them, had a
maddening allure. Some houses were of wood and many of brick, and
where the brick was painted white and the paint had flaked there were
speckled patterns, sometimes overlaid with the additionally speck-
ling shadows of vines or leafy branches. Eccentricity intermingled.
One beautiful wide house along the way was not only ivy-covered on
the outside, but the ivy had found its way through the upstairs windows, then climbing the windows on the inside, looked out, pressing
against the panes. In the northern part of the neighborhood were
estates of several acres, some suavely groomed, others overgrown,
suggesting a family that had drifted away from the present world.

It is the custom in Georgetown not to draw the shades, and, furthermore, the main floor of most houses was at ground level. In daytime the interiors were semidark; still, one might glimpse the shape
of a table or an object picked out by a ray of sun. On my way home
in the evening, however, rooms were lit and on full display. Kitchens
in Georgetown are often in the front, affording a glimpse of people
cooking supper, or, through other windows, a study or library: book-
shelves full of books, a painting in a frame on the wall, sometimes
even a person reading in an armchair. All this added up to a sense
of elaborately interlocking interior and exterior enclosures, intricate
and continuous, of which the streets and the alleys behind the houses
as well as the architecture itself and the gardens were a part. All was
perfectly scaled to the human body and, in that, conducive to a sense
of safety, of being at home in a known world.

Like the oldest parts of many American cities, much of Georgetown had, by the early twentieth century, become a largely black
neighborhood, in this case an established community of mixed economic levels, but thought by some to be a slum. Also, as in other

cities, some of the oldest and finest architecture in the city was to be found in this historic core. During the Depression, Rooseveltian policy wonks, lured by that architectural charm, began moving into the neighborhood, along with other New Dealers whose mass arrival in Washington was driving up housing prices, especially in Georgetown. After the war the trend continued. J.F.K. chose Georgetown as a young man, ran for the Senate from there, and, after he and Jackie married, moved into a modest house on Dent Place, and later a big one on N Street. Prominent Cold Warriors also chose Georgetown: Averell Harriman and Chip Bohlen under Ike, and McGeorge Bundy and Paul Nitze, who under Kennedy and Johnson advised on nuclear policy. The group, which included journalists Stewart and Joseph Alsop, and *The Washington Post* Grahams, became known as the Georgetown set. It had a reputation for blue-bloodedness and indeed there was more than a tinge of that in the group that managed the Cold War. Old architecture feels ancestral to blue bloods, setting an old eastern establishment tone.

By my time Georgetown was long established as one of the most fashionable neighborhoods in Washington, its soothing old qualities lovingly preserved by a community that was almost entirely white, the old black community in evidence only on Sundays as a well-dressed congregation from elsewhere attending a Georgetown church to which it had ancestral ties. Sometimes on my walks I thought about how many of the people who handled Cold War policy lived in this place where the beauty and intimate scale of the physical environment amounted to as powerful a denial of the condition of nuclear standoff as one could find. Why did the people who guided us through the Cuban missile crisis choose this extremely traditional neighborhood? Looking into one of those book-lined rooms of an evening I would imagine a member of the Georgetown set sitting in a chair under a landscape in a gilded frame with a report having to do with the policy of Mutual Assured Destruction in his lap. In a blink the whole neighborhood would be whisked up, like a little town in a string bag in a Christmas stocking, and where the man was then I couldn't say. But I didn't feel I was in a position to be critical of the Georgetown set for their choice of neighborhood. I, after all, had also chosen Georgetown for refuge from the discomforts and confusions of atopia, hardly to be compared to the strains of managing the Cold War—though perhaps the two were not altogether unconnected, as revealed by Tobin's article.

Tobin quoted Eugene Rabinowitch, the editor of the *Bulletin of the Atomic Scientists*, and one of its founders, who wrote in 1951: "In the absence of international control, dispersal is the only measure which could make an atomic super Pearl Harbor impossible." A reader sees quickly that the ideal defensive pattern would be complete dispersal across national territory, not that anyone suggested that, as it would have been politically impossible. However, relocation to areas outside but still near cities, where the jobs were, was, perhaps, feasible. Businesses, too, could be encouraged to leave cities. The National Security Act of 1947 included the creation of the National Security Resources Board, the purpose of which was to advise the president concerning the coordination of military, industrial, and civilian mobilization, including advice regarding "the strategic relocation of industries, services, government and economic activities, the continuous operation of which is essential to National Security" in the case of atomic attack. Many planning experts, Tobin showed, were also calling for dispersal from cities for safety reasons.

All this was the common sense of people thinking about defense at the time—and defense, in these early days of the Cold War, was a pressing issue. But a big problem in implementing this common sense was that it was impossible in a democracy to coerce people into changing their way of life. Suburban living was still a minor trend; most planners and policy makers assumed that people preferred to live in cities and would resist moving outward. Tobin quoted the economist and statistician Winfield Riefler, who had written in 1947 that decentralization would require, for most of us, changes "in our way of life so complete as to exceed our capacity of the imagination to envisage them and to paralyze the will to adopt them." How blind we are when we stare into the future! How fast settlement preferences—so basic to a way of life—can change! Cities had been in decline for some time, as economic energy seeped away from the old cores to the edges, partly because new factory technology such as the forklift and the assembly line needed sprawling single-story plants, which required lots of cheap land. Downtown Albuquerque, created in the 1920s, was the last central city downtown to be built in the United States. It's not that there was no suburban growth: what we see as old suburbs now, such as Brookline outside of Boston or Shaker Heights outside of Cleveland, had been appearing for a while. But the residential population of cities was still on the rise after World War II, to the point that planners could not envision the preference for cities changing on a large scale. I was surprised by this, partly because of the nineteenth- and early-twentieth-century urban reform movements, which were directed at horrendous urban conditions—crowded tenements, disease, filth—and argued for airy green environments for the poor. But the Tobin piece gave me a sense that this was the antiurban structure of feeling of social idealists, that mainstream attraction to cities remained strong, so strong that even the threat of holocaust was deemed insufficient to persuade people to leave them. Tobin quotes R. E. Lapp, a nuclear physicist: "The American people will react vigorously against any attempt to force decentralization and any premature or ill-considered program will probably meet sufficient resistance to render it useless."

Tobin does not go into this, but a major impediment to achieving a defensive dispersal was that our central government—unlike that of any other developed nation—has no constitutional land-use powers with which to reconfigure how Americans live. The government has certainly done a lot to shape our society spatially: but it has done so indirectly, as through the Federal Housing Administration's redlining for purposes of mortgage eligibility. It's one of the oddest aspects of the most powerful nation in the world, as we were just becoming then, that our federal government has lacked direct control over the use of its own terrain, even though, as the nuclear danger brought home, terrain is the essence of a nation. But here in the United States land-use powers are lodged in the states, and state sovereignty was sacred. Furthermore, in many states that power was left largely unused, ceded to more local governments—counties, townships, and even, in some cases, villages—that, in turn, often restrained themselves in deference to the rights of individual property owners. Over time, this fierce individualism where the use of land was concerned has come to be deemed basic to the American character.

But one way the federal government could have an effect on settlement patterns was by locating itself outside of cities. Tobin notes that under President Harry S. Truman a committee of representatives from all military branches, plus the State Department, the General Services Administration, and the Bureau of the Budget recommended that "agencies not required to be in Washington should be moved out of the region" and that "those remaining should be moved to a radius of 20 miles, into Maryland and Virginia," a plan Truman submitted to Congress though no legislation was passed. As far as I'm aware, no thought was given to moving the Capitol or the White House out of Washington permanently, although later an underground—way underground—bunker was developed in Colorado, the Cheyenne Mountain complex, from which generals and politicians could govern in the case of apocalypse. The site for the Pentagon building in Arlington County, across the Potomac, had been designated before World War II, so that decision cannot be attributed to these concerns. The CIA was a postwar agency but I don't know if its location outside the District, in Virginia, had anything

THE ABSENT HAND

to do with a fear of atomic attack. (In those days the effects of an atomic bomb on Hiroshima were the measure of disaster.) Tobin does document that the Truman administration developed a policy of pressuring industry to relocate outside cities, explicitly for civil defense purposes in 1951. However, there was no way of compelling businesses to move out, and indeed Republicans resisted the policy as an interference in free-market forces.

But the federal government did wield the indirect pressure of taxation. In 1954, President Dwight D. Eisenhower, though a Republican, successfully pushed for using additional tax incentives—some were already in place—through the Office of Defense Mobilization, the successor to the National Security Resources Board, to get businesses to move. As Tobin puts it, "The granting of rapid tax amortization ultimately became the principal means of influencing the dispersal of industry." The government had a great deal of leverage with the defense industry, which was dependent on government contracts as it grew into a military-industrial complex. Although Tobin shows no direct pressure from the federal government on defense contractors, I have long puzzled over the fact that, in many places that later became heavily suburbanized, defense plants appeared well in advance of residential development—GE Aerospace to King of Prussia, for example, or Grumman and the military-electronics company Hazeltine to rural Long Island. Tobin's tale, while not explaining the phenomenon explicitly, provided a context in which it makes sense.

In *Dead Cities*, Mike Davis, a left-wing historian, identified other connections between suburbia and the government's concern with nuclear holocaust—for example, that tests were conducted in the Nevada desert to determine what domestic structures could best withstand an atomic blast. That turned out to be the ranch house. Venetian blinds were also found to stand up to heat tests better than other shades. Whether these styles became popular in suburbia as a result of government influence on the housing industry Davis leaves unclear. An explicitly Cold War–related feature of suburbia that also had overt support from federal government authorities on civil defense was the family bomb shelter stocked with canned soup—a mini version of the suburban home, underground. This feature of civil defense entered the popular imagination at the time, and is to this day well remembered.

As a believer in the deep coherence between our landscapes and the evolving human condition, I had long wondered how the quietly domestic, famously conventional, and complacent culture of suburbia fit with the nuclear terror. Tobin's revelations were a partial answer. Davis's research on design features added a touch. To say it was satisfying to find the connection might seem an extreme indulgence of suburbophobia. But condemnation of suburbia is not where this connection takes me; the plotted trajectories of ready-to-fire missiles affected the meaning of all landscapes. Suburbia is the one that appeared during the Cold War and is therefore the one that most directly expresses that condition. We hardly escape the condition by rejecting suburbia. However, I do speculate that suburbophobia itself may have originated in an aversion to the Cold War reality, though subconsciously. The attitude is, after all, to this day the quirk of intellectuals, artists, and cosmopolitans—almost always politically progressive; we who tend to believe ourselves more sensitive, more perceptive than the "common man." Perhaps in this case we were. Perhaps while the thick-skinned "common man" got practical with his bomb shelter, we sensitive ones recoiled into denial of the shifting of responsibility for earthly hospitality into human hands, transferring our horror to suburbia rather than facing this development, a demonization that reinforced the romance with cities when that began to set in.

Collective psychoanalysis aside, Tobin, in connecting suburbia and a defensive reaction to the nuclear threat, and in identifying the government's overt defensive instinct for dispersion, does reveal that the radical reconfiguration of our landscape through suburbanization did, in part, reflect latent Cold War violence. In doing so, she broke through the impenetrable banality that became the perceived hallmark of suburbia. The Tobin story is hardly the only historical factor reflected in the suburban landscape, but once you have glimpsed that piece it seems integral and even, in a way, enlivening. To back up and leave it out impoverishes the scene.

As both the dangers and the range of radiation became better understood, the whole idea of civil defense melted away before its evident futility. In the later '60s, the "plot" of nuclear holocaust as in *Dr. Strangelove* disappeared from literary novels and film, too, replaced by catastrophes of unspecific origin, which put apocalypse at an emotional distance, making it allegorical. Clearly historical memory also blipped out the connection between government support of decentralized development and nuclear threat. For as long as Cold War conditions prevailed, after all, to remember would only be to remind ourselves of how vulnerable we actually were, with no alternative solution on hand. Even bomb shelters were forgotten as the arms race increased the scale of possible apocalypse to a point where you didn't want to be reminded of it by obviously inadequate boltholes.

By the 1980s, the purely domestic nature of suburbia, alongside its economic dependence on the city, began to change, too. As corporate offices began to appear out in what had been thought of as suburban sprawl, as the famous one-way pattern of the rush hour into the city in the morning and out of it in the evening was getting shuffled into traffic in all directions at almost all times, as the looser, haphazard, fall-as-it-may atopian pattern of postindustrial development, a flying wardrobe of all possibilities, was tossed farther and farther from the old central city—past the beltways, sometimes all the way to the next beltway—the pattern of perfect dispersal wished for by defense officials in the early days of the Cold War began to be realized to an extent far greater than had been imaginable before. What this reflected was that in this new age work could be done anywhere. Theoretically, at least, the perfect dispersal wished for as the perfect defense was becoming possible just as the Cold War was about to end. Actually, business success in the global economy, according to Garreau, requires an international airport no more than a half hour away: not a city but the ability to leave in a trice that cities provide.

Somewhere along the way in this long history, a loathing of cities, once the posture of political idealists concerned with the conditions in which the poor lived, took root in mainstream suburban culture, alongside a political evolution in the conservative direction. As suburban sprawl evolved into metropolitan areas that were more and more independent of cities—drawing enterprise as well as population out, further dooming cities—progressive dislike of the decentralized settlement pattern intensified. The rise of environmental concerns only reinforced this aversion: it became a powerful structure of feeling. For their part metro dwellers were increasingly able to avoid cities altogether as they threaded their ever more personal routes through their Alice in Wonderland landscape in which urban amenities like restaurants and shopping opportunities were ever more available. (Indeed stores associated with suburban malls were invading the city.) A saving stroke of genius on the part of urbanists in the late 1980s was to give up the dream of restoring cities to dominance, to overcome their disapproval of spreawlian, and to make the argument that metropolitan areas could not survive with black holes at their center. By casting cities as entertainment centers for the metropolitan area, they shifted the antiurban attitude into a vision of city as funfair. In many cases, this strategy has been so successful that the old one-way suburban rush hour has reappeared on weekends as metro dwellers travel into cities for a day of entertainment, and out again, often late into the night.

The need for a defensive pattern of dispersal in response to the nuclear threat is long past. If there is a defensive reason for dispersal today, it has to do with terrorist attacks—a new danger reflecting the closeness of all the world in our tightly netted global enclosure. Though lethal in limited ways, terrorism depends on the fear it instigates rather than actual damage, which, as nations go, is minimal. For maximum effect, dramatic, symbolic targets are required, and these are still to be found principally in the compact old city. Our scattered atopian landscapes, in contrast, tend to have few symbolic landmarks. In this they represent the best possible defensive settlement pattern for an age of terrorism. It is a defensive pattern that is the exact opposite of the walled city—and yet its descendant. Neither planners nor defense experts have focused on this, as far as I know, but firms that had had offices in the World Trade towers didn't need directing. Having been attracted to the towers for their prestige in the global theater, many dispersed outward into the metro area after the attack. After all, they didn't really need to be in the city. Spreawlian was much safer, though I am guessing that accessibility to the entertainment center of New York was essential to attracting and holding talented young employees.

That this scatteredness is a defense against both nuclear attack and contemporary terrorism is not a total coincidence, vastly different in consequences though these acts of aggression might be. Both express the condition of global enclosure that, militarily speaking, has replaced the city wall. The military armature of that enclosure was inaugurated by the Cold War of which our present armature of electronic communications was, at the beginning, a part. That one is so violent and the other so peaceful lifts the matter of the changes in our world out of the realm of good and evil, exposing the shift in the relationship of ourselves to our surroundings as a matter to be understood in itself, outside the realm of morality, or of fear: as a matter, one might say, of art, of form; of imaginative adjustment.

come up with a plan. The Gallatin plan, Lacey writes, "would have bound together the Union with roads and waterways linking the entire national domain as of 1808, tying it into a whole, including the Northwest and Louisiana Territories which were under federal jurisdiction, and the most advanced projects that were underway within . . . the states." This, he wrote in another passage, would form "an intricate interconnected system of transport and communication that bound together every state and territory east of the Mississippi."

Because the Constitution allocated power over territory to the states, Jefferson had already asked Congress to draw up an internal improvements amendment to the Constitution permitting the federal government to make this kind of plan across state lines. The need for this was something on which fierce adversaries agreed. But after that initial request, no further pressure came from the White House. Both the Gallatin plan and the amendment initiative died.

Something similar happened with James Madison, Jefferson's immediate successor. During the debates over the Constitution, in *Federalist* No. 14, Madison had argued that the central government should have authority over planning. As president, he strongly supported a bill for a national internal-improvements plan overseen by Washington. Nevertheless, as Lacey puts it, "to the surprise of all, on his last day in office, Madison vetoed the bill on constitutional grounds, declaring his support for its objectives, but insisting that an amendment to the Constitution was necessary first." President James Monroe, Madison's successor, in his turn, supported the measure, but got cold feet at the last minute, too, calling for an internal improvements amendment and then vetoing a bill establishing funding for it. Some uncoordinated federal efforts had already begun, such as building the Cumberland Road, but Monroe, with regret, also vetoed a bill that would have enabled the government to finance the road by collecting tolls—again on the grounds that there was no internal improvements amendment to the Constitution. While his lengthy veto message was largely a catalog of rebuttals to arguments for federal planning powers, he ended it with a passionate call for an amendment that would give the central government those powers, saying that the benefits would be "almost incalculable." Lacey notes that all three of these presidents were slaveholders, whose way of life was protected by state sovereignty, and that to shift power over land use to the federal government would implicitly weaken that protection. So far this is unproven, but it's a theory that fits. Rationally, each believed that the federal government ought to have control over land use, but, at the eleventh hour, one after the other, as if caught in an undertow, could not bring himself to see it through, passionate as each was about the need.

John Quincy Adams, Monroe's successor, who had been an active proponent of federal planning powers as a senator, was, as president, unambivalent as to the need and believed no amendment was necessary. But, by the time Adams was president, the political climate had changed. A populist movement had arisen, fueled by anger at the emergent northern industrial elite. Populists feared that a federal government given land-use powers would be manipulated by the mercantile barons to their own ends, to the detriment of the common people. The angry mood ran strong. Adams was unable to get a planning measure through Congress. He ran for a second term against the populist Andrew Jackson, whose movement had from the beginning virulently opposed the "American system," as the idea of nationwide, federally directed development was known. Jackson won the 1828 election: there would be no federal oversight of industrial development in the United States.

The reasons behind these successive failures to vest planning powers in the central government were many and complicated, Lacey points out. At the beginning of his piece, he attributes the ambivalence of Jefferson, Madison, and Monroe to an unresolved resistance in their mind to cooperative federalism, a vision of close collaboration between the state and federal governments, versus dual federalism that envisioned the two levels of government, state and federal, from operating independently—even in opposition to each other at times. Despite well understanding the obvious benefits of a cooperative system, Jefferson, Madison, and Monroe were instinctively attracted to dual federalism, in a way that was not, Lacey suggests, closely examined. He leaves it unsaid that the instinct might have had its roots in fear that the slaveholding way of life would become vulnerable under cooperative federalism. We don't know what lay behind that instinct and, for sure, it was not one thing. But at the end of this part of his history he writes of the one president involved in the issue who was not a slaveholder, that "Adams attributed the failure of national planning ultimately to the underlying problem of race." Lacey then quotes an address Adams made to his congressional constituents in 1842 (he served in the House of Representatives after being president), in which he clearly identified a link between the failure of the planning initiative and slavery, describing first how such powers would have generated prosperity, and how this, in turn, would have created a kind of political popularity for the Federal powers that would have weakened beliefs in state sovereignty. "And then the undying worm of conscience twinges with terror for the fate of *the peculiar institution*. [A southern euphemism.] Slavery stands aghast at the prospective promotion of the general welfare, and flies to nullification [states' rights] for defense against the energies of freedom, and the inalienable rights of man."

With federal planning powers dead, we still faced the dilemma of how to build a national infrastructure. By default, the job fell to the states. But without coordination from above, the states failed miserably. Legislators jockeyed for road and canal routes that favored local interests rather than interstate efficiency. Some roads didn't even

while dooming a whole roster of places, from cities down to small
towns, that were passed by. But there was a certain order in this nonetheless; it served industrial work. The hand of work, therefore, as had
been true since the beginning of time, was still designing the landscape, not only in the creation of transcontinental railroad routes,
which dramatically redesigned the nation, but in the character of
the industrial city—for example, the emergence of extensive residential neighborhoods in which domestic life was separated from noisy
polluting factories. The size of newly central cities itself reflected the
manpower needed to run the factories, as did semideserted rural areas. Suburbs, in turn, were laid out in concentric circles around those
cities as factory work moved to city edges. While the hand of man was
perhaps a lot more forceful in this age, it was still in close collaboration with nature, or that which had been provided: the ore in the hills,
rivers for the factory processes, and later cheap land at edge of cities
to accommodate the assembly line and the forklift—tools of work.
The grand archetypes of city and country held, with those parts of the
country capable of production on a scale equal to feeding the cities becoming ever more industrial themselves. But still, there was in this a
strong grammar of collaboration with the underlying order of nature.
Meanwhile, though in many ways man was subjugating nature with
tools that extended the power of muscle, the Romantic movement got
busy representing the magnificent mystery of nature, and the older
forms of pastoral life, powerfully asserting the sensibility of transcendence, and the importance of awe, while deploring the predations of
industrialism as the opposite of those. We now romanticize the obsolete landscapes of industrial times, because, to us, by comparison
with our present situation, they represent a collaboration between the
hand of man and the hand of nature: what landscapes have always
been. For us, the abandoned city on the river, the millworks against
the sunset, are scenes of a kind of connection that we are hard put to
find in the landscapes contemporary work is creating.

There is no such link between the physical world and the kind of work that reigns today, work that is done with tools that extend the powers of mind rather than muscle and therefore has no particular relationship to place. We still exist in bodies, so we have to do this work somewhere, but the patterns created as we do so are haphazard—can be anything. The hand of work, in other words, has been withdrawn from the design of landscape. Or, to put it another way, the design of landscape is up to us alone. This is a new role we have not yet learned to fill, especially here in America, where we have never developed a strong sense of collective responsibility for our physical environment. As a result, most of our contemporary landscapes are haphazard, seemingly meaningless in comparison to older places, but in fact directly expressing our new way of work, this new separation, and the worldwide collapsed space in which we have come to live. It's right there before us in the atopian scene.

With the designing hand of work withdrawn, we also, for the first time, see the full effect of the Founding Fathers' failure to establish central planning powers and responsibilities—the absence of the hand of the central government in land planning reflecting the interests of perpetuating slavery to at least some degree. With no hand of work to make order, we see that lapse clearly at play for the first time. In the resulting chaos, in other words, the chaos of atopia, we see slavery at play. There are many other factors but there is that too. If one adds into that the also shadowy but decentralizing momentum of nuclear defense, a complex mirror of ourselves as a culture comes into view. In one sense our atopian landscape is just laissez-faire without the hand of work. But if I refer back to the lesson of those grand American nineteenth-century paintings, so boring in the very beauty of their subjects until one saw the tensions in the scenes on the canvas—that is to say, the underlying depredations of industrialism and the divisiveness of slavery as civil war loomed—then I can see through the seeming banality and even ugliness in our

contemporary landscape to a similar underlayer of vitalizing meaning. There I find a dramatic, unpredictable, and even moving expression of our predicament today, a scene that pulses with the two ways
in which we are a truly exceptional nation, our history of slavery and
our role in the introduction of nuclear weapons to the world. There
I find the tragedy of human nature, but also, its ability to question
itself, its promise. These haphazard secenes reflect another kind of
preservation, you might say, a slow building role of landscape in our
self-understanding, a harboring of revelations that appear only when
we need to take on new registers of national identity: waiting until
we are ready.

Herbert Hoover's Hand

A last bit of history lies curled inside the evolution of suburbia, one
in which the federal government did in fact have a directly shaping
hand in the creation of the suburban landscape of the mature industrial age, but under cover of boosting the economy, without a sense of
responsibility for the physical results, much less the impact of those
on society. Llewellyn Park in West Orange, New Jersey, designed by
A. J. Davis in 1957, and Frederic Law Olmsted's Riverside, Illinois,
are generally acknowledged as laying down the suburban ideal. Both
were for the wealthy with a cultivated pastoral appearance, albeit in
different ways. Lewellyn Park had a more rustic character, and is said
to have been a model for Olmsted's Central Park. Riverside is more
obviously landscaped. Other planned communities followed, on up
into the twentieth century. This is a well-known history.

A less well-known part of the story is haphazard and individu-
alistic in spirit. It begins with the introduction of the balloon frame
in Chicago in the 1830s. As opposed to age-old post-and-beam construction, made of heavy timber, the balloon frame was light, made

of two-by-fours on which walls could be hung. The idea of walls hung on a frame rather than weight bearing would be the radical innovation that, together with manufactured steel, later made skyscrapers possible. But the technique instigated another landscape-altering effect. As Kenneth Jackson notes in *Crabgrass Frontier*, two men could erect a home using the balloon frame, and many immigrants in this way were able to construct their own free-standing dwellings in the city, using light two-by-fours and nails. Nails are essential to balloon-frame construction and as mass-produced nails became progressively cheaper in the decades after the Civil War, home building by individuals with one helping hand became ever more possible.

Two other developments converged after the war. First, as Dolores Hayden tells it in *Building Suburbia*, was the invention of the mail-order kit, popularized by Sears, Roebuck, which made it even easier to construct your own house. The second was that railroad companies began to make a killing on real estate by buying up land before they laid rails, whereupon the value would shoot up. Because the locomotive took time to get up to speed and more time to stop, these early suburbs along railroads tended to be a few miles apart with open country in between. Before the age of the automobile, all houses had to be within walking distance of the station, giving these first suburbs the qualities a traditional settlement: they were relatively compact and surrounded by country. Most of the railroad commuter lines served wealthy suburbs. When the electric trolley companies came along, they, too, saw a big opportunity in real estate speculation, developing commuter lines after buying up land, and selling it to the "common man" who could avail himself of a mail-order kit. Sears actually offered mortgages, though the mortgages did not cover building costs and had balloon payments at the end. Foreclosure was common. Trolleys could stop and start easily so that, while development clustered around stations, stops were much closer to each other. Builders got into the act, developing tracts of mail-order houses. In the 1890s, banks began to cautiously issue short-term mortgages: long-term loans were forbidden by law. Building and loan associations grew up. Mail-order houses came in a variety of styles and were often erected haphazardly, creating chaotic, unregulated scenes quite unlike the railroad suburbs. Though land was plentiful, because trolleys required a certain volume of traffic for profitable operation, the standard lot size was one-tenth of an acre. This was a movement tailored to people of modest means. As Kenneth Jackson puts it, "For the first time in the history of the world, middle-class families in the late nineteenth century could reasonably expect to buy a detached home on an accessible lot in a safe and sanitary neighborhood." It was this more reasonably priced type of development that would be the model for twentieth-century postwar suburbia to come, including discrimination: African Americans built their own homes in the cities but were excluded from purchasing real estate along the rail and trolley lines.

After the automobile became available, development was freed from the rails, and suburbs did begin to develop in concentric rings around the city. But home building slowed down during the Depression, and ways of life change slowly in any event: the popular preference for the city remained strong. Suburbanization would not go mainstream until after World War II and even then it seemed improbable to the officials who wanted to get people out of cities for reasons of defense.

Republicans, however, took an interest in suburban development as early as the 1920s. A leader in this regard was Herbert Hoover, a man committed to fostering economic growth. His great vision was that housing could be a national industry. The land outside cities was by far the more likely arena for big business home building, but an obstacle was that each municipality had its own building codes. This made construction the purview of local contractors who knew the ropes. In effect, local codes kept building local, whether you were an individual building from a kit or a contractor. Hoover envisioned standardized codes that would open the way for his vision of housing as big business. Toward that end, he helped form an organization called Better Homes in America, of which he became president.

When Warren Harding became president of the United States in 1921, he made Hoover secretary of commerce. As secretary, Hoover kept up his involvement in Better Homes, serving on its National Council. Hoover described Better Homes as "a sort of collateral arm to the Housing Division of the Department of Commerce." Dolores Hayden calls Better Homes "a coalition of over seven thousand local growth machines composed of bankers, builders, and manufacturers supporting government aid to private real estate development as a national economic strategy to boost consumption."

So here was the federal government meddling in land use, but through the back door and with no accountability for the physical results of that meddling. It was all about aiding the growth of big business and stimulating consumption. Did anyone see in this a strategy to boost Republican votes? I found no evidence that this was so but it had that effect. The Democrats had a political lock on the cities. But sometimes people switched parties when moving to the suburbs as a way of leaving behind an immigrant past, with which the corrupt city machines were associated. I am speculating—my evidence is mere shreds here and there. But it makes sense that to move to the affordable suburbs was a way to move up into a more American, more privileged identity, and becoming Republican would be one way to reinforce that. What clearly motivated Hoover, however, was promoting a national housing industry, and as secretary of commerce he furthered that vision by seeing to it that the national building codes which made the creation of mass-produced suburbia possible were established.

There was, actually, some thought on Hoover's part about what the physical character of suburbia should be. Under his leadership at

Commerce, the department issued model zoning ordinances that encouraged local governments to separate commercial and residential establishments, and to exclude multiple dwellings. The Hooverian ideal would become the archetype after World War II. In the meantime, an organization called the National Association of Real Estate Boards was lobbying for two measures Hoover favored: federal guarantees of mortgages and building loans, and for mortgage-interest payments to be tax deductible. At this time mortgages were still short-term: the standard loan being for from five to ten years, advancing one-third to one-half of the value of the home. For all the optimism of the do-it-yourself movement, these financial restrictions were a deterrent. In 1929, Hoover became president of the United States. Then the crash came and the Hooverian vision went on hold, though he got a few measures through, including a bill to establish a federal credit reserve to back up mortgage lenders to builders—a way to create jobs in home construction: that was the rationale. Then, in November 1932 he was swept out of office by an FDR landslide.

To a new president who had inherited a desperate economy, there were attractive aspects of the Hooverian vision: that accelerating home building might create jobs, first of all. The idea of development outside of cities was also appealing: it was an opportunity to relieve pressure on the cities and also to implement progressive visions starting from scratch, although the visions themselves were different from Hoover's. The New Dealers wanted new towns set in rural landscapes with clear borders, offering factory jobs and other opportunities to work, and with a variety of housing. Few were built: Greenbelt, Maryland; Greendale, Wisconsin; Arthurdale, West Virginia; and Greenhills, Ohio, are the best known. The towns meant to serve as models for a nationwide pattern of development that would check the growth of monstrously large cities, in which it was almost impossible to maintain health and social services. Rex Tugwell, an economist with a specialty in planning, was the New Dealer behind the conception, which reflected the planning consensus of the time. The "Tugwell towns" were also deemed by some critics as "communistic boondoggles." In retrospect the Tugwell town looks pretty good—as against what happened later.

A New Deal measure that did shape the future was the federally backed mortgage, a policy that Hoover had taken some steps to establish. In 1933 FDR got bipartisan support for his own version, in the form of the Home Owners' Loan Corporation (HOLC), which refinanced "tens of thousands of mortgages in danger of default or foreclosure" according to Kenneth Jackson's account, and even reversed foreclosure in many cases. This was government getting into housing for the first time, in response to widespread homelessness brought on by the Depression, and it was aimed at urban homes: the Emergency Farm Mortgage Act authorized a similar agency for rural foreclosures. According to Jackson, "between 1933 and 1935 alone, the HOLC supplied $3 billion for over one million mortgages, or loans for one tenth of all owner occupied non-farm residences in the United States." These mortgages were different from what had been available from the private sector in the 1920s, short-term loans that required a home owner to reborrow, an impossibility if the money market was tight, and one of the causes of foreclosures. The HOLC loans were twenty years in duration, with set payments distributed over the term of the loan, calculated to entirely pay off the loan by the end.

This went a long way toward stabilizing home ownership for many ordinary Americans: while aimed at urban home owners, this type of mortgage would be essential to the growth of suburbia after the war. But who would get mortgages on these terms? The government was taking risks with the long terms that banks were not willing to take: how to assess candidates responsibly? After all, it would be the taxpayer who would be left holding the bag if home owners defaulted. Standards would have to be universal: a method of appraisal applied in one place should be the same as in another. And those standards would be the taxpayers' protection against foreclosures.

But the government had no housing experts, no experience. So the New Dealers turned to the part of the private sector that did have experience, namely, the bankers. An elaborate, four-tiered system was developed that determined loan-worthiness based not only on the individual applicant's ethnicity and occupation, and the state of repair of his home, but also the neighborhood in which the home in question was located, the predominant ethnicity, and the general state of the housing stock there, apart from the home in question. Four categories were devised, with desirability identified, in declining order by numbers and letters but, most famously, colors: green, blue, yellow, and red. Because the two divisions were "city" and "country," suburban candidates fell under "city." Bankers had favored the suburban environments as lower risk, especially for new homes, because of ease of building on farmland, which had good drainage and was far from the dangers of urban decay. So the ideal (green) candidate was white with a new home on the outskirts of the city. In retrospect we can see the postwar suburban explosion loaded into the future in the HOLC provisions. We can see a federal government with no land-use powers putting in place a mechanism that would bring about landscape changes more extensive than any I can think of implemented by a government in the history of the world but done blindly, without thoughts to the effects on the existing landscape, let alone on the ways those physical changes would reconfigure society.

Of the ways in which society was changed, from the vantage of hindsight the racial restriction was the most fateful aspect of this dependence on the bankers' rules of thumb for home loans. What is most tragic in retrospect is how much power the government had at this point to actually change the course of our history with respect to race. I have found no trace of anyone in the New Deal registering the injustice of this, much less a sense of progressive possibility in dropping the racial restriction. Eleanor Roosevelt objected to segregation everywhere, including in the Works Progress Administration, but not, insofar as I have been able to determine, to the implicit segregation built into the HOLC loans. Historians tell me that to do so would have been so far beyond the common sense of the time as to have seemed ridiculous. But the New Dealers did not stick religiously to the bankers' template in other respects. The long-term mortgage, for example, was a risky innovation only the government could shoulder. It's also true that, at that point, large numbers of black southerners, put out of work by the invention of the cotton picker, were only then beginning their migration to northern industrial cities. So it was perhaps not so easy to foresee how black those cities would become, let alone the mass impact on black residents of northern cities of these exclusive standards. It remains that black urban applications would systematically be rated red on several counts—ethnicity, neighborhood, and state of repair of surrounding homes. The government continued to redline black inner city areas until the middle 1960s, by which time it had become very obvious what the effects were—and that they were greatly accelerating urban decline and social isolation. Unrealistic as it might be to wish the New Dealers had been more foresightful, I can't help imagining how different postwar history would have been if the government had changed the bankers' standards with respect to race. To the extent that white flight from the neighborhoods where the newcomers got a footing was motivated not by racism but by fear that the value of the homes in those neighborhoods would go down, that fear was realistic, because decline in value was institutionalized by government standards that systematically excluded candidates, including white candidates, whose homes were in neighborhoods where African Americans lived.

Many, in government and out, believed that when World War II was over the Depression would set in again. Millions of returning GIs who would need jobs were a factor in this prediction. So when

Truman succeeded FDR, generating work was a high priority. At hand was the Hooverian idea that a national housing industry would boost the economy, along with the mortgage program—all set for building outside of cities. By this time, many city dwellers, disturbed by the influx of black southerners or, fearing that the value of their property would sink because of their presence, were far more inclined than formerly to consider suburban living. When Eisenhower took office, the fear of depression was still strong, and he, too, viewed the housing industry as a stimulus. He was also, as we have seen, very focused on the need to get people out of cities for defense reasons.

As a result of this concern, the Housing Act of 1954 required all government agencies whose work had any bearing on housing to use their powers to reduce "vulnerability of congested urban areas to nuclear attack." Redlining, of course, helped insure that new housing would not be built in cities, though I know of no affirmative acknowledgment of this. Ike also initiated construction of the interstate highway system as another big way to create jobs, and defensive dispersion was an overt purpose here, too. According to Kathleen Tobin, when Eisenhower signed the Interstate Highway Act, in 1956, he observed that "in case of atomic attack on our key cities, the road net must permit quick evacuation of target areas." The interstate system, of course, greatly facilitated suburbanization, a form of permanent evacuation from cities, making it possible to commute from much farther out into urban centers. Tobin mentions a later shift toward "circumferential highways" that would allow traffic to bypass urban areas in case of attack, as well as encouraging industry and residential development farther away from cities: the beltway pattern that has become a standard feature of our landscape. Industry was actively encouraged to leave the city, bringing jobs close to if not into suburbs, seeding the landscape of the succeeding era—our atopian time— with the earliest corporate émigrés from the urban downtowns. That white homeowners wanted to get away from black neighbors is well

design. Their brave experiment reveals the pitfalls and paradoxes of taking on the landscape solo. To suggest actually building in evil sprawl defied the very strong structure of feeling among architects and urbanists at the time. To embrace traditional aesthetics on top of that was almost suicidally heretical. The association of traditional designs with class-stratified societies of the past—the old ideology of the modernist architectural aesthetic—was still strong enough to tar the New Urbanists with political conservatism, not a popular association in a generally progressive profession. But Duany and Plater-Zyberk argued that we have built well in the past, that we love our old places, and that we should let them guide our hand; that these new designs would be both practical and beautiful; that, being compact, they were easier on the natural environment and, in mixing levels of income, were also more democratic and community-fostering than the standard, homogenous suburban enclave. The New Urbanists put their money where their mouth was and actually went out and built in atopia, getting their hands dirty, as it were, and making money, too, giving opponents the opportunity to brand them as merely greedy. But that was not all they did. They continued to develop their ideas and held yearly "congresses" to which, despite all the resistance, there was an enormous and enthusiastic response by architects and planners of various aesthetic leanings. At the two I attended the very air was electric. If nothing else, the response to the New Urbanist congresses revealed on the part of all sorts of people involved with our physical surroundings a wide and deep desire for an arena in which to grapple with the question of how to build in our new era. The congresses perhaps fell short of their full potential because of a doctrinaire tendency on the part of the New Urbanists, a resistance to ideas other than their own, but that is perhaps to quibble with what was an enormously constructive initiative.

As for what those ideas were, the New Urbanist vision was in some ways similar to that of the New Deal planners, favoring variety in home size and clear edges to developments, for example. The newer ideal, however, was intensively traditionalist, drawing directly on a variety of American models, from eighteenth-century settlements like Georgetown to Victorian seaside towns. Duany had a reputation as a micromanager, and indeed the New Urbanist rule book was fat and reached down into tiny details, such as the permitted width of streets, the inclusion of corner stores, even if they had to be subsidized, and suggesting, further, seemingly happenstantial elements, such as that an old dog be acquired to sleep on the floor of the store for atmosphere. Masters of imitation, the New Urbanists could also convincingly re-create the intricate variety that place acquires as it naturally evolves—the odd scrap of land that serves as an impromptu passage, the quirkily shaped barn turned into a residence that gives character to a corner, the eccentric placement of a cottage next door to an attached town house. Moreover, they got it right to the point of blurring the line between the real thing and the imitation: to the point that it can be hard to tell the difference.

The most famous New Urbanist developments are both in Florida: the resort town of Seaside, which to my eye is mostly Edgartown, Martha's Vineyard, and Celebration, which draws heavily on traditional 1920s-era Florida Panhandle towns, although it included houses in coastal, classical, colonial revival, and French Normandy styles. Both Seaside and Celebration were privately owned, so that elaborate New Urbanist zoning restrictions could be imposed without interference. Celebration, however, was sponsored by the Disney company using New Urbanist principles, and some of it was shoddily built. In contrast, deep thought and care went into Seaside. Everything about it declared it was the real thing. Hollywood captured what is disturbing in that eerie authenticity. In the movie *The Truman Show*, the town is actually a stage set, although Truman, the hero, played by Jim Carrey, doesn't know that. He thinks it's a real town. Nor does he realize that America is watching his life on TV.

The movie is witty. Why is it that it almost seemed too easy to send up Seaside in this way?

Some criticize New Urbanist developments for being like Disneyland, which is accurate in that they have a fantasy quality about them: you feel you are in a cute world in which there is no dark side and everyone is nice. But Disneyland settings would never be mistaken for reality. The castle in the Orlando Disney park is clearly cartoonish, the Western street undersized in a way that lets you know it's for fun. In contrast, Celebration, built nearby, strives to be as close as possible to a real old-fashioned town. The same is true—even more so—of Seaside. The Truman show stretches credibility not in that Truman believed that his town was real but that one doubts a stage set could be as good as Seaside. And yet it was in fact fabricated from whole cloth as a stage set is. In a New Urbanist environment, the visitor knows it's real, of course, but almost automatically wonders, "Could this be true?" As if fearing one might be a fool like the deceived Truman, one's eye scans for signs of inauthenticity. Slips are not easy to spot. The New Urbanists are masters at what charms us in the old world. If you care a lot about those charms, though—if you think their age and slowly acquired beauty means something—you don't like being fooled. You don't want to know that these seemingly mysterious qualities can be successfully faked. So well do the New Urbanists capture what we yearn for—that which is disappearing from the world—that, almost enragedly, I, for one, can become obsessed in one of their environments with trying to pinpoint how they have failed.

Though much of the architectural establishment was resistant to New Urbanism, postmodern starchitects had been moving toward an imitative aesthetic too, though in an ironic mode. Most famous perhaps is Phillip Johnson's "Chippendale Building," a skyscraper topped with a motif taken from classic eighteenth-century cabinetry. It went up in midtown Manhattan in 1980, a hoot for the skyline and a radical departure from the modernist stricture against ornament. Michael Graves's work was less funny but nevertheless playfully ornamental while remaining modernist in tone. This trend was followed by a straightforward embrace of traditional proportions and motifs, especially by Robert Stern, who borrowed from classic design without irony, sometimes whole hog, a practice repudiated by some in the architectural establishment as "Disneyfication," the same charge leveled at New Urbanism. New Urbanism is essentially a planning approach, a vision of how whole communities should look as opposed to the single great building, but it is at this point that trends in mainstream architecture came close to converging with scorned New Urbanism: indeed both Michael Graves and Robert Stern contributed to Celebration. There is nothing simple about the swirl of resistance and defiance, of snobbery and fear, around New Urbanist design.

Suspicions of crypto-conservativism notwithstanding, people who bought into Celebration, in particular, shared the progressive aspect of New Urbanist ideals—they wanted a community and a diverse one at that, economically and ethnically. The whole New Urbanist idea, after all, was a rebellion against classic suburbia. But economic diversity was difficult to achieve, because New Urbanist construction is expensive. As for ethnic diversity, middle-class African American prospects were scarce, which suggests that somehow an old Southern town might not be an attractively humanistic model to all people.

It's fun to make fun of the New Urbanists. My favorite poison-pen jab is to call them the Ralph Lauren of architecture; another is to describe what they do as a Shake 'n Bake of good taste. But I have come to know that this hostility really expresses my own resistance to our movement into a new age and the loss of a sense of safety in place that that entails. While offering a kind of homage to all we have loved in place, the New Urbanists actually deepen our sense of exposure in an uncanny way. In the very perfection of their imitations, they only underscore what is no longer available: the designing hand of work and the complex levels of meaning worlds built by it have. New Urbanist developments do not have those layers of meaning. But this is not, I think, the fault of the New Urbanists.

The power of architectural computer programs is partially accountable for the ability of New Urbanist designers to produce large, varied settlements at less than astronomical cost. It's a power that can be seen less artfully used all over atopia. Where previously architectural ideas had to develop from nothing, pencil meeting blank paper, with computer programs all possibilities are right there at an architect's fingertips, instantly realizable on the screen, ready to be manipulated according to any whim. CAD, as the program is called, is actually supposed to be a drafting tool, not a design tool, but it gives a sense of its capacity that with it anybody can design a house. Well-heeled newlyweds who have never given a thought to design can sit down with a contractor and choose a Tudor façade, a Palladian library, a Victorian porch in back. They can even arrange furniture in the rooms if they want to. (The contractor has a licensed architect somewhere in the offing to put an official seal on the plan.) In amateur uses of traditional motifs, a kind of indecision can linger in the results, sometimes giving the impression of a trick house in which you wouldn't be totally surprised if the living room snapped up into a wall and the ceiling came down with a kitchen. The smorgasbord approach in itself is not new. An architect friend points to eighteenth-century Englishmen returning from the Grand Tour and ordering up, as he put it, "a Venetian dining room, a library based on Pompei, and a drawing room in Louis XIV." Well, yes. But, again, the sheer ease of implementation, so great that even untrained people can do it, changes the contemporary version. There is an almost thoughtless discontinuity in many contemporary smorgasbords, an offhandedness: it might be traditional but doesn't really seem to be reminding us of anything, much less expressing reverence. I remember one I happened to visit that definitely had that do-it-yourself feel, though who knows? The feature that really stayed with me was a door in a Palladian library—a room with vast shelves but almost zero books, and a little too narrow and too high to be comfortable—that gave on to a vast pool in a churchlike enclosure: perfect atopia.

There is a difference in quality between communities designed in this way and those that were not, but even among those that came into being in the CAD era there can be a huge difference. Seaside, for all its eerie perfection, was actually the work of many offices, the coherence of the ultimate design evolving out of rigorous guidelines. Much easier for one office to design a whole community and CAD certainly facilitates that. But over time it seems to me that ease has prevailed over difficulty, over deep thought, that a certain absence of creative intensity—of the struggle entailed in making something out of nothing—has left architecture somehow not mattering the way it once did. Even when a building is designed by an aesthetically brilliant architect, and there are plenty of those, the rejected possibilities can hang in the air, a tiny telltale aura of "whatever," a sense that in the end it doesn't matter whether the designer chose classic, Spanish, or edgy modern. This gives even imperious buildings a strangely lightweight air. You can see that "whatever" in masterpieces sometimes, though you have to look hard: it's much more obvious in the junk that makes no attempt to hide its arbitrariness. New Urbanist architecture is so meticulously nailed down style-wise that often it takes hard work to spot the "whatever." To put it another way, a lot of thought goes into their work and it's this that produces the verisimilitude that provokes dislike. Maybe it's our capacity for reproduction itself, implicit in New Urbanist environments, that upsets us by telling us that the world has changed and there is nothing outside ourselves to relate to as we design: no dance between us and what is given, no wild blue yonder in our circumstance, no blank page on which aesthetic transcendence can appear if we open ourselves to it, making it harder to forget that we live an enclosed environment of our own extended minds.

Kentlands is a New Urbanist development in the Baltimore–Washington Metropolitan Area. One day, when I was living in Georgetown, I headed out there. It's a big development in the municipality of Gaithersburg, Maryland, not far from I-270, the multilane artery that takes you north through rural Montgomery toward Pennsylvania. Kentlands consists of big-porched wooden Victorian-style houses with heavily Georgetown-like sections, too. In the period I visited, it was still partially under construction, which was steadying, in that you could see plainly that it was make-believe, not the real thing. Still, I had to scan for tell-tales in the completed sections. The only one I could spot was that town-house windows were actually single sheets of glass that were made to look as if they consisted of many panes by pretend mullions pasted on from inside.

This querulous nit-picking made me feel ungenerous, for Kentlands was downright lovely. Large maples had been left standing, and they blazed on that fine October day. Back alleys, created to keep cars out of the way, gave streets a quiet located feeling. Late-blooming flowers grew in small front yards, some surrounded by a picket fence. But there was almost no one about on those quiet streets on a fine autumn weekend. For all its loveliness, after a while this wholesome place began to take on a noir quality, as in movies in which you know murder is about to happen in the sunny scene.

I visited Kentlands several times, and each time I was enchanted at first and then after about four hours claustrophobia would set in. Though large sections looked uncannily like Georgetown, this sense of suffocation never happened to me at home. I wondered why. I went out there with an architect once. She began to have the same claustrophobic feeling: she wanted to get to the edge of it, she said. So we found our way there and saw, well, normal hodgepodge atopian sprawl. She pinned what was wrong with New Urbanism on the fact that it doesn't solve the larger landscape problem. The style of Kentlands suggests a classic landscape lies around it, but it doesn't. Really, Kentlands was just part of the sprawl, is what she said when we got to the edge. It's true that when you get to the edge you see how deeply fake it is. Sprawl is full of mismatched elements jumbled together: Kentlands was just one part of the jumble. I saw her point, but I also knew we were both fighting something in ourselves, not in Kentlands. After all, if you walk to the edge of Georgetown, other than the river side you find not a classic rural landscape but extending development, older than that around Kentlands perhaps, but outside-D.C. sprawl nonetheless.

Regularly, in flight from Kentlands after reaching the four-hour mark, I found myself actually glad to be on I-270, not a usual reaction for me. One time I turned off the highway into an ordinary development that manifested all that was deplorable in spreawlian: nearly identical houses of inflated size, on about half an acre each, one after another; conformity combined with excess. Two-car garages facing the street: no back alleys here. People were unloading groceries from their oversized SUVs in front of their houses. It was as if I—deep-dyed suburbophobe though I was—could finally breathe.

Strangest of all, however, was the effect on reentering George-town. The first time I expected the relief of the "real thing," because it is that, surely, in all its inimitable quirkiness: the motley pattern of old paint on brick, the ancient rose, the strange house with the ivy looking out at you through the windows. The New Urbanists, clever as they are, cannot reproduce that! (Don't count on it.) And yet, for a terrible but ineradicable five minutes, on my return, every time, Georgetown seemed to be Kentlands. Reverse colonization had taken place. Atopia triumphant.

An irony that befell the New Urbanist movement, as it also befell critics of malls, is that ordinary profit-driven commercial ventures, ever hungry for novelty, absorbed its ideas. Traditional design—though usually without the mixture of dwelling sizes or the finer quirky touches—has become the hallmark of high-end spreawlian developments. The tasteful enclave that the Duke had had a hand in, for example, with its large trees but no graveyards, was a New Urbanist knockoff. This is perhaps a good thing, in that the style, though more mechanically varied in commercial developments, is preferable to the monotony of industrial-age suburban sameness. But what this spread of ideas really brings home is the problem of planning from the top in the absence of the hand of work. The problem has to do with the limits of individual imagination. Enough of these knockoffs have appeared that we see that—varied, tasteful, communal, and overall brilliant as the New Urbanist template is— had we, by magic, suddenly developed strong land-use powers in our central government, and had that agency been turned to the New Urbanists, the most successful planners and designers of contemporary development, with a mandate to implement a responsible and aesthetically pleasing national landscape, we might all have ended up living in Andrés Duany's mind.

One day I decided to go to Haymarket. When learning about the Disney fight, I had pictured Haymarket as a picturesque little town in a classic Virginian landscape, well beyond the obvious encroachment of Balt–Wash. What I found was a threadbare place, rural but visibly more than half subsumed into global space already. I-66 roared close by; there was a strip mall on the periphery, the old rural center was in visible decline, and around it—and to an extent in it—a schizoid juxtaposition of metropolitan prosperity and rural poverty had grown up.

Several developments, built since the Disney fight, were New Urbanist knockoffs—Disneyfied, you could say. Fieldstone, Georgian windows, brass knockers, lanterns. Hispanic gardeners worked on "landscaping." Down the road, shacks, trailers, old cars in the yards. The hangover of extreme disappointment was strong. I felt sorry for the people of an economically stressed town who had come so close to a windfall. At the post office, SUVs and battered pickups. On the side streets some fine old wooden houses with porches and lawns, some 1950s-style bungalows sinking back into the greenery, and then a stretch—again—of spanking new town houses with round arch windows, black shutters, sidelights in the door frames.

In Haymarket a mixture of ennui and sorrow set in. There was the luxury, there was the trailer, there was the tasteful traditional stone building spanking new. I found a stretch of country road outside town: a sensation of quiet, the lines of collapsed stone walls running through the woods and the sound of a rushing stream. I got out of the car to drink it in and noticed a bit of brightness flashing through the trees: the stream perhaps. On closer look, this was the sun bouncing off cars on the interstate, the source of the sound I had taken for that of a stream. Some farming was going on: here a field dotted with bales, and next a turf farm where ready-made lawns were rolled up like carpet. I felt a jarred slipperiness of location, by now familiar. American emptiness, that threadbare feeling of that's all there is: our modern-day Hopper. The real thing.

4

The Inverted Cradle

Wherever I find myself, I like to figure out where I am, in the sense of the four points of the compass, in the sense of a spot on the map, but Towson was conducive to a subjective state in which orientation didn't matter. In my early years at the Sheraton, a whiff of location came through in the distinctive Baltimorean accent of the African American housekeeping staff, a sweetness conveying the funny, sorry loveliness of the human pickle and our connection to one another in it. All that in a simple "Good morning." The sight of the sun setting over the mall roof one evening told me I was looking west, which took me mentally to D.C., prompting the realization that I was in my old Balt–Wash schoolroom, of which Towson was a floating piece. More natural was to sink back into the dreamlike state of personal routes.

A dejected supermarket across an eight-lane intersection from the Sheraton offered basic supplies. One day I spotted some crab cakes in a deli there. They looked good, though the careless surroundings made me doubtful. The boy behind the counter told me that they were made on-site. He spoke about them with a solemnity that reminded me of watermen on the Eastern Shore of the Chesapeake. I asked the boy to heat two crab cakes. He was a little confused—the request wasn't usual. I am staying at the Sheraton, I explained. He saw my predicament. Pointing to a venerable, large, odd-looking steam device behind him, he said he couldn't guarantee that my crab cakes wouldn't explode if he put them in there. I said go ahead. It turned out all right. I took my crab cakes back across the intersection, all the way to my room, where I ate them in a throne-like office chair at my blond desk: simple and delicious—I was in the Chesapeake Bay region.

Once I realized I was close to the Eastern Shore, I got into the habit of visiting a friend out there in the middle of my Towson sojourns. There was, in the voyage, a sense of hurling myself across an abyss in a capsule. The capsule was a flimsy rental car. The abyss was a brutal bit of beltway. I'm a good driver, but on this trip I'd feel nervous. Probably this was just the dependency one develops living in a hotel for days on end: you don't do for yourself in a normal sense, and that engenders a feeling that you can't.

But then I would be across the Chesapeake and on back roads through fields in their August fullness, and I would lower the window and feel the good air on my face and see its easy movement through the full-grown corn and the soybeans, barns settled knowingly in the swales, silos gone hatless, sprouting out the top, others confabulated with mechanistic extensions: all an inland scene, sweet smelling, and then a flash of blue, and this always made me sit up in my little car. The blue would be a pond. From the pond would issue a stream. The stream would eventually widen into a tidal creek that would find its way to a small tidal river that would itself widen and then empty into a larger estuarial river that in its own turn would widen and flow into the bay. The bay itself was estuarial, fed by the Susquehanna River, its principal freshwater source with headwaters in Ostego Lake in upstate New York. As it approached the Bay, the Susquehanna widened dramatically, becoming estuarial, that is to say tidal, near Baltimore, where it flowed into the bay, a form taken by all the lesser rivers and even smaller creeks flowing into the bay, all the way down to Hampton Roads, the sea passage between the bottom of the Chesapeake peninsula and the mainland, where the bay meets the ocean.

My friend's house was on the Corsica, a middle-sized river. On arriving I would greet him, and we would chat. But as soon as politeness permitted I would put a kayak into the Corsica and head off downstream—not because I didn't want to see my host but because after a week in the Sheraton I felt subhuman and had to recover myself before I could really be present to his company. The Corsica there is in the dramatically widening stage. The headlands in the distance downstream on a sunny day are bright and inviting. Nevertheless, I would soon turn into the mouth of a smaller creek. The journey upstream would be the story in reverse, the serial narrowing of the Chesapeake formation. The allure is the source, the innermost place to which one is drawn as to a place of perfect peace and still awareness.

A long, narrow dock that had been picked up by a storm, twisted like a ribbon, and then set down again stretched nearly to the middle of the mouth of the creek in those years. At the outer end, ospreys had built a big, crazy-twigged nest. When there were chicks in the nest, the parents would frantically dive at a person passing nearby in a boat. Even when the nest was empty, I'd give the nest a wide berth, going for the far shore. All Chesapeake waters have been brown since plows were put to land, though the water near the far shore would look black, as in a woodland pond.

The shore itself was lakelike—grasses and wild irises, bees and butterflies. But the tides made their way in, secretly undermining trees until they fell over into the water, then lived on providing leafy bowers to passersby. Eventually dying, the trees then were stripped by the weather until they became silvery and essential, pointing outward over the creek with long-tapering fingers with which they made exquisitely precise points. Herons, extended through long necks to similarly didactic beaks, favored these preaching trees as perches and, being also gray, were so like the trees I didn't always see them until they rose creakily, with prehistoric croaks, and glided up the creek sublimely.

One Towson sojourn, I spotted a handwritten notice on an index card posted in a Starbucks about a lecture nearby, sponsored by the Chesapeake Bay Foundation (CBF). The notice was old, the lecture long given. But it recalled to me the recent history of the bay. The foundation was formed, in 1967, as a private effort to reverse the bay's advancing deterioration. The goal at the time was to restore the bay to a pristine wilderness state, with clear waters as found by European settlers. In the mid-1970s, the new, moon-shot-inspired Environmental Protection Agency (EPA) using the data gathered by the foundation began compiling an extensive report on the bay, consisting of five parts that were made public in the early '80s. The report made clear that to reverse the deterioration of the bay, the entire watershed would have to be regulated. This would mean convincing at least the four principal watershed states—Maryland, Virginia, Pennsylvania, and New York—as well as the District of Columbia to enact laws governing what went into the tiniest stream. State cultures with regard to land-use regulation varied wildly. Maryland was progressive. In Virginia, property rights trumped. The headwaters of the Susquehanna, in Otsego Lake in western New York, were so far from the bay that a felt sense of the Chesapeake was close to nonexistent.

All the states, and D.C. eventually, fell in line, passing pollution-control legislation, though of varying stringency, with New York coming in last, signing on fully to the Chesapeake Bay Agreement only in 2014. By that time the goal of perfectly restoring the bay was rolled back to one of arresting deterioration and attaining an ecological balance between the needs of man and of marine life. Even that has had its disappointments and scandals. Virginia, predictably, had been more loathe than other states to restrict developers. But I have sat in hearings in atopian Fairfax at which a big-time builder of a new batch of condominiums was held to account for how construction would affect a small underground stream. Perhaps not all hearings are as fastidious as the ones I attended. But there can be no question that the Chesapeake Bay initiative made the watershed not only a topographical entity in the public imagination but into a felt political jurisdiction that cut across deep-set traditional boundaries. It had done this much more successfully than a lot of metropolitan councils and boards focused on fostering economic prosperity across fixed jurisdictions.

The Chesapeake Bay initiative was an environmental one, which saw itself in terms of restraining economic ventures in order to protect what had been given to us by nature. The fundamental assumption, in other words, was that human prosperity and the integrity of nature operated in different spheres which belonged on different planes and were in many ways opposed. The idea of the watershed, for example, had long been an esoteric unit belonging to ecological science, having little to do with economic development, which was governed by states with their different land-use laws and political cultures. However, in the meantime, the movement out of the industrial age and into our present one was redefining the relationship between terrain and work. Already in the 1990s, but ever more so through the '00s, a connection was emerging between large watersheds and the more diffuse settlement pattern of our digital global age, which had different spatial needs. For, ethereal as the work of the digital age is, as irrelevant as distance has become in so many ways, physical proximity still has a role, especially at the top levels. We have seen it in the gentrification of New York, the most centralized major city on earth, we have seen it in the high price of real estate in Silicon Valley, and we have seen it in the fact that edge cities do not in fact pop up in the corn fields of Kansas but, more or less, near other edge cities, even if the central city close by has become a hollowed core.

But the proximity requirements in a global, electronically facilitated economy are larger-scaled than those required by traditional industrial work. To the extent that central cities still act as centers to which large enterprises, however loosely, hove, the resources of two or three cities are now required to create the productive synergy of success in our time. For example, the global enterprise of today often requires several research universities near its headquarters, or even its significant outposts, to supply both innovation and the quantity of highly educated employees that are the backbone of today's top tier of work. In other words, the spatial unit of work has become more regional than defined by a single big city, as we have seen in the ambi- and trivalent place names that have become common. The form of our times is regional, rather than city-centered. The landscape pattern created by work in our time is, interestingly, more like the old agrarian one: it has many centers like a painting by Kandinsky. "Region" is indeed an old word, going back to "kingdom," a time when boundaries were a bit vague, as defined by culture more than law, and, in many cases, topography, especially mountains. Regions are still recognized today as cultural units. But though there is no exact, political definition of region, there is, in many cases, a topographical one, and that is the large watershed, very precisely delineated today through scientific surveying methods. Especially where there are mountains, big watersheds often define the regions within which the engines of the far-flung global economy work in concert. So, as it turns out, the large watershed, the natural unit of ecological health, is also sometimes the spatial unit of economic prosperity in the present era.

What is most interesting about this to me is the way in which the seeming opposition between economic prosperity and ecological health begins to dissolve. This has everything to do with the nature of work in our new age. The overlap between large watersheds and the clusters of resources needed to participate successfully in the worldwide economy includes, perhaps above all, the need for highly educated, talented employees. This is where environmental and economic health converge. For such people are choosy about where they live. To draw them, companies must be located near vibrant cities—this is where the recovery of old cities really matters—but also in places that, in the wider sense, are attractive. And that means ecologically healthy. This is why the rust belt staggers in its recovery: the industrial heyday left a degraded environment behind. The right wing still opposes environmental regulation on the grounds that it suppresses growth. Putting aside, for the moment, the ultimate issue of how climate change threatens prosperity at its root, looking only at the requirements for short-term success at the regional level, the fact is that, with the rise of mind-work, it has come to pass that a clean environment fosters rather than represses economic growth. This happy calculus, which somehow has not yet infiltrated political culture, has, however, an infernal underside: the healthier the ecology of a region, the more people and businesses it attracts. This, in turn, puts ever more pressure on the environment, escalating the challenge of protecting it. In my Georgetown years I followed a study, the Loudoun County Environmental Indicators Project, a five-year program conducted at George Washington University that was tracking change down in the grass roots—the actual grass roots, in part—as the county developed, especially in Eastern Loudoun, focusing on pollution from residential sources such as road runoff and lawn fertilizers, ever increasing, and impacting the natural environment in stealthy but cumulatively destructive ways.

When, just after moving to D.C., I was assimilating regional points of reference for my own sense of orientation, side trips would help me expand and then consolidate what seemed like a physical relationship with the landscape. I remember in particular the experience of Harpers Ferry, where the Shenandoah dramatically joins the Potomac River: this became a reference point to the west. Visiting a friend on the Rappahannock near Fredericksburg became a reference to the south. In my basement study in Georgetown I sometimes activated this slow-forming internal map by thinking outward with my body—toward Harpers Ferry, toward Fredericksburg—to see how far it sensed itself in place: a kind of somatic mapping. It seemed to me that somatic distance was perhaps marked by how far the body could imagine walking while retaining a sense of being in range of home, though that would be a rather fictional body, since an actual walk from Georgetown to Fredericksburg was not likely. Utterly unreliable as all this was, it seemed to engage a faculty of some kind. I valued the balance these intimations provided to more abstract research. In my study there was a low window that looked out on the back garden but was crowded by leaves. One day rain spattered on the leaves and the glass causing me to look up from my work, and my awareness automatically leapt to a forest place high in the Alleghenies, where rain was also falling.

The Chesapeake Bay itself quickly became such a felt reference. But when I became aware of the watershed—through learning the history of the foundation rather than going places—the somatic map seemed to coincide with the watershed boundaries. If I thought I was tapping into some ancient instinct this was purely fanciful, since, old as watersheds are, people didn't really think in terms of them commonly until recent ecological awareness. The watershed is more of a scientific concept than a lived one. But when the Chesapeake watershed became a subject of study for me, as a container of the atopian landscape of Balt–Wash, my informal somatic-mapping experiments came along. It kept me from getting too abstract. It kept me with at least one foot in the simple fact of our whereabouts—in bodies on the ground.

Along the way I acquired a poster-sized Landsat image of the watershed. There was no writing on it. As for boundaries, only state lines were represented and those so faintly they could hardly be seen. Baltimore and Washington, D.C., were just gray smudges, easy to miss. But the jiggly edge of the watershed was prominently marked with a white line, which stood out in high contrast to the dark greens, dull reds, and browns of the land. You could see from the intricate irregularity of the line that very sophisticated surveying equipment, or perhaps computerized satellite information, had been used for the detailed denotation of the watershed boundary on irregular land. The outline of the watershed came together as a centaurish dancing giant, his scraggy head thrown back ecstatically in western New York, his hands clasped on his chest in prayer, bestial thighs through the mid-Atlantic states, his right hoof—the tip of the Chesapeake Peninsula—en pointe like a ballerina as the slopes of the Alleghenies flew out behind him like tattered skirts: a figment of our unblinking collective, informational eye, on the outermost edge of our manmade enclosure of ourselves.

When, on the creek off the Corsica river, I disturbed the herons on their perches, they glided upstream to a place where the wooded shore stretched straight across, as if the creek ended there. But the herons would take a sharp right, as I would, too, in turn, following them into a suddenly narrowed waterway, secretively winding between tall reeds. Next came a moderate opening, where a grass-covered earthen dam extended from one shore toward, but not quite meeting, the other, connected to it by a dilapidated wooden structure with a once movable panel in it. This apparatus, I speculated, was for purposes of controlling the mixing of saltwater from the sea and freshwater from the upper reaches of the stream, for purposes of cultivation. The panel had long ago been left in a half-open position, leaving a space just big enough to get through in a kayak if you crouched.

Then I'd find myself in a wide labyrinth of cressy islands with a periphery of mature woodland. The herons, disturbed again, this time from live trees just the other side of the dam, would head for a particularly tall copse on the far side, the likely fall line of the fresh-water stream that they would follow, fishing, right on up to the head-water pond, somewhere in the interior. I knew from experience that even at high tide I could not follow. The idea of the innermost recess, the still place at the source, had strong allure, but never had I succeeded in finding my way to a source-pond by following an Eastern Shore creek. I did once find the source of a creek but that was by car: it turned out to be a pond enclosed in chain link with a vent protruding from the middle. In the cressy place, as was my custom, I made no attempt to reach the stream, but instead moved along the shore on my right, where the water was deep, to a commodious bower near a half-overgrown landscape in which a pentimento of past agricultural uses still showed through. The bower would provide still point enough. Ten minutes and I would be restored from the depredations of Towson.

And then it would start: the layers, the contradictions, the imperative of what had become an implacable curiosity about the complex and largely unimagined character of the world as it was becoming, infiltratively atopian, the fiction of escaping Towson notwithstanding. But each year I found myself more at ease with this truth, more fluent in atopian, more accepting. Each year my curiosity about the new world was a little stronger, my old romances a bit less interesting. Each year the shift from restorative escape to explorative probing was easier, more natural, but the actual upshot was not a replacement of one experience by another, not a contest between false and true, but rather a swinging back and forth between perspectives that always seemed to get me closer to reality than when I embraced one or the other alone. All along I had known both were there.

Even as I set out on the Corsica, I knew that if I turned upstream I would immediately see a slew of perfectly schizoid McMansions that looked like images cut out of magazine advertisements and pasted on the air. The glimpse of gorgeous fields down to the shore on my chosen route was inseparable from knowledge that this landscape was an artifact of Maryland land-use policy, their beauty an economic factor in the region that kept real estate values high. If I forgot that the Chesapeake Bay had become a not totally successful artifact of protective law, an unfamiliar algae bloom would remind me.

Who is to say what nature is to us under these conditions? You go out into it and there it is, glorious beyond comprehension, spookily numinous, blowing away the intellectual plane of consciousness, transforming you in an instant as if you had been struck by lightning: that isn't false. But it's also true that, whatever this man-made enclosure is from which we can't escape, nature is in there with us. It's reduced and contained, as in a terrarium of our own making. But, on the other hand, in its new roguishness it's more enormous than we have ever known. We thought we had conquered it: now it's threatening us in a way that requires a resourcefulness we have not yet found in ourselves. It's the ground beneath us out of which we arose and in which we are still embedded inextricably. And yet it is also our ward. Nature is salving still and yet it has also become inherently alarming: most of all because we know that what is alarming is our own doing. We are entrapped in nature, and also unbearably exposed there: exposed to ourselves. Nature used to be the thing outside society; now it's inside society. So because we have so far failed as effective stewards, yet are as dependent as ever, nature also represents our ungovernedness: our inability in this very basic matter of self-preservation to take care of ourselves.

Always there is this despair in nature for us now, that we have put ourselves in a position of responsibility with respect to it that was formerly attributed to God, but without acquiring godlike powers. Our old romantic relationship with nature provided a language for our emotions and our ideals: inner storms and tranquillity, freedom, democracy—all metaphor. Now we see our own hand in all nature, together with our human limits, literally, not metaphorically: our hubris, our greed, our helplessness over ourselves, our ingenuity, our imbeddedness. Once we saw nature as flecked with glory: divinity even, to which we responded with an awe and humility that became an inherent part of our humanity. Glory still shines out, but mixed in is the gleam of haywire: laid there by us. Sometimes a natural disaster occurs that is in no way traceable to our own doings. What a relief it is to be frightened—and awed—by the effects of a volcano. Terrible as a major earthquake is, there is simplicity in rushing to the rescue, merely heroic, doing our creaturely best to help one another in the face of what insurers call "an act of God": an event beyond our control. Now some small earthquakes are said to be caused by fracking. How different the meaning of a natural and fracking-caused earthquake.

Over the years, the housekeeping staff at the Towson Sheraton has changed: it consists now mainly of immigrants from cultures entirely unlike our own. One rarely hears the Baltimorean accent in the hotel anymore. The dreary supermarket has gone, too: one year it was replaced by a construction site, the next by a sophisticated and appealing enterprise, the Fresh Market, with a vast deli but no kid, no strange steam-heating device. Sometimes crab cakes, pretty good. I have not gone to the Eastern Shore for a while because my friend with awful quickness took ill and died, before his time. His ashes were thrown out over the water, and the breeze lifted them and they expanded a little, caught by the sun in a moving shape, before dispersing and falling. Sometimes the improvised ritual exceeds anything tradition can provide. But what I have found in this loss is that my ritual creek passage has become installed in my Sheraton room.

Just as Towson was there on the creek, so now the creek has become a part of Towson.

To my mind, the despair that we feel in relation to nature has less to do with our failure to protect nature than with our failure to protect ourselves. The despair is humanistic, not technical: we have not yet figured out how to govern ourselves effectively enough to become good custodians of nature. That is perhaps the darkest feature of this despair, and yet there is also hope in it: the answer lies within ourselves. It's natural to want to protect ourselves, so it doesn't seem foolish to hope that we will. But our relationship to nature is not the only instance in which we are unable to respond in a self-protective way to a self-made situation that reflects our brilliance, and even power, but could also doom us, reflecting our helplessness before ourselves in the same fateful way. The coordinates of our nature problem are almost exactly the same as those created by the Cold War, while molecular biology may well present us with a similar paradox of triumphant achievement and boundless disaster in the future. Who among us would be astonished if tomorrow some other unforeseen predicament with the same coordinates appeared?

It might seem to compound despair to point this out. But to my mind the connection between predicaments is positive. It shows us to be on a threshold that, extending across a spectrum of facets of life, may be susceptible to the same political solution. This order of problems seems to require the development of a capacity in ourselves, an interior shift. The outcome would be political, but first a deep reimagining of ourselves and our situation would be necessary, as I have been attempting to do in a small way here. Always behind my readings of landscapes are the questions, Where are we? What is our relationship to one another? and What is our relationship to our surroundings now? Political effectiveness under drastically new circumstances must start with basic questions of this kind. The equivalent might be the imaginative leap that broke past belief in the divine right of kings toward the possibility of shared power. I have sometime thought of our situation in this period as like that of the English just before the Magna Carta was written. But on a visit to the British Museum in the midst of these long studies, I saw, to my amazement, that there were, actually, several Magna Cartas. It wasn't a simple dawn. It was a messy repetitive struggle, of power but also of imagination, such as we are engaged with in the present period as we fumble our way toward a society reconfigured to our circumstances, our needs.

A common aspect of our multiple contemporary predicaments, again, is that we have acquired godlike responsibilities but without godlike powers. To put it another way, we have to find a human way to develop self-governance in areas that previously did not require it. Meanwhile the idea of a deity who will magically come down and rescue us has become downright dangerous, in that it suggests that we are not, in fact, really responsible for ourselves in these new ways. A dilemma is that each of these predicaments also contains immeasurable stakes: the end of civilization, the upending of the cradle of providence. The stakes transcend all other human concerns. But how does one comprehend stakes beyond measure, how can one even bear to really engage fully with such predicaments without an internal sense of transcendence—something larger than our situation, which is exactly what has been taken away by the predicament itself? Some say all sense of transcendence is childish invention that should be relegated to the ash heap of primitive delusions. But there is a difference between religion as we have known it, which does seem out of joint with our times, and the capacity to conceive of transcendence, out of which religion arose. Surely that capacity is a power, not a weakness. Surely to be without that is no advance.

As we face predicaments that present us with immeasurable stakes, and that require a kind of collective internal change, a stretching and development of our nature rather than our know-how, our ability to conceive of the immeasurable, would surely seem to be a part of the human instrument we should cultivate rather than discard. The problem is similar to that of seeing past the glorious Romantic archetypes of landscape to what landscape is and means today. The question in relation to transcendence is how to cultivate it in response to an entirely new situation, learning from the superb traditions that gave us Chartres and the Blue Mosque, and yet free enough from stupendously well-developed expressions of this capacity to find the infant response that is true to our present situation. Because I think the capacity is a gift essential to our humanity, I am certain that civilizations of the future will find ways to express and develop it. But in the meantime, as we strive to secure that future, our best course might be to cultivate an open faith without doctrine, a faith of no footing, accepting for now just the naked capacity itself as our footing in the midst of uncertainty and contradictions. This wouldn't be faith in a deity but rather faith in life itself: that we have within us the ability to respond effectively to any situation we ourselves created—to grow into it: not that we *will* respond successfully, but that we could.

I believe that keeping our sense of transcendence in play is likely to expand our imaginative growth as we grapple with enclosure, rather than diminishing it. But this argument, like the others, is based on the conviction that our ability to conceive of transcendence is a gift and a power rather than a form of whistling in the dark. Let me emphasize again that my focus here is on human capacity and not an idea of a deus ex machina coming down to change the course of human events. To my way of thinking, a faith of no faith is far more useful, and more empowering, and also probably more truthful to our circumstances than either the hubristic belief that we can geo-engineer our way out of problems, or the righteous, all-knowing posture of despair. At the bottom, what I care about most is the imaginative creativity necessary for political reinvention. While we face great dangers, we may find the foundations for a great new civilization in our response to them. It's this that can fire our ambitions, our hopes. We must relentlessly and realistically appraise our situation but, lest we become paralyzed by fear and despair, we must also think past catastrophe to what a successful engagement with dangers might produce. I think we need our intimations of an unknowable and unmeasurable dimension to existence to get there. Never yet has there been a great civilization that did not cultivate those intimations—because there is no full humanity without them.

Sometimes the spread of the global economy is seen as a kind of Americanization. This is a big exaggeration. But the world is now having an experience similar to one we have lived with for a long time in America: the unrelenting unraveling of tradition and the way that unraveling rips out context, exposing people to the emptiness of life without deep culture. Because of the long American commitment to inclusion, and therefore growth, we are used to that emptiness here. It is our cornerstone of no cornerstone, our culture of no culture. It is, you could say, a kind of faith of no footing. The great paradox of the worldwide enclosure is that, while bringing prosperity to previously poor parts of the world, it also undermines the value of what has been accumulated, stealing cultural inheritance, leaving people bereft of the great webs of connection and collective human depth that cultures provide. I am reluctant to characterize Americans as special in any regard, because that has gotten us into so much trouble. Yet we may have a special role in this unfolding planetary situation, not as a people excepted from the tragic laws of history, as we are wont to believe, but as one long used to cultural loss, to vulnerability, to exposure, to emptiness—to keeping faith in a fragile experiment, rampant evidence of failure notwithstanding. We come to the worldwide enclosure long inured to the emptiness that this new stage of humanity is now imposing on all peoples. So in our familiarity with that, we might be especially able, among peoples, to contribute something about how to live in this new wilderness with its dangers

Acknowledgments

I had so much help from different quarters along the way, and such abiding support from friends, family, and colleagues over a long span that I could never be sure I have named all. I will be lucky if this is the half of it.

Editors: Richard Todd Jr., Jack Shoemaker, Susan Kamil, Sam Nicholson.

My agents Andrew Wylie and Jeff Posternak.

Trusted readers at crucial moments: Susan Chase, Daphne Merkin, Vincent Virga, Cynthia Zarin.

Tactical support: Kathleen Furey, Elizabeth Macklin, the N2 fact-checking team, Neda Semnami.

Research support: Marvin Bilotsky, Phillipa Dunne, Robert Fishman, Bruce Katz, Steve Lagerfeld, Janet Spikes, Ken Storms, Sam White.

Moral support: Mary Barnes, Katherine Bowling, Karan Branan, Tally Brennan, Deborah Burns, Chris Burrill, Virginia Cantarella, Judy Collins, Blanche Cooke, Clare Cos, Barbara Dudley, Phillippa Dunne, Kennedy Fraser, Josh and Carol Friedman, Robert Ganz, Bernadette Grosjean, Constance Gutske, Felicia Kornbluh, Lis

Harris, Steve Kurtz, Susana Leval, Jacob Levenson, Beverly Lowry, Heather Dune Macadam, Mary Macy, James McCourt, Celia Morris, Barbara Mowat, Paul Multimear, Peter Neill, Fairlie Nicodemus, Molly O'Neil, David Payne, Leonard Peters, Didi Rae, Peter Rand, Elizabeth Barlow Rogers, Sylvia Shorto, Tom Smith, Clay Sorrough, Catherine Stimpson, Phillippa Strum, Helen Tworkov, Mary Lee Stein, Lorin Stein, Anna Stein, and Beverly Willis.

A special salute to my students who kept me lively and growing.

Material support: Louis Jaramillo, Fred Leebron, Honor Moore, Peggy Pierrepont, Robert Polito, Leslie Rubinkowski, Patsy Sims.

A special thanks to Margaret Adams.

Institutional support: The Anthony Lukas Foundation Prize Project; the Brookings Institution; The Huyck Preserve in Rensselaerville, New York; The Jenny Moore Fellowship at George Washington University; The Logan Residency for Non-Fiction writers; The Nation Institute; Pioneerworks; The Whiting Foundation; Woodrow Wilson International Center for Scholars; the Yaddo Foundation; and Diana Hume-George and all of the Goucher MFA in Nonfiction faculty over the years.

Without whom nothing: my partner, Noel; my son, Julian; my mother, Alida; my sisters Hester Lessard, Griselda Healy, Sophie Lessard, Laura Lessard, and Jenny Lessard.

As always: Charlie Peters and William Shawn.

© Christine Burrill

SUZANNAH LESSARD is the best-selling author of *The Architect of Desire: Beauty and Danger in the Stanford White Family*, a *New York Times* Notable Book. A founding editor of *The Washington Monthly* and a staff writer at *The New Yorker* for twenty years, she is a recipient of the Whiting and Lukas Awards and has received fellowships from the Woodrow Wilson International Center for Scholars and George Washington University. Find out more at suzannahlessard.com.

Printed in the United States
by Baker & Taylor Publisher Services